SÃO PAULO
HETEROTOPIA
URBANE RÄUME IN DER SCHWEBE
URBAN SPACES IN SUSPENSE

ARCHITECTURE | VOLUME 68

HERAUSGEBER PUBLISHER	Ulrike Böhm, Katja Benfer, Cyrus Zahiri
TITELBILD COVER PHOTO	SESC 24 de Maio, São Paulo, Brasilien © Nelson Kon 2017
VERLAG PUBLISHER	transcript Verlag, Bielefeld www.transcript-verlag.de
	© 2022 transcript Verlag, Bielefeld
	All rights reserved. No part of this book may be reprinted or reproduced or utilized in any form or by any electronic, mechanical, or other means, now known or hereafter invented, including photocopying and recording, or in any information storage or retrieval system, without permission in writing from the publisher.
PRINT ISBN	978-3-8376-6575-8
PDF ISBN	978-3-8394-6575-2
	https://doi.org/10.14361/9783839465752
ISSN OF SERIES	2702-8070
EISSN OF SERIES	2702-8089
	Bibliographic information published by the Deutsche Nationalbibliothek. The Deutsche Nationalbibliothek lists this publication in the Deutsche Nationalbibliografie; detailed bibliographic data are available in the Internet at http://dnb.d-nb.de

ULRIKE BÖHM, KATJA BENFER, CYRUS ZAHIRI (HG./EDS.)

SÃO PAULO
HETEROTOPIA
URBANE RÄUME IN DER SCHWEBE
URBAN SPACES IN SUSPENSE

Wir streben eine genderneutrale Sprache an. Angelehnt an die Empfehlung des Bundesverwaltungsamtes (Merkblatt M19), sollen dabei Verständlichkeit und Lesbarkeit der Texte nicht beeinträchtigt werden. Ausnahmsweise wird auf die Form des maskulinen Substantivs zurückgegriffen, wenn genderneutrale Personenbezeichnungen fehlen oder eine gehäufte Verwendung der Paarform vermieden werden soll.

We strive for gender-neutral language. As per the recommendation stated in the M19 leaflet, issued by the Federal Office of Administration, the comprehensibility and readability of the texts should not be impaired in the process. As an exception, the form of the masculine noun is used if gender-neutral personal designations are missing or a frequent use of the pair form is to be avoided.

1	**ÜBERBLICK / OVERVIEW**	**7**
	EINFÜHRUNG	8
	INTRODUCTION	10
	PRESTES MAIAS PLANO DE AVENIDAS	12
	PRESTES MAIA'S PLANO DE AVENIDAS	16
	GALERIEN: ÖFFENTLICHER RAUM UND PRIVATE GRUNDSTÜCKSENTWICKLUNG	22
	GALLERIES: PUBLIC SPHERE AND PRIVATE REAL ESTATE DEVELOPMENT	26
	ÖFFENTLICHER RAUM UND HETEROTOPIE	30
	PUBLIC SPHERE AND HETEROTOPIAS	34
2	**PROJEKTE / PROJECTS**	**41**
	GALERIA METRÓPOLE	42
	GALERIA METRÓPOLE	50
	GALERIA DO ROCK	56
	GALERIA DO ROCK	63
	GALERIA NOVA BARÃO	72
	GALERIA NOVA BARÃO	81
	SESC 24 DE MAIO	86
	SESC 24 DE MAIO	97
	PRAÇA DAS ARTES	106
	PRAÇA DAS ARTES	116
	MASP UND MIRANTE	124
	MASP AND MIRANTE	138
	MINHOCÃO	146
	MINHOCÃO	157
	CENTRO CULTURAL SÃO PAULO	166
	CENTRO CULTURAL SÃO PAULO	174
3	**ANHANG / APPENDIX**	**187**
	QUELLEN / SOURCES	188
	INTERVIEWS / INTERVIEWS	192
	BILDQUELLEN / IMAGE SOURCES	194
	IMPRESSUM / IMPRINT	198

1
ÜBERBLICK
OVERVIEW

EINFÜHRUNG

Öffentliches und Privates, Verkehr und Freiraum, Geplantes und Spontanes - unsere Stadtvorstellung ist geprägt durch Gegensätze. Dagegen illustrieren die im Buch vorgestellten Stadtbausteine, dass sich diese Pole auch bewusst verknüpfen lassen. Das Ergebnis zeigt sich in unerwartet eigenwilligen Stadtszenen: Tanzen entlang der Schnellstraße, Flanieren durch das Steinarchipel, Planschen vor der Stadtsilhouette ...

Auffällig ist, dass viele dieser Räume verknüpft sind mit Ideen des brasilianischen Architekten und Stadtplaners Francisco Prestes Maia. Der im europäischen Raum weitgehend unbekannte Planer entwickelte in den 1930er Jahren Konzepte zur Neuordnung und Modernisierung des Stadtgefüges von São Paulo. Ein Blick in seine Bibliothek zeigt, dass Prestes Maia gewissenhaft die zeitgenössischen Diskurse zum Städtebau verfolgt hat. Dabei bleibt seine Entwicklungsstrategie für São Paulo aber sehr eigenständig.

Prestes Maias ‚Plano de Avenidas' sieht ein übergeordnetes Gerüst aus Schnellstraßen vor, das Kernstadt und Vorstädte mit dem Umland São Paulos verbindet. Seine Stadtvorstellung illustriert er anhand von Ideenskizzen zu besonderen Knotenpunkten in diesem Gerüst. Beispielhaft verknüpft er dabei Freiräume, Hochbauten und Verkehrsbauwerke zu komplexen Stadtbausteinen.

Ergänzend formuliert Prestes Maia städtebauliche Festsetzungen, die Bauwillige dazu motivieren sollen, innerstädtische Freiräume mitzuentwickeln. Als Anreiz wird ihnen dazu eine höhere Grundstücksausnutzung in Aussicht gestellt. Das Ergebnis sind Galeriebauten, die Freiflächen, Wohn- und gewerbliche Nutzungen miteinander verbinden.

Die folgende Projekt-Zusammenstellung illustriert das Potenzial von Prestes Maias Ansätzen. Die Auswahl umfasst Beispiele aus seiner Amtszeit als Bürgermeister São Paulos, aber auch aktuelle Projekte, die Aspekte seiner Ideen aufgreifen und weiterentwickeln.

Der Knotenpunkt MASP-Mirante illustriert beispielhaft das Verknüpfen von Freiraum, Architektur und Verkehr. Die Projekte Galeria Metrópole, Galeria Nova Barão und Galeria do Rock sind das Ergebnis städtebaulicher Festsetzungen. Zu den zeitgenössischen Ansätzen, die Prestes Maias Ideen neu interpretieren, gehören die Projekte Centro Cultural São Paulo (CCSP), Praça das Artes und Serviço Social do Comércio 24 de Maio (SESC).

Den Abschluss der Sammlung bildet die Via Elevada Presidente João Goulart, eine aufgeständerte Schnellstraße aus den frühen 1970er Jahren. Das im Volksmund ‚Minhocão' genannte Verkehrsbauwerk ist eine Antithese zu Prestes Maias Ansatz, Verkehr, Freiraum und Gebäude zu integrieren. Ursprünglich ausschließlich dem motorisierten Verkehr vorbehalten, wird die Trasse inzwischen abends, an Wochenenden und Feiertagen zum Flanieren und Radfahren in Anspruch genommen. Zeitnah geplant ist der Ausbau zu einem Park.

PERSPEKTIVEN

Wer entwirft und plant, orientiert sich an Bekanntem, an Referenzen und Vorbildern. Dagegen stellt die vorliegende Sammlung Stadtbausteine vor, die Ungewohntes versuchen. Anstoß dazu boten die besonderen sozioökonomischen Bedingungen von São Paulos Centro Novo und die damit verbundenen Folgen für Strassen-, Platz- und Parkräume.

Entstanden sind Projekte, die öffentliche Räume erweitern und ersetzen, die sich aber selbst - streng genommen - nicht eindeutig dieser Raumkategorie zuordnen lassen. Gerade dadurch erlauben sie einen frischen Blick auf die Grenzen und Qualitäten des Begriffs ‚öffentlicher Raum'.

Die Sammlung erlaubt es zudem, Facetten der Arbeit des brasilianischen Planers Prestes Maia vorzustellen. Sein Ansatz Verkehr, Freiraum und Architektur zusammenzudenken, ist angesichts anstehender Planungsaufgaben überraschend aktuell.

Er bietet wichtige Anregungen im Umgang mit wachsenden Städten, insbesondere durch die Verknüpfung baulich-räumlicher Dichte mit gemischten Nutzungen und innerstädtischen Freiräumen.

METHODE

Die Projekte werden anhand von Plänen und Fotografien vorgestellt. Trotz intensiver Suche ist es nicht immer gelungen, historische Unterlagen für die einzelnen Projekte zu beschaffen.

Um ihre Entstehung und ihre Nutzungen näher zu beschreiben, fanden vor Ort Gespräche mit unterschiedlichen Personengruppen statt. In Form von offenen Interviews wurden Fragen gestellt zur Vergangenheit des Projekts, zum Alltag sowie zu Vorstellungen für die Zukunft. Befragt wurden Planerinnen und Planer, aber auch Personen, die die Projekte nutzen, mieten oder verwalten. Die folgenden Beschreibungen basieren daher zum Teil auf ihren Aussagen.

An der Untersuchung beteiligt waren Studierende und Lehrende der Faculdade de Arquitetura e Urbanismo da Universidade de São Paulo, der Escola da Cidade São Paulo, der Leibniz Universität Hannover sowie der Universität Stuttgart.

Vorbereitet wurde die Untersuchung durch Seminarveranstaltungen an der Leibniz Universität Hannover (Lehrgebiet Darstellung in der Landschaftsarchitektur) und der Universität Stuttgart (Fachgebiet Freiraumgestaltung). Die Dokumentation der Fallbeispiele und die Befragung erfolgte vor Ort durch gemischte Teams aus brasilianischen und deutschen Studierenden.

DANKSAGUNG

An dem vorliegenden Buch und der begleitenden Ausstellung haben eine Vielzahl von Fachleuten und Institutionen mitgewirkt. Ihnen sei an dieser Stelle für ihre Unterstützung und ihr Engagement gedankt. Ein besonderer Dank geht an:

Abbildungen und Pläne
- Melhoramentos
- Arquivo Histórico Municipal - Secretaria Municipal de Cultura de São Paulo
- Nelson Kon, Fotograf
- brasil arquitetura
- Hereñú & Ferroni Arquitetos
- MMBB arquitetura e urbanismo
- Paulo Mendes da Rocha
- SIAA Arquitetos Associados
- Management Galeria Metrópole
- Management Galeria do Rock
- Management Mirante 9 de Julho

Universidade de São Paulo
Faculdade de Arquitetura e Urbanismo
- Ana Castro, Prof. Dr.
- Eduardo Costa, Dr.
- Sabrina Studart Fontenele Costa, Dr.

Escola da Cidade
Faculdade de Arquitetura e Urbanismo
- Sebastian Beck, Prof. Ms.
- Juliane Bellot Rolemberg Lessa, Prof.
- Pedro Beresin, Prof. Ms.

Studierende
- Marcelo Baliú Fiamenghi, Maria Luiza Belo, Luísa Gonçalves, Elis Macedo, Marina Rigolleto, Gabriela Yumi Takase[1]
- Joana Andrade, Sofia Boldrini, Tamara Crespin, Paula Mattos, Luísa Moreno, Beatriz Oliveira, Louise Rodrigues[2]
- Lea Dirmeier, Willie Sauerborn, Florian Stiegler[3]
- Matthias Bierschenk, Jacob Fielers, Anna Finn, Santiago Guerrero Koch, Roya Haghparast Keyhani, Hanna Höhne, Jasper Nöhren, Leander Olkner, Zhiyuan Peng, Lina Reulecke, Josef Schacht, Florian Schlossmacher, Josefine Siebenand, Jonas Teuber, Felix Wagner[4]

[1] Universidade de São Paulo Faculdade de Arquitetura e Urbanismo
[2] Escola da Cidade Faculdade de Arquitetura e Urbanismo
[3] Universität Stuttgart Städtebau Institut
[4] Leibniz Universität Hannover Institut für Landschaftsarchitektur

INTRODUCTION

Splashing in front of the city skyline, strolling through the stone archipelago, dancing next to the expressway... São Paulo's urban spaces are unexpectedly idiosyncratic - places that surprise your senses.

These spaces attempt the unusual: they combine aspects that we often think of separately: public and private, traffic and open space, the planned and the spontaneous.

It is striking that many of these spaces are connected to ideas of Brazilian architect and urban planner Francisco Prestes Maia. Mostly unknown in Europe, he developed concepts for reorganising and modernising São Paulo's urban fabric in the 1930s. One look into his library demonstrates that Prestes Maia diligently observed contemporary urban development discourse. Still, his development strategy for São Paulo remains highly original.

Prestes Maia's 'Plano de Avenidas' envisions a superordinate motorway framework connecting the city core and the suburbs with São Paulo's surrounding region. He illustrated his idea of a city using sketches for ideas regarding particular nodes in this framework. In an exemplary manner, he connected open spaces, buildings and traffic structures to form complex urban modules.

In addition, Prestes Maia articulated urban design rules intended to motivate investors to contribute to developing inner-city open spaces. As an incentive, they were promised a greater degree of property utilisation. This resulted in gallery buildings combining open spaces, residential and commercial uses.

The following compilation of projects illustrates the potential of both approaches. It includes projects from Prestes Maia's term as mayor of São Paulo as well as current projects which further develop aspects of his ideas.

The node MASP-Mirante, for instance, demonstrates the combination of open space, architecture and traffic.

Galeria Metrópole, Galeria Nova Barão and Galeria do Rock as projects represent the result of urban design rules. Contemporary approaches acting on Prestes Maia's ideas and developing them further include the projects Centro Cultural São Paulo (CCSP), Praça das Artes and Serviço Social do Comércio (SESC) 24 de Maio.

The compilation is concluded by the Via Elevada Presidente João Goulart, a raised motorway from the early 1970s. The structure, commonly referred to as Minhocão, is an antithesis to Prestes Maia's approach of integrating traffic, open space and buildings. Originally reserved for motor traffic, the route is now used by pedestrians and cyclists in the evenings, on weekends and on bank holidays. A conversion into a public park is in the planning stage.

PERSPECTIVES

Those who design and plan use established references and examples as orientation. In contrast, this compilation introduces projects which attempt the unfamiliar. The spaces presented were motivated by the special socio-economic conditions of São Paulo's Centro Novo and the related consequences for street, square and parking spaces.

The result are projects that expand and replace public spaces, but which themselves - strictly speaking - cannot be clearly assigned to this category of space. Precisely because of this, they allow us to take a fresh look at the limits and qualities of the term 'public space'.

The compilation also allows us to introduce facets of the work of Prestes Maia in more detail. His approach of combining traffic, public space and architecture is surprisingly current in the light of upcoming planning tasks. He provides important impulses regarding the handling of growing cities - particularly by connecting spatial density with mixed uses and open spaces.

METHOD

The projects are introduced using plans and photographs. Despite an intensive search, it has not always been possible to obtain historical documents for the individual projects. In order to describe their development and their uses in more detail, interviews were conducted on-site with various groups of people. These included architects, users, owners, commercial tenants and representatives of the building administration. In the form of open interviews, questions were asked about the project's past, everyday life and ideas for the future. The following descriptions are therefore based in part on the statements of those interviewed on-site.

The study was conducted by students and teachers of Faculdade de Arquitetura e Urbanismo da Universidade de São Paulo, Escola da Cidade São Paulo, Leibniz University Hannover and University of Stuttgart.

Preparations for the study took place in the course of seminars at Leibniz University Hannover (Institute for Landscape Architecture) and at University of Stuttgart (Chair of Landscape Architecture). Case studies documentation and surveys were conducted on-site by mixed teams of Brazilian and German students.

ACKNOWLEDGEMENTS

Numerous experts and institutions participated in the present volume and its accompanying exhibition. We would like to express our gratitude for their support and commitment.
A special thank you goes to:

Images and plans

- Melhoramentos
- Arquivo Histórico Municipal - Secretaria Municipal de Cultura de São Paulo
- Nelson Kon, Photographer
- brasil arquitetura
- Hereñú & Ferroni Arquitetos
- MMBB arquitetura e urbanismo
- Paulo Mendes da Rocha
- SIAA Arquitetos Associados
- Management Galeria Metrópole
- Management Galeria do Rock
- Management Mirante 9 de Julho

Universidade de São Paulo
Faculdade de Arquitetura e Urbanismo

- Ana Castro, Prof. Dr.
- Eduardo Costa, Dr.
- Sabrina Studart Fontenele Costa, Dr.

Escola da Cidade
Faculdade de Arquitetura e Urbanismo

- Sebastian Beck, Prof. Ms.
- Juliane Bellot Rolemberg Lessa, Prof.
- Pedro Beresin, Prof. Ms.

Students

- Marcelo Baliú Fiamenghi, Maria Luiza Belo, Luísa Gonçalves, Elis Macedo, Marina Rigolleto, Gabriela Yumi Takase[1]
- Joana Andrade, Sofia Boldrini, Tamara Crespin, Paula Mattos, Luísa Moreno, Beatriz Oliveira, Louise Rodrigues[2]
- Lea Dirmeier, Willie Sauerborn, Florian Stiegler[3]
- Matthias Bierschenk, Jacob Fielers, Anna Finn, Santiago Guerrero Koch, Roya Haghparast Keyhani, Hanna Höhne, Jasper Nöhren, Leander Olkner, Zhiyuan Peng, Lina Reulecke, Josef Schacht, Florian Schlossmacher, Josefine Siebenand, Jonas Teuber, Felix Wagner[4]

[1] Universidade de São Paulo Faculdade de Arquitetura e Urbanismo
[2] Escola da Cidade Faculdade de Arquitetura e Urbanismo
[3] University of Stuttgart Institute of Urban Planning and Design
[4] Leibniz University Hannover Institute for Landscape Architecture

PRESTES MAIAS
PLANO DE AVENIDAS

STADTENTWICKLUNG SÃO PAULO

Ende des 19. Jahrhunderts verfügt São Paulo über ein sternförmiges Eisenbahnnetz, das die Kaffeeanbaugebiete im Umland mit der Stadt und dem nahegelegenen Hafen Santos verbindet. In Folge eines ‚Kaffee-Booms' und des Zuzugs von Arbeitskräften, dehnt sich die Stadt stark in Richtung Norden und Nordwesten aus. Dabei führen die topographischen Bedingungen sowie das Bedürfnis nach Abgrenzung zu einem Nebeneinander aus Siedlungseinheiten, denen Verknüpfung und Zusammenhang fehlen.

Zur Modernisierung dieses Gefüges entwickelt der Architekt und Planer Prestes Maia eine Reihe von weitreichenden Entwurfsideen. Seine Konzeption fasst er 1930 in der Publikation ‚Plano de Avenidas' zusammen. Zwischen 1938 und 1945 sowie 1961 und 1965 hat Prestes Maia als Bürgermeister die Gelegenheit, Teile seiner Vorstellungen umzusetzen.[1]

PRESTES MAIAS STADTVORSTELLUNG

Prestes Maia versteht sein Planwerk als Gesamtkonzeption, das die Stadterweiterung São Paulos langfristig trägt.[2] Bausteine dazu sind die Anpassung des Stadtgefüges an die Anforderungen des motorisierten Individualverkehrs, Maßnahmen zur Regulierung von Überschwemmungen[3], das Bereitstellen eines angemessenen Freiflächenangebots[4] sowie Vorgaben zum Umgang mit hohen baulichen Dichten. Seine Planung sieht dazu ein Radialsystem vor, das über hierarchisierte Straßen den Stadtkern mit dem Umland verknüpft.[5] Dazu werden der Rio Tietê und der Rio Pinheiros verrohrt und ihr Flussbett jeweils als übergeordnete Schnellstraßen ausgebaut.

Prestes Maias Stadtvorstellung lassen sich besonders gut an seinen Perspektiven und Schnitten ablesen. Die Zeichnungen illustrieren wichtige Schnittstellen innerhalb seines Gesamtkonzepts.

Seine Vorschläge konzentrieren sich auf eine Verbesserung von Verkehrsverbindungen und dabei insbesondere auf Maßnahmen zum Überwinden topographischer Hindernisse. Dabei folgt Prestes Maia aber nicht den Stadtmodellen der Moderne der 1920er Jahre. Stattdessen kombiniert er für die Entwurfsaufgaben jeweils Elemente des europäischen und US-amerikanischen Städtebaus der Vormoderne. Dazu gehören eine starke bauliche Verdichtung, die Ausbildung von großzügigen Stadträumen sowie vertikale Akzentsetzungen.

An wichtigen Knotenpunkten und Übergängen sieht Prestes Maia multifunktionale Hybridbauten vor, die die trennende Wirkung des Automobil-Verkehrs mindern sollen. Die Projekte haben die Aufgabe, Stadträume zu fassen und zu akzentuieren. Sie verbinden dazu verkehrliche und räumlich-gestalterische Anforderungen des Kontexts.

Bemerkenswert an seinen Zeichnungen ist, dass diese Projektvorschläge immer auch die Maßstäblichkeit von Fußgängern berücksichtigen. Seine Entwurfsideen verknüpfen dazu Hochbauten, Ingenieurbauwerke und Freiraumelemente.[6] Für Prestes Maia bieten Straßen-, Brücken- und Tunnelprojekte stets Anlass für ein zusätzliches Angebot an öffentlichen Räumen.[7] Ziel ist es, unbelebte Transiträume zu vermeiden und das Spektrum an innerstädtischen Freiflächen zu ergänzen.

Je nach Aufgabe sind Grünflächen, Plätze, Terrassen, Kolonaden oder Stadtloggien jeweils wichtiger Bestandteil des Entwurfs und keine nachgeordnete Zutat.[8] Neben Bewegungsräumen sind daher immer auch Aufenthalts- und Rückzugsbereiche für Passanten vorgesehen. Dabei werden Fußgänger und Automobile als gleichberechtigte Verkehrsteilnehmer aufgefasst. Das moderne São Paulo soll störungsfreies Fahren ermöglichen, dabei aber gleichzeitig eine Stadt des Flanierens bleiben.

---

[1] Costa (2010): S. 52

[2] Erste Ansätze werden zwischen 1934-1938 unter dem Bürgermeister Fábio Prado umgesetzt; Costa (2010): S. 52

[3] Prestes Maia (1930): S. V

[4] Prestes Maias veröffentlicht eine Liste von Großstädten, geordnet nach ihrem Grünflächenanteil. Dabei liegt São Paulo im Schlussfeld; Prestes Maia (1930): S. 346, Figure 230

[5] Prestes Maia (1930): S. 52, Figure 37

[6] Die Entwurfsskizzen erinnern an Ideen des US-amerikanischen Architekten Hugh Ferriss; Ferriss (1929): S. 66

[7] Prestes Maia (1930): S. V, 139, Figure 3

[8] Prestes Maia (1930): S. 4

1 **Praça Pedro Lessa**
(S. 13 / p. 13)

rasantes Stadtwachstum
rapid urban growth

2 **Hybridbau mit Terrasse**
Hybrid building with terrace

Perspektive
Perspective

3 **Trennung Verkehrsarten**
Separation of transport modes

Querschnitte
Cross sections

4 **São Francisco Viadukt**
São Francisco Viaduct

Längsschnitt
Longitudinal section

5 **Hybridbau auf Viadukt**
Hybrid building on viaduct

Ansicht
View

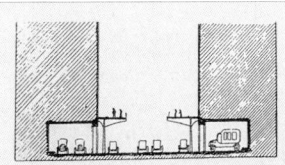
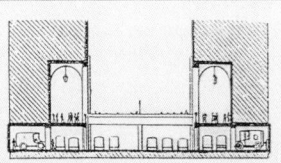
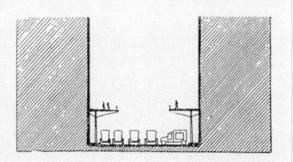

PRESTES MAIA'S PLANO DE AVENIDAS

URBAN DEVELOPMENT OF SÃO PAULO

At the end of the 19th century, São Paulo featured a star-shaped railway network which connected the coffee-producing areas in the hinterland with the city and the nearby harbour Santos. Following a 'coffee boom' and the influx of workers, the city expanded significantly to the north and northwest. Topographical conditions as well as the need for boundaries led to a coexistence of disjointed settlements lacking connection and cohesion.

To modernise this urban structure, architect and planner Prestes Maia developed a series of extensive planning measures in 1930. He summarised his concepts in the publication "Plano de Avenidas". Between 1938 and 1945 as well as 1961 and 1965, Prestes Maia had the opportunity to implement parts of his ideas as mayor of São Paulo.[1]

PRESTES MAIA'S IDEA OF THE CITY

Prestes Maia understood his plans as an overall concept supporting São Paulo's long-term urban expansion.[2] Its components were adapting the urban structure to requirements of private vehicle traffic, measures for regulating flooding[3], providing a suitable amount of public spaces[4] and establishing specifications for handling areas of high urban density. His plans envisaged a radial system with hierarchically organised streets connecting the city centre to the surrounding region.[5] To this end, Rio Tietê and Rio Pinheiros were to be encased, and their riverbeds were to be developed into superordinate motorways.

Prestes Maia's idea of the city can be observed particularly well in his planning sketches for partial areas.

His suggestions were focused on improving traffic connections, with an emphasis on measures for overcoming topographical obstacles. However, Prestes Maia did not follow the urban models of the modern era of the 1920s. Instead, he combined elements of European and North American urban design concepts of premodern times. They include significant urban densification, ample urban spaces and vertical accents.

At important urban junctions, Prestes Maia envisaged multifunctional hybrid structures to mitigate the divisive effects of car traffic. In addition, the projects are intended to form urban spaces and support orientation. To achieve this Prestes Maia combined traffic and spatial design requirements of the context.

What's remarkable about his sketches is that his projects always factor in pedestrian perspective and scale. This means a combination of superstructures, engineering structures and open-space elements.[6] For Prestes Maia, road, bridge and tunnel projects always provide opportunities for additional public spaces.[7] This aims at avoiding lifeless transit spaces and increasing the availability of inner-city open spaces.

Depending on the design task at hand, green areas, squares, terraces, ambulatories and loggias respectively are components of the design and not subordinated additions.[8] Besides access spaces, there are always public spaces provided where passers-by can linger and recover. Pedestrians and cars are understood as equal participants in traffic. The modern São Paulo should facilitate undisturbed driving while remaining a city of flâneurs.

---

1. Costa (2010): p. 52
2. Initial measures were implemented between 1934 and 1938 under mayor Fábio Prado; Costa (2010): p. 52
3. Prestes Maia (1930): p. 5
4. Prestes Maia ranked major cities according to their portion of green spaces. São Paulo came in near the bottom; Prestes Maia (1930): p. 346, figure 230
5. Prestes Maia (1930): p. 52, figure 37
6. The designs evoke ideas of US-American architect Hugh Ferriss; Ferriss (1929): p. 66
7. Prestes Maia (1930): p. 5, 139, figure 3
8. Prestes Maia (1930): p. 4

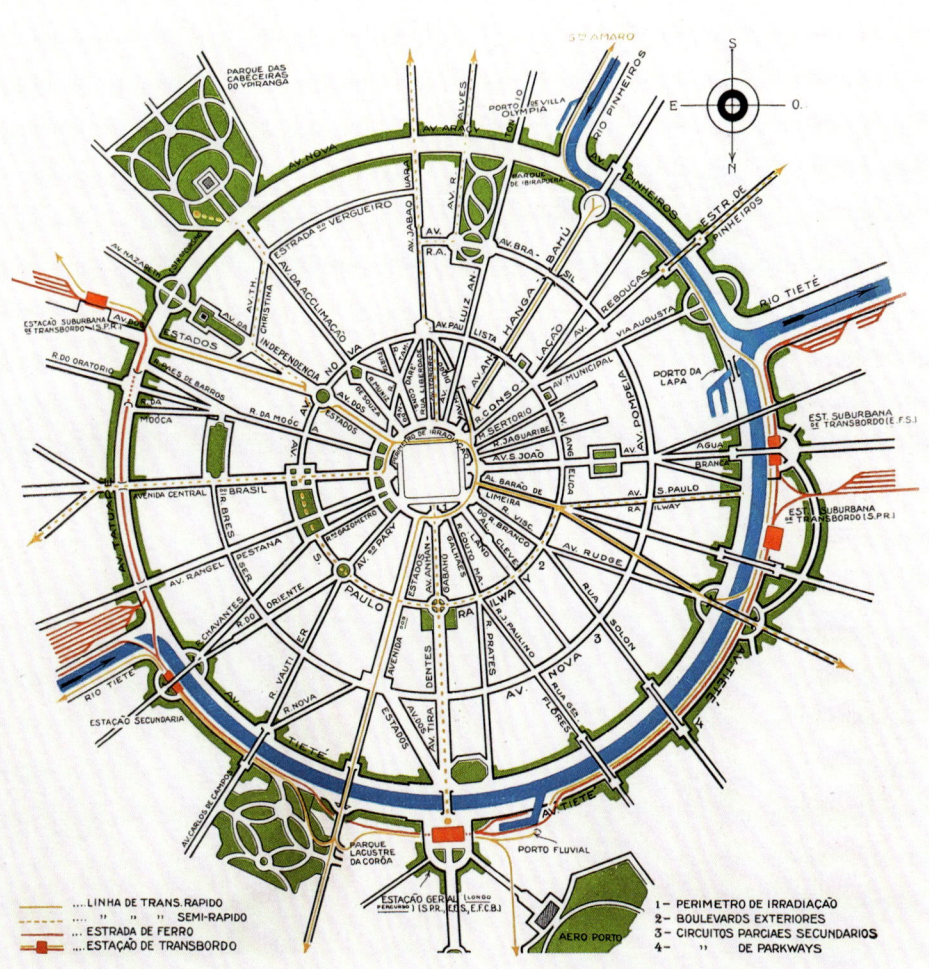

6   Plano de Avenidas
    da Cidade de São Paulo
    (S. 17 / p. 17)

    Erschließungsschema
    Traffic scheme proposal

    Prestes Maia (1930)

7   Plano de Avenidas
    da Cidade de São Paulo

    Vorstudie
    Preliminary study

    Prestes Maia (1930)

8 **Tunnelmund Mirante**
Tunnel entry Mirante
Avenida Anhangabaú
Entwurf
Proposal
Prestes Maia (1930)

9 **Erdarbeiten**
Earthworks
Anhangabaú-Tal
Anhangabaú valley

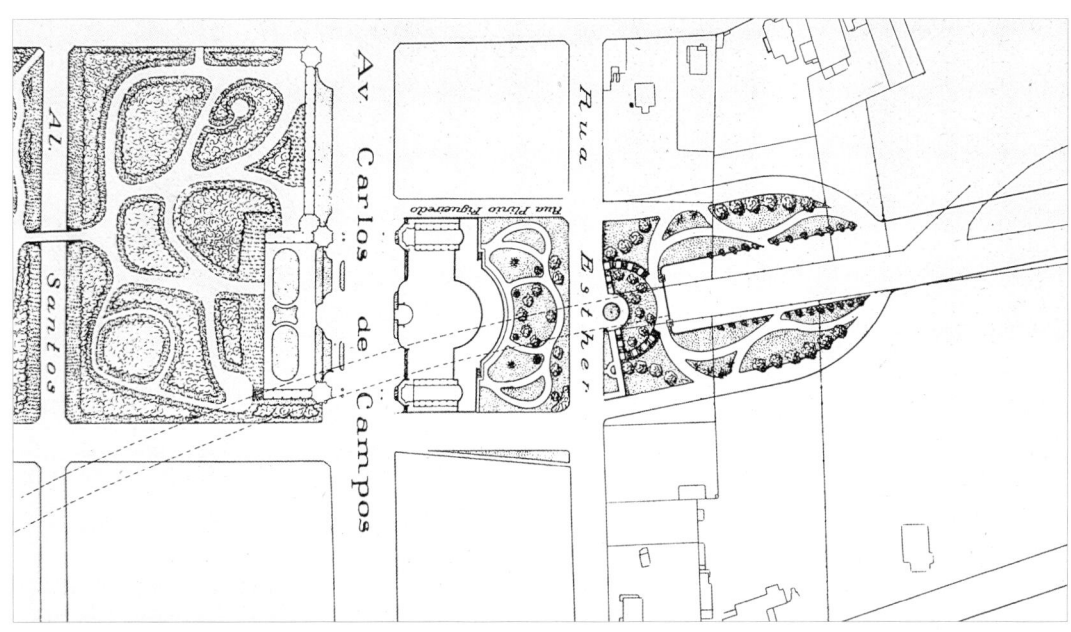

10 **Belvedere do Trianon**

Aussicht zum Anhangabaú-Tal
View facing Anhangabaú valley

11 **Entwurfszeichnung
Proposal**

Tunnel und Mirante Trianon
Tunnel and Mirante Trianon

Prestes Maia (1930)

12 **Belvedere do Trianon**

Tunnelmund und Aussichtsturm
Tunnel entry and observation tower

GALERIEN: ÖFFENTLICHER RAUM UND PRIVATE GRUNDSTÜCKSENTWICKLUNG

GALERIEN UND STÄDTEBAULICHE REGELN

Für Prestes Maia kann das historische Zentrum São Paulos ab den 1920er Jahren den Anforderungen an eine sich rasch modernisierende Stadt nicht mehr gerecht werden. Er schlägt daher vor, zentrale Nutzungen in das westlich angrenzende Centro Novo zu verlagern. Für ihn sind diese Funktionen nicht unbedingt an den alten Stadtkern gebunden. Er ist überzeugt, dass ihre Lage viel eher beeinflusst wird durch den Charakter und die Erreichbarkeit eines Ortes, besonders in wachsenden Städten.[1]

Prestes Maias Planungen sehen ein System aus Schnellstraßen vor, das direkt an das Centro Novo anschließt. Im Gegensatz zum Stadtkern verfügt der Stadtteil über ein großzügig zugeschnittenes städtebauliches Gerüst.

Die Maschenweite des Erschließungssystems, die Breite der Straßenprofile und der Besatz mit öffentlichen Räumen entsprechen Prestes Maias Vorstellung von zeitgemäßen und repräsentativen Stadträumen. Damit bestehen ideale Voraussetzungen für die Weiterentwicklung des Stadtteils zu einem hochwertigen Standort für Dienstleistungsangebote und Kultur.

Bereits Ende der 1920er Jahre wird im Bereich der Innenstadt die Entwicklung durch ortsbezogene städtebauliche Regeln gesteuert. Sie regulieren die bauliche Dichte, die Gebäudehöhe und sie bestimmen die Ausbildung von Straßenprofilen.[2]

Für repräsentative Bereiche des Centro Novo schlägt Prestes Maia eine neue Festsetzung vor.[3] Sie verknüpft die zulässige Gebäudehöhe mit dem Flächenmaß öffentlich zugänglicher Erdgeschossflächen. Mit dieser Festlegung verbindet er mehrere städtebauliche Ziele:

- Das öffentliche Erschließungssystem wird als fein verzweigtes Netz in den Gebäudeblocks weitergeführt.
- In der Innenstadt steht mehr Fläche für den Fußgängerverkehr zur Verfügung.[4]
- Es entstehen immissions- und witterungsgeschützte Fußgängerbereiche.
- Mit dem erweiterten Erschließungssystem vervielfachen sich gleichzeitig auch die Flächen für Läden und Dienstleistungsangebote.[5]
- Schrittweise steigt damit die Attraktivität des Centro Novo.[6]

Mit der neuen Festsetzung gewinnt der Stadtteil ein Alleinstellungsmerkmal als neues innerstädtisches Zentrum - gegenüber anderen Stadtteilen São Paulos, aber auch im Vergleich zu konkurrierenden Großstädten. Gleichzeitig wird damit ein wichtiger Anreiz formuliert, der Investitionen im Centro Novo stimulieren soll, und damit die bauliche Entwicklung des Zentrums vorantreibt.[7]

Für diese Festsetzung greift Prestes Maias auf Vorbilder zurück. Dazu gehören die historischen Galerie-Bauten in italienischen und französischen Großstädten sowie der nicht realisierte Entwurf der ‚Galeria de Crystal' des Architekten Jules Martin. Martins 1890 veröffentlichter Plan sah vor, vier Baublocks in der Altstadt São Paulos miteinander zu verbinden.[8]

1938 wird die städtebauliche Festlegung zur Ausbildung von einheitlich geschlossenen Baufluchten gestrichen. Stattdessen treten 1940 und 1941 Ersatzregeln in Kraft. Das Dekret Nr. 41 beschränkt sich zunächst auf Neubauten entlang der Avenida Ipiranga. Es verlangt die Ausbildung von durchlässigen und durchquerbaren Erdgeschossbereichen. Gebäude mit mehr als 20 Etagen müssen im Erdgeschoss einen Übergang als Portal, Galerie, Kolonnade oder offene Arkade ausbilden. Die Bauteile dürfen eine Breite von 3,5m und eine Fläche von 30m² nicht unterschreiten.

---

[1] Prestes Maia (1930): S. 55

[2] Die Phasen der jeweils unterschiedlichen Festsetzungen lassen sich heute noch stellenweise im Stadtgrundriss ablesen. Beispielsweise reagiert das Lei n. 3.427 (Código de Obras Arthur Saboya) auf potentiell entstehenden Hochhausbauten. Ab 1929 sind zulässige Gebäudehöhe und Geschosszahl jeweils mit bestimmten Straßenzügen verbunden; Costa (2010): S. 110

[3] Hugh Ferriss illustriert 1929 das stadträumliche Potential des New Yorker Zoning Laws von 1914/18.; Ferriss (1929); vgl. dazu auch Koolhaas (1999); Zahiri (2013). Prestes Maia verweist auf unterschiedliche städtebauliche Regelwerke, u.a. auch auf das New-Yorker Zoning-Law; Prestes Maia (1930): S. 181 f.

[4] Prestes Maia (1930): S. 55 f.

[5] Costa (2015): S. 4

[6] 1938 müssen gemäß Lei n. 1.366 die Fassaden entlang der Rua Marconi zugunsten einer Ensemblewirkung einer einheitlichen gestalterischen Linie folgen; Costa (2010): S. 110

[7] Aleixo (2005): S. 141

[8] Der Entwurf sieht eine Abfolge aus Galeriebauten vor, die die Baufelder zwischen Rua São Bonifácio und Rua Quinze de Novembro durchqueren. Das Areal liegt südlich des Anhangabaú-Tal. Prestes Maias Festsetzung gelten dagegen für den nördlich anschließenden Stadtbereich; Toledo (1996): S. 60

Sie müssen zudem mindestens 1/3 der Gehwegseite des Grundstücks einnehmen und dürfen für Außengastronomie in Anspruch genommen werden. Projekten, die diese Anforderungen erfüllen und deren Höhe 39m nicht überschreitet, können Vergünstigungen eingeräumt werden.[9]

Das 1941 verabschiedete Dekret Nr. 92 fordert schließlich für alle Gebäude im Centro Novo die Ausbildung von Durchgängen im Erdgeschoss.[10] Entlang von 18m breiten Straßen beschränkt die Vorschrift die zulässige Gebäudehöhe auf eine Skala zwischen 50m und 80m.[11] Beginnt der Hauptbaukörper dagegen oberhalb einer öffentlich zugänglichen Erdgeschosszone, darf die Gebäudehöhe 80m überschreiten. Die zulässige Überbauung der Grundstücksfläche im Erdgeschoss ist abhängig vom Grundstückstyp. Überbaut werden dürfen bei Standard-Grundstücken 25% der Grundfläche, bei Eckgrundstücken bis zu 30% sowie bei Solitärbauten bis zu 35%.[12]

GALERIE ALS GEBÄUDETYP

Ab den 1930er Jahren entstehen im Stadtteil Centro Novo erste Galeriebauten.[13] Dabei wird die Ausbildung des Gebäudetyps durch unterschiedliche Faktoren beeinflusst. Neben den städtebaulichen Festsetzungen gehören dazu Grundstückslage und -zuschnitt, Marktanforderungen sowie das zur Verfügung stehende Investitionsvolumen. Ende der 1950er Jahre tragen Wettbewerbsverfahren dazu bei, den neuen Gebäudetyp zu präzisieren.[14]

Die städtebaulichen Festsetzungen verlangen ein weitgehend offen zugängliches Erdgeschoss, unabhängig vom Grundstückszuschnitt. Auf langgestreckten Parzellen entstehen zunächst Durchgangspassagen; ein Rückgriff auf das in Europa historisch bekannte Galeriemotiv.

Ein weiterentwickelter Gebäudetyp nutzt das offene Erdgeschoss als Auftakt für ein dreidimensionales Erschließungsgefüge.

Die dazu notwendigen Verbindungselemente müssen die Stadtebene und die darüber liegenden Geschosse prägnant und spannungsvoll verbinden. Schließlich sollen die Passanten motiviert werden, die über dem Erdgeschoss liegenden Ebenen zu erkunden. Eingesetzt werden dazu Erschließungssysteme aus Treppen, Rolltreppen und Rampen. Kombiniert werden diese Elemente mit mehrgeschossigen Gebäudeöffnungen, Lufträumen, Lichthöfen, Stadtloggien, großzügigen Fassadenöffnungen sowie bewegten Fassaden. Stellenweise sind auch die Dachebenen als Freiflächen und Dachgärten einbezogen.

Die Galeriebauten unterscheiden sich in ihrer räumlichen Konzeption und ihrem Nutzungsgefüge. Sie besitzen aber auch einige gleichbleibende Merkmale. Im Stadtbild machen die Gebäude auf sich aufmerksam. Dazu öffnen sich die Erdgeschoss- und Galerieflächen zu den umgebenden Straßen- und Platzräumen. Der Anteil an Erschließungs- und Bewegungsflächen ist häufig so großzügig dimensioniert, dass die kommerziellen Nutzungen nicht dominieren. Entsprechend laden die Bauten zum Betreten und Erkunden ein.

In den 1960er Jahren entstehen Betreiberkonzepte mit Bezeichnungen wie ‚Grandes', ‚Presidente' oder ‚Metrópole'. Die Galerien bieten dazu einen Mix aus Kultur- und Konsumangeboten, der sich überwiegend an die Mittel- und Oberschicht São Paulos richtet. Dazu gehören insbesondere exklusive Modegeschäfte und Buchhandlungen, ergänzt durch Großkinos, Bars, Cafés und Restaurants. Neben rein gewerblich genutzten Projekten entstehen auch gemischte Komplexe, die Läden, Gewerbe- und Büroflächen mit Wohnungen kombinieren.

IMAGEWANDEL DES CENTRO NOVO

Ab Mitte der 1960er Jahre verliert das Centro Novo schrittweise sein positives Image.[15] 1964 beschränkt die Militärregierung Treffen in öffentlichen Räumen sowie zulässige Nutzungen.

---

[9] Costa (2014): S. 3

[10] Somekh (1997): S. 129; Aleixo (2005): S. 140; Costa (2010): S. 108, 114, 121

[11] Von dieser Bindung sind Gebäude ausgenommen, die städtebaulich prägnante Stellen besetzen; Prestes Maia (1930): S. 76

[12] Costa (2010): S. 108 f.

[13] Costa (2015): S. 1

[14] Dazu gehören die Wettbewerbe zur Galeria Metrópole sowie zum Sede Social Jockey Club; Ferroni (2008): S. 161; Ferroni, Shundi Iwamizu (2013): S. 149 f. sowie Acrópole 259/4 (1960): S. 159. Zur städtebaulichen Qualitätssicherung lobt Prestes Maia ergänzend einen Preis aus, der die „schönsten Gebäude der Stadt" auszeichnet; Lei n. 1.573; in Costa (2010): S. 115

[15] Costa (2015): S. 6

[16] Rupf (2015): S. 77

[17] Rupf (2015): S. 88

[18] Rupf (2015): S. 80

[19] Operação Urbana Centro (Lei 12.349 de 6 de Junho de 1997 do Município de São Paulo)

[20] Lei n. 12.350; in Rupf (2015): S. 90

[21] Coy (2001): S. 285

Die Durchlässigkeit der Galeriebauten und ihr Angebot an Clubs, Bars und Kinos widersprechen diesen Auflagen. Zudem ist der Stadtteil besonders belastet durch die rasche Zunahme des Automobilverkehrs. Zeitgleich verschiebt sich der Entwicklungsschwerpunkt vom Centro Novo zur Avenida Paulista.

Ab den 1970er Jahren unternimmt die Stadt unterschiedliche Versuche, um die Attraktivität des Centro Novos zu erhöhen. Zwischen 1975 und 1979 wird der Revitalisierungsplan zur Aufwertung des zentralen Bereichs verabschiedet. Der Ausbau der U-Bahn-Linie in Ost-West-Richtung dient dazu, die Erreichbarkeit des Zentrums mit öffentlichen Verkehrsmitteln zu verbessern. Ergänzend werden ausgewählte Straßen zu Fußgängerbereichen umgewidmet. Die Maßnahmen sollen auch dazu beitragen, neue Investitionen für die Immobilienentwicklung zu gewinnen.[16]

Das 1993 gestartete Programm ‚Pro Centro' sieht zur Revitalisierung der Bereiche Sé und República eine Aufwertung von ausgewählten öffentlichen Räumen vor. Dabei werden teilweise Fußgängerbereiche wieder für Fahrzeuge geöffnet.[17] Über öffentlich-private Partnerschaften fördert das Programm auch die Vermietung von Galerieflächen an Nutzende mit alternativen Nutzungskonzepten. Trotz dieser Maßnahmen steigt der innerstädtische Leerstand in den 1990er Jahren weiter an.[18]

Ende der 1990er Jahre versucht die Stadt verstärkt öffentlich-private Partnerschaften zu initiieren. Dazu wird 1997 das Gesetz ‚Operação Urbana Centro' verabschiedet.[19] Es zielt darauf ab, die Innenstadt durch eine größere Nutzungsvielfalt wiederzubeleben und sieht dazu eine finanzielle Förderung von Bestands- und Neubauten vor. Gefördert werden Projekte mit öffentlichen Nutzungen in den Bereichen Kultur, Bildung und Freizeit. Das zeitgleich verabschiedete Fassadengesetz sieht vor, denkmalgeschützte Gebäude von der städtischen Grundsteuer (IPTU) zu befreien.[20]

In der Zusammenschau bleibt die Wirksamkeit der unterschiedlichen Programme jeweils hinter den Erwartungen zurück. Das Initiieren von Maßnahmen zur Revitalisierung der Innenstadt São Paulos stellt damit weiterhin besondere Anforderungen an Planung, Politik und Stadtgesellschaft.

GALERIEN UND REVITALISIERUNG

Um den Abwertungsprozess des Centro Novos abzumildern, haben Betreibende von Galerien und Läden über einen längeren Zeitraum hinweg ihre Nutzungskonzepte verändert und angepasst. Dabei erweist sich die Kombination von auffälliger Architektursprache, großzügigen Erschließungssystemen und kleinteilig aufteilbaren Gewerbeeinheiten als Vorteil.

Die meisten Betreibenden haben ihr Waren- und Dienstleistungsangebot inzwischen auf bestimmte Zielgruppen ausgerichtet. Entsprechend ist ihr Angebot stark spezialisiert und richtet sich dezidiert an eine wiederkehrende Kundschaft und ihre Präferenzen. Die jeweils angebotenen Dienstleistungen und Produkte sind in typischen Einkaufszentren nicht zu finden.[21]

Je nach Nutzergruppe etabliert sich ein jeweils spezifischer Angebotsmix, unterlegt mit ergänzenden Angeboten wie Restaurants, Cafés oder Dachgärten. Dabei sorgt die besondere Gestaltsprache der Galeriebauten für eine einprägsame Adresse. Entsprechend hat inzwischen eine neue Schicht an Stadtbewohnern die Galerien für sich entdeckt.

Die Maßnahmen zur Revitalisierung der Innenstadt zielen darauf ab, das weitgehend kommerziell geprägte Nutzungsgefüge des Centro Novo durch Kultur- und Freizeitangebote anzureichern. Im Rahmen dieser Anstrengungen sind das Kulturzentrum SESC 24 de Maio und die Praça das Artes entstanden. Beide Projekte greifen Elemente des historischen Galerien-Konzepts auf und interpretieren diese mit zeitgenössischen Mitteln.

GALLERIES: PUBLIC SPHERE AND PRIVATE REAL ESTATE DEVELOPMENT

GALLERIES AND URBAN DEVELOPMENT RULES

For Prestes Maia, the historic centre of São Paulo was incapable of meeting the requirements for a rapidly modernising city. Alternatively, he suggested shifting uses connected to the old city centre to the adjacent western Centro Novo. In his view, central uses were not necessarily tied to the city centre. Their future location could be influenced by the character of a place as well as its accessibility, particularly in growing cities.[1]

Through its direct connection to the planned motorway system, Centro Novo would be excellently connected in the future. In contrast to the city centre, this part of the city featured a generously dimensioned urban structure. The mesh of its access system, its street profile and the equipment with public areas corresponded to Prestes Maia's ideas of modern and representative urban spaces. Therefore, conditions were ideal for a further development of the quarter into a diverse and high-quality location for service providers and cultural uses.

As early as the late 1920s, development in the inner city was controlled by site-specific urban design regulations. They determined urban density, building height and also the shape of street profiles.[2] In a departure from this, Prestes Maia suggested for certain areas of Centro Novo an alternative rule.[3] It linked permissible building height to the surface measure of a publicly accessible ground floor area. Through this regulation, he combined several urban design aims:

- The public access system will be extended through a finely branching network inside the urban fabric.
- Pedestrian traffic gains more space.[4]
- Immission- and weather-protected pedestrian areas are created.
- The extended access system simultaneously multiplies the available space for shops and service providers.[5]
- Overall, the regulation intends to increase the appeal of Centro Novo as a new inner-city centre.[6]

Gradually, a complex urban fabric emerges - singular among other quarters of São Paulo and compared to competing major cities. With this urban design rule, the district would gain a unique selling point; compared to other districts of São Paulo, but also compared to competing large cities. At the same time, an important incentive is formulated to motivate capital investments, which in turn would drive the urban development of Centro Novo.[7]

For this setting, Prestes Maia drew on models. These include the historic gallery buildings in major Italian and French cities, as well as the unrealised design for the 'Galeria de Crystal' by architect Jules Martin. Martin proposed to connect four building blocks in the historical centre of São Paulo.[8]

In 1938, the urban design regulation regarding uniform street shapes was discarded. Instead, Prestes Maia's replacement rules went into effect in 1940 and 1941. Decree no. 41 was initially limited to new buildings along Avenida Ipiranga. It required the formation of permeable and traversable ground floor areas. Buildings with more than 20 floors would have to include a ground floor passage in the shape of a portal, gallery or colonnade. Structural parts could not be narrower than 3.5m or smaller than 30m^2. Also, they had to take up at least one third of the pavement side of the plot. Their use as outdoor gastronomy was permitted. Projects fulfilling these requirements at less than 39m of building height could be granted benefits.[9]

Finally, Decree no. 92 from 1941 required all buildings in Centro Novo to feature passages at ground level.[10]

---

1 Prestes Maia (1930): p. 55

2 The phases of the varying specifications can still partially be seen in the city's layout today. For instance, Lei n. 3.427 (Código de Obras Arthur Saboya) reacted to potentially emerging high-rise buildings. From 1929, permissible building heights and number of floors were tied to certain streets; Costa (2010): p. 110

3 In 1929, Hugh Ferriss illustrated the urban space potential of the New York zoning laws of 1914/18; Ferriss (1929); cf. also Koolhaas (1999); Zahiri (2013). Prestes Maia referred to various urban development regulations, among others the New York zoning law; Prestes Maia (1930): p. 181 f.

4 Prestes Maia (1930): p. 55 f.

5 Costa (2015): p. 4

6 In 1938, the facades along Rua Marconi had to follow a uniform design concept intended to create an ensemble effect according to Lei n. 1.366; Costa (2010): p. 110

7 Aleixo (2005): p. 141

8 The design stipulated a sequence of gallery buildings crossing the plots between Rua São Bonifácio and Rua Quinze de Novembro. The area is located south of the Anhangabaú valley. Prestes Maia's specifications apply to the urban area adjacent to the north; Toledo (1996): p. 60

9 Costa (2014): p. 3

10 Somekh (1997): p. 129; Aleixo (2005): p. 140; Costa (2010): p. 108, 114, 121

13 **Galeria Metrópole**
(S. 23 / p. 23)

Blick aus dem bepflanzten
Innenhof in die Galeria Metrópole
View from the planted courtyard
into the Galeria Metrópole

14 **Galeria de Crystal**

Jules Martin (1898)

Perspektive
Perspective

15 **Galeria de Crystal**

Jules Martin (1898)

Lageplan
Site plan

Along streets with 18m width, buildings had to be between 50m and 80m high.[11] However, if the main building structure only started above the ground floor zone, exceeding the maximum building height of 80 m was permissible. Permissible superstructures for the ground floor plot area depended on the plot type. In standard plots, 25% of the floor space could be covered; in corner plots 30% and with detached buildings up to 35%.[12]

GALLERY AS A BUILDING TYPE

From the 1930s, various gallery buildings were created in the Centro Novo quarter.[13] The development of the building type was influenced by various factors. In addition to the urban design regulations, these included plot layouts and sizes, market requirements as well as the available investment volume. In the late 1950s, a series of competitions contributed additionally to the specification of the new building type.[14]

The urban design rules required an open and accessible ground floor regardless of plot layout. On elongated plots, passageways were initially created; a recourse to the gallery motif historically known in Europe.

A further developed building type used the ground floor as a prelude to a three-dimensional access structure. The connecting elements required for this had to link the ground level and the floors above it in a concise and exciting way. After all, pedestrians were to be motivated to explore the higher floors. To achieve this, escalators and ramps were employed. These elements were combined with generous facade openings, atriums, urban loggias and curved facades. In places, the roof levels were also incorporated as open spaces and roof gardens.

The resulting gallery buildings can be distinguished by their spatial concepts and use arrangements. Beyond that, they also feature a series of consistent characteristics. As ensembles with an open concept, they attract attention in the streetscape.

Their portion of access and movement spaces is generously dimensioned, ensuring commercial uses are not dominant. Accordingly, they invite people to enter and explore.

In the 1960s the gallery buildings provided a mixture of culture and consumer venues, mainly targeting São Paulo's middle and upper classes. This included in particular exclusive fashion boutiques and bookshops, supplemented by multiplexes, bars, cafés and restaurants. Besides projects with exclusively commercial use, there were also mixed complexes which combined shops and commercial or office spaces with residential apartments.

CENTRO NOVO IMAGE CHANGE

In the late 1960s, Centro Novo gradually lost its positive image.[15] From 1964, the military government regulated gatherings in public spaces and permissible uses. The permeability of the gallery buildings and their provision of clubs, bars and cinemas conflicted with these stipulations, which led to a plunge in visitor numbers. Additionally, the quarter was particularly burdened by the rapid increase of vehicle traffic. Simultaneously, the development emphasis shifted from Centro Novo to Avenida Paulista.

From the 1970s, the city made various attempts at enhancing the attractiveness of Centro Novo. Between 1975 and 1979, a revitalisation plan was passed to upgrade the central area. An expansion of the east-west underground line served to improve access to the centre via public transport. Also, selected streets were transformed into pedestrian areas. These measures were also intended to win new investors for real estate developments.[16]

The programme "Pro Centro" started in 1993 aimed at upgrading selected public spaces to revitalise the areas Sé and República. It partially reopened pedestrian areas to vehicle traffic.[17] Through public-private partnerships, the programme also promoted the leasing of gallery spaces to users with alternative use concepts.

---

11 Buildings occupying significant spots in the city in terms of urban development were exempt from this obligation; Prestes Maia (1930): p. 76

12 Costa (2010): p. 108 f.

13 Costa (2015): p. 1

14 This included competitions such as the one for the Galeria Metrópole or the Sede Social Jockey Club. Ferroni (2008): p. 161; Ferroni, Shundi Iwamizu (2013): p. 149 f. as well as Acrópole 259/4 (1960): p. 159. To ensure urban development quality, Prestes Maia additionally offered a reward for the 'most beautiful buildings' of the city; Lei n. 1.573; in Costa (2010): p. 115

15 Costa (2015): p. 6

16 Rupf (2015): p. 77

17 Rupf (2015): p. 88

18 Rupf (2015): p. 80

19 Operação Urbana Centro (Lei 12.349 de 6 de Junho de 1997 do Município de São Paulo)

20 Lei n. 12.350; in Rupf (2015): p. 90

21 Coy (2001): p. 285

In spite of these measures, inner-city vacancies kept rising during the 1990s.[18] In the late 1990s, the city increasingly attempted to initiate public-private partnerships. To this end, the bill "Operação Urbana Centro" was passed in 1997.[19] It aimed at revitalising the inner city through a greater variety of uses and stipulated financial support for existing and new buildings. Support was available for projects with public uses in culture, education and leisure. The simultaneously passed facade bill stipulated exempting landmarked buildings from the municipal real estate tax (IPTU).[20]

Viewed together, the effect of the various concepts fell behind expectations. Initiating suitable measures for revitalising São Paulo's inner city therefore continues to pose a particular challenge for planning, policymakers and urban society.

GALLERIES AND REVITALISATION

In order to overcome the devaluation process of Centro Novo, gallery and shop operators have to adjust their use concepts over an extended period of time. A combination of conspicuous architectural expression, representative access systems and small sized commercial units has proven to be a benefit.

Most operators at this point have geared their range of goods and services to certain target groups. Accordingly, their ranges are highly specialised and decidedly address a returning customer base and its needs. Services and products offered in these places cannot be found in typical shopping centres.[21] Depending on specific user groups, a certain mix of uses emerges and is supported by additional offers such as restaurants, cafés or rooftop gardens. The particular appearance of the gallery buildings creates a memorable destination. By now, a new class of urbanites have discovered the galleries for themselves.

In the context of the city's effort to revitalise the inner city and to enrich it with cultural and leisure uses, SESC 24 de Maio and Praça das Artes have emerged over the past years. Both projects reference elements of the historical gallery concept and interpret them with contemporary means.

ÖFFENTLICHER RAUM UND HETEROTOPIE

Europäisch geprägte Städte werden strukturiert durch öffentliche Räume.[1] Platz-, Park- und Straßenräume sollen für alle zugänglich sein[2] und dabei ohne Kontrolle und Nutzungsbestimmung[3] auskommen. Was aber, wenn diese Ordnungsvorstellung zusammenbricht?

São Paulos Stadtteil Centro Novo eignet sich gut, um die Konsequenzen näher zu betrachten. Während öffentliche Räume in Europa meist zu beliebten Treffpunkten der Stadtgesellschaft gehören, werden sie in São Paulo vielfach gemieden. Inzwischen hat sich ein Teil der Platz- und Straßenräume in reine Transitflächen verwandelt. Nach Ladenschluss und bei unübersichtlichen Verhältnissen wirken sie unsicher. Entsprechend werden sie rasch durchquert oder grundsätzlich ausgeblendet.

Stellenweise sind dazu Ausweichräume entstanden. Zu den Beispielen gehören die Galeriegebäude Metrópole, do Rock, Nova Barão sowie die beiden neu gebauten Projekte SESC 24 de Maio und Praça das Artes. Die Gebäude werden jeweils von privaten Sicherheitskräften überwacht. Zudem stellen die Grundstücksverwaltungen Hausregeln auf. Damit wird den Besuchenden nicht nur Schutz, sondern auch mehr Bewegungsfreiheit eingeräumt. Die hier beschriebenen Projekte übernehmen aber nur teilweise die Funktionen öffentlicher Räume. Als Zufluchtsorte und als Orte des Experiments[4] lassen sich ihre Merkmale besser mithilfe des Begriffs ‚Heterotopie'[5] fassen.

SÃO PAULO: ÖFFENTLICHE RÄUME VS. HETEROTOPIEN

Foucault führt die Bezeichnung ‚Heterotopie' in den 1960er Jahren ein, um auf eine alternative Raumkategorie zu verweisen. Als „realisierte Utopie"[6] verbindet sie Merkmale privater und öffentlicher Räume.[7] Heterotopien sind häufig zunächst unsichtbar,[8] von ihrer Umgebung isoliert und in ihrer Zugänglichkeit kontrolliert.[9]

Darüber hinaus etablieren Heterotopien meist eigene Vorschriften[10], die dazu dienen, abweichendes Verhalten zu schützen.[11] Das Spektrum möglicher Heterotopien ist kulturabhängig. Im Laufe der Zeit können sie verschwinden, aufgelöst oder ersetzt werden.[12]

Die hier vorgestellten Projekte weisen unterschiedliche Merkmale von Heterotopien auf. Am ausgeprägtesten gilt das für die Projekte SESC 24 de Maio (SESC) und Centro Cultural São Paulo (CCSP), in abgeschwächter Form auch für die historischen Galeriebauten und die Verkehrsräume Minhocão und Mirante. Die Projekte illustrieren damit eine Reihe von sozialräumlichen Merkmalen, die für das Funktionieren von öffentlichen Räumen maßgeblich sind, im Kontext europäischer Städte aber weniger sichtbar werden.

Öffentlich

Öffentliche Räume stehen allen offen - so ein wichtiges Paradigma zur europäischen Stadt. Dabei bleibt umstritten, auf welche Weise für die Nutzenden ein ausgleichender Ordnungsrahmen entsteht. Jacobs und Feldtkeller zufolge etablieren sich ausgleichende Verhaltensregeln, wenn öffentliche Flächen durch unterschiedliche Nutzergruppen in Anspruch genommen werden.[13] Dagegen liegt für Habermas die Verantwortlichkeit für das Durchsetzen eines Ordnungsrahmens bei den Sicherheitskräften.[14]

São Paulos Freiräume zeigen, dass das freie Interagieren unterschiedlicher Sozialgruppen nicht unbedingt ausgleichend wirkt. Sind Ordnungskräfte abwesend, bestimmt die stärkste Gruppe die örtlich geltenden Verhaltensregeln. Wer nicht zu dieser Gruppe gehört, muss sich mit den Auswirkungen arrangieren. Alternativ werden öffentliche Räume gemieden, erst zeitweise und schließlich dauerhaft.

---

[1] Feldtkeller (1995): S. 52, 67
[2] Feldtkeller (1995): S. 57, 68, 88
[3] Feldtkeller (1995): S. 40 f., 58 f., 89
[4] Foucault (1978): S. 95, 228; Fraser (1992): S. 122 f.; Cenzatti (2008): S. 83
[5] griech. ‚hetero'= anderer, griech. ‚topos'= Ort
[6] Foucault (1966): S. 10
[7] De Cauter und Dehaene (2008): S. 91, 94
[8] Foucault (1992): S. 38
[9] Foucault (1966): S. 18 f.
[10] Foucault (1966): S. 21
[11] Foucault (1966): S. 12
[12] Foucault (1966): S. 13
[13] Jacobs (1963): S. 28 f. und Feldtkeller (1995): S. 37, 59, 71
[14] Habermas (1965): S. 11, 41

16 **Grandes Galerias**
Werbeanzeige
Advertisement
Alfredo Mathias (1960)

17 **Grandes Galerias**
Innenraum
Werbeanzeige
Inner Space
Advertisement
Alfredo Mathias (1960)

Offenbar ist für ein gelingendes Miteinander im öffentlichen Raum ein schützender Rahmen erforderlich. Dieser Rahmen kann nicht allein durch die Nutzenden hergestellt werden. Allerdings können auch Ordnungskräfte auf Dauer keine übergeordneten gesellschaftlichen Konflikte lösen, die sich im öffentlichen Raum als Sicherheitsprobleme artikulieren. Dies ist Aufgabe von Politik und Verwaltung.

Zugang und Regeln

Ein wesentliches Merkmal öffentlicher Räume ist ihre Zugänglichkeit für alle Gesellschaftsgruppen.[15] Dagegen sind das CCSP, das SESC, aber auch die historischen Galeriebauten nur eingeschränkt zugänglich. Das Betreten der Grundstücke wird über kontrollierbare Ein- und Ausgänge gebündelt.[16] Zusätzlich ist der Zugang jeweils auch zeitlich eingeschränkt.

Darüber hinaus unterliegen die Nutzungen vor Ort bestimmten Regeln. Neu Hinzukommende übernehmen diese Verhaltensregeln freiwillig, überwiegend durch das Beobachten der bereits Anwesenden. Dazu gehört es u.a. nicht zu stören, gemeinsam genutzte Flächen sparsam in Anspruch zu nehmen oder von erlaubten Nutzungen nicht abzuweichen. Ordnungskräfte sind hauptsächlich im Hintergrund präsent. Sie greifen erst bei andauerndem Fehlverhalten ein. Sie können Störende verwarnen oder ein Hausverbot aussprechen.

Die durch alle Anwesenden antizipierten Regeln bieten Schutz und beeinflussen die Aufenthaltsqualität des Ortes. Erst darauf aufbauend, lässt es sich sorgenfrei lesen, tanzen, recherchieren, diskutieren oder sich ausruhen.

Nutzungsvielfalt

Für Feldtkeller ist die Nutzung öffentlicher Räume „weitgehend unvorhersehbar".[17] Besteht für möglichst viele Gesellschaftsgruppen die Chance zur Teilhabe, führen ihre unterschiedlichen Bedürfnisse und Wünsche zu einer großen Bandbreite an Nutzungen.[18] Diese Vielfalt trägt wesentlich zur Lebendigkeit öffentlicher Freiräume bei.[19]

Eine gemischte Gruppe Nutzende mit einer großen Bandbreite an Wünschen und Interessen setzt eine tolerante Gesellschaft voraus, denn das mögliche Nutzungsspektrum wird durch die Normen und Wertvorstellungen der Mehrheitsgesellschaft bestimmt. Davon abweichende Gruppen sind unerwünscht und können ausgegrenzt werden. Habermas zufolge sind öffentliche Räume deshalb immer auch exklusive Räume.[20]

Entsprechend fehlt Personen, die abweichende Interessen verfolgen, die Möglichkeiten sich im öffentlichen Raum zu entfalten. Heterotopien erlauben es, diese Nutzungen in geschützte Räume zu verlagern. Als Zuflucht und sicherer Hafen[21] bieten sie einen ‚Erlebnisraum', der „den Einzelnen gesellschaftsfähig hält".[22]

Projekte wie das CCSP, das SESC und die Galeria do Rock ermöglichen Praktiken, die sich im direkten Umfeld der Nutzenden nicht oder nur sehr eingeschränkt verfolgen lassen. Dazu gehören beispielsweise Tanz, Musizieren und Sport, aber auch grundlegende Bedürfnisse wie Schutz vor Witterung, Orte zum Ausruhen und Lernen oder sichere Spielbereiche für Kinder.

Keines der vorgestellten Projekte schließt den Zutritt von Randgruppen aus. Klassenzugehörigkeit spielt hier keine Rolle. Die Anwesenheit von sehr unterschiedlichen Gesellschaftsgruppen macht deutlich, dass ein vielfältiges Miteinander einen schützenden Rahmen braucht.

Ästhetik

Heterotopien bieten eine Auszeit gegenüber dem Alltäglichen.[23] Sie interpretieren dazu Vorstellungen einer idealen Welt.[24] Als Orte der „Kompensation"[25] bieten sie einen Raum der Illusion, der jeden realen Raum, alle Orte, in denen das menschliche Leben aufgeteilt ist, als illusorisch entlarvt. Oder sie formulieren eine Alternative, die „so perfekt, so akribisch, so übersichtlich, wie unserer Raum ungeordnet, schlecht gebaut und durcheinander ist".[26]

Die im Buch vorgestellten Projekte spannen jeweils einen eigenen ästhetischen Rahmen auf, der die Nutzer in ein charakteristisches Raumerlebnis einbindet. Dazu gehören ein spezifisches Raumangebot sowie besondere Ausblicke auf die angrenzenden Stadträume.

Darüber hinaus formulieren die Projekte aber jeweils auch spezifische Themen. Beispielsweise ist das SESC als verfeinerter Rohbau konzipiert. Das Projekt nutzt die Betonkonstruktion eines Vorgängerbaus mit. Großzügig eingefügte Öffnungen rahmen Ausschnitte angrenzender Gebäude. Im Durchgehen entfaltet sich damit ein Nacheinander unterschiedlicher ‚Stadtbilder'. Auf dem Weg entsteht zugleich eine Collage, die Ausschnitte von unterschiedlichen Nutzungen wie Tanz, Sport und Bibliothek verknüpft. Den Abschluss bildet das Dach-Schwimmbad, das an die Ausstattung eines Kreuzfahrtschiffs erinnert.

In ähnlicher Weise entfalten auch die übrigen Projekte jeweils eigene ästhetische Programme:

---

[15] Habermas (1965): S. 11, 98 f.
[16] Foucault (1966): S. 18
[17] Feldtkeller (1995): S. 89
[18] Jacobs (1963): S. 91
[19] Feldtkeller (1995): S. 51; Gehl (2012): S. 37; Jacobs (1963): S. 97
[20] Siebel (2004): S. 27
[21] De Cauter und Dehaene (2008): S. 97
[22] Schäfer-Biermann et al. (2016): S. 87
[23] De Cauter und Dehaene (2008): S. 92
[24] Faubion (2008): S. 31 f.
[25] Foucault (1992): S. 45
[26] Muzzio und Muzzio-Rentas (2008): S. 146
[27] Foucault (1992): S. 39
[28] Schäfer-Biermann et al. (2016): S. 83
[29] De Cauter und Dehaene (2008): S. 4

- Das Verkehrsbauwerk Minhocão durchzieht die Stadt in sanften Wellenbewegungen. Die Trasse ist aus der hektischen Stadtebene herausgehoben und bleibt frei von Nutzungen. Von hier aus lässt sich das Stadtgefüge mit einem ‚landschaftlichen Blick' neu entdecken.
- Das Kulturzentrum CCSP liegt als langgestrecktes ‚Schiff' an der Hangkante des Rio Itororó Flusstals. Die Nutzungen sind auf unterschiedlichen ‚Decks' verteilt und untereinander durch Stahlgangways und -treppen verbunden. Auf der Dachebene befindet sich ein Sonnendeck und eine Wiesenfläche.
- Die Gebäude des SESC und der Praça das Artes wirken jeweils wie unfertige Rohbauten. Damit betonen sie die Schmuckfassaden der angrenzenden Bebauung. Als große, begehbare Plastik bieten sie unerwartete Sicht- und Wegezusammenhänge. Zudem erlauben sie das Durchqueren der sonst überwiegend geschlossenen Baufelder des Centro Novo. Beim Entdecken des Blockinneren entfaltet sich ein sonst unsichtbares Gefüge.
- Die Galeria do Rock verknüpft psychedelische und surrealistische Gestaltelemente miteinander. Decken und Fassadenflächen sind fließend artikuliert und perforiert.

Heterotopie als Werkstatt

Jedes der vorgestellten Projekte hat Komponenten einer „realisierten Utopie"[27]. Sie ermöglichen den Nutzenden eigene Arten des Miteinanders zu erproben und verändert ihre Beziehung zu ihrer Umwelt.

- Die Hochstraße Minhocão kehrt probeweise die Hierarchie zwischen motorisiertem Individualverkehr und Fußgängern um.
- Vom Aussichtspunkt Mirante aus wird die tieferliegende Schnellstraße zu einem landschaftlichen Canyon.
- Im CCSP ruhen sich Wohnungslose und Touristen nebeneinander aus.
- Im Zwischengeschoss des SESC zeigen die Straßenkinder den Bildungsbürgern, wie Planschen geht.

Als ‚Orte der Andersartigkeit' greifen sie bestehende Gesellschaftsverhältnisse auf und ermöglichen es gleichzeitig, diese Verhältnisse infrage zu stellen.[28] Damit lassen sie sich auch als ‚Werkstätten' verstehen, um alternative Praktiken zu etablieren.[29]

Ausblick

Bemerkenswert ist, dass sich São Paulos Stadtgesellschaft selbst Ersatz schafft für fehlende oder unbenutzbare öffentliche Räume. Das Phänomen unterstreicht, dass funktionierende Platz-, Straßen- und Parkräume unverzichtbar sind. Zu hoffen ist, dass die mit den Projekten jeweils gesammelten Erfahrungen auch zu einer Wiederbelebung der öffentlichen Räume der Stadt beitragen.

PUBLIC SPHERE AND HETEROTOPIAS

Cities with European influence are structured by open spaces.[1] Squares, parks and streets are intended to be accessible to all[2] and do without terms of use[3]. However, what happens when this idea of order collapses?

São Paulo's Centro Novo quarter is a good place suited for taking a closer look at the consequences. The urban spaces in Centro Novo are comparable to squares and street spaces in European cities in terms of layout and design. While urban spaces in Europe usually are among the popular meeting points in urban societies, they are often avoided in São Paulo. A portion of the public spaces have transformed into mere transit areas at this point. After business hours and in unclear conditions, the spaces appear to be dangerous. People cross them quickly or ignore them as a matter of principle.

As a reaction to these circumstances in some places, alternative spaces have emerged. Particularly the gallery buildings Metrópole, do Rock, Nova Barão and the two new constructions SESC 24 de Maio and Praça das Artes have become established as fallback spaces. These spaces are monitored by private security staff. In addition, the property management establishes house rules. This way, users not only receive protection, but also more freedom of movement.

However, the projects described here only partially assume the functions of public spaces. As places of refuge and places of experimentation[4], their characteristics can be better described using the term 'heterotopia'.[5]

SÃO PAULO: PUBLIC SPACES VS. HETEROTOPIAS

French philosopher Michel Foucault introduced the term 'heterotopia' in the 1960s to refer to an alternative category of space.

As a 'realized utopia'[6] it combines features of private and public spaces. Heterotopias are often isolated from their surroundings[7] and access to them is monitored.[8] Beyond that, heterotopias usually establish further regulations[9], which serve to protect deviant behaviour.[10] Over time, these codes can be amended or redefined. The spectrum of possible heterotopias depends on the respective culture. Over time, heterotopias can disappear, be suspended or replaced.[11]

The projects presented here feature various characteristics of heterotopias. This applies most of all to SESC 24 de Maio (SESC) and Centro Cultural São Paulo (CCSP) and to a lesser extent also to the historic gallery buildings and the traffic spaces Minhocão and Mirante. The projects thus illustrate a number of socio-spatial characteristics that are relevant for the functioning of public spaces, but are less visible in the context of European cities.

Public sphere

Public spaces are open to everyone - a central paradigm for European cities. However, the manner in which a balancing framework of order is established is still disputed. According to urban theorist Jane Jacobs and city planner Andreas Feldtkeller, balancing codes of conduct are established when public areas are used by people from all parts of society.[12] German philosopher Jürgen Habermas, however, sees the responsibility for enforcing a framework of order with law enforcement.[13]

São Paulo's open spaces demonstrate that suitable codes of conduct cannot emerge simply through the free interaction of different individuals. Where law enforcement is absent, the strongest group determines the applicable code of conduct in the space. Other users have to come to terms with the consequences.

---

1 Feldtkeller (1995): p. 52, 67
2 Feldtkeller (1995): p. 57, 68, 88
3 Feldtkeller (1995): p. 40 f., 58 f., 89
4 Foucault (1978): p. 95, 228; Fraser (1992): p. 122 f.; Cenzatti (2008): p. 83
5 Greek 'hetero' = other, Greek 'topos' = place
6 Foucault (1966): p. 10
7 Foucault (1992): p. 38
8 Foucault (1966): p. 18 f.
9 Foucault (1966): p. 21
10 Foucault (1966): p. 12
11 Foucault (1966): p. 13
12 Jacobs (1963): p. 28 f. and Feldtkeller (1995): p. 37, 59, 71
13 Habermas (1965): p. 11, 41

18　Galeria Nova Baraõ

„Bald zugänglich, eine parallele Strasse zur Rua Marconi"

"Soon to be opened, a parallel street to Rua Marconi"

Werbeanzeige
Advertisement

Alfredo Mathias (1962)

14	Habermas (1965): p. 11, 98 f.
15	Foucault (1966): p. 18
16	Feldtkeller (1995): p. 89
17	Jacobs (1963): p. 91
18	Feldtkeller (1995): p. 51; Gehl (2012): p. 37; Jacobs (1963): p. 97
19	Siebel (2004): p. 27
20	De Cauter and Dehaene (2008): p. 97
21	Schäfer-Biermann et al. (2016): p. 87
22	De Cauter and Dehaene (2008): p. 92
23	Faubion (2008): p. 31 f.
24	Foucault (1992): p. 45
25	Muzzio and Muzzio-Rentas (2008): p. 146
26	Foucault (1992): p. 39
27	Schäfer-Biermann et al. (2016): p. 83
28	De Cauter and Dehaene (2008): p. 4

Where user groups are imbalanced, the safety of certain societal groups can be challenged. Gradually, these groups will then avoid public spaces - at first occasionally, then permanently.

It appears that a protective framework is required for successful cohesion in public spaces. This framework cannot be formed by the users themselves. However, law enforcement also cannot resolve superordinate societal conflicts which manifest as safety issues in the public space in the long term. This is a task for policymakers and administrators.

Access and rules

A central feature of the public sphere is its continuous accessibility to all societal groups.[14] In contrast, CCSP, SESC and also the historic gallery buildings are only accessible under controlled conditions. Entering the property is bundled via controllable entrances and exits.[15] In addition, access is also limited to certain hours.

Beyond that, on-site uses are each subject to certain rules. New users adopt these codes of conduct voluntarily, mainly by watching those who are already present. Rules include not disturbing anyone, making sparing use of commonly used space, or not deviating from permissible uses. Security staff is merely present in the background and only intervenes in cases of obvious misconduct. They can caution or ban disruptors.

Rules anticipated by all users provide safety to those present and impact the quality of stay in the place. Only on this basis, individuals can read, dance, research, discuss or relax in a carefree way.

Variety of uses

For Feldtkeller, the use of public spaces is "mostly unpredictable"[16]. However, where the greatest possible number of societal groups has the opportunity to participate in a public space, varying needs and desires lead to a great range of uses.[17] This variety significantly contributes to the liveliness of public open spaces.[18] Accordingly, it also works in favour of a balance in terms of dominance and interests.

A mixed user group with a great range of desires and interests requires a tolerant society, since the possible spectrum of uses is determined by the norms and values of the majority group. Groups deviating from those are unwanted and can be excluded through various mechanisms. According to Habermas, public spaces therefore are also always exclusive spaces.[19]

Consequently, users with deviating interests lack the opportunity to express themselves in the public sphere. Heterotopias make it possible to move these uses to protected spaces. As a refuge and safe haven[20], they provide a 'space for experience' which "keeps the individual socially acceptable".[21]

Projects such as the CCSP, the SESC, and the Galeria do Rock enable practices that cannot be pursued in the users' immediate environment, or only to a very limited extent. These include, for example, dancing, music-making and sports, but also basic needs such as protection from the weather, places to rest and study, or safe play areas for children.

None of the projects presented excludes access of marginalised groups. Class affiliation does not play a role here. The presence of greatly different societal groups emphasises that cohesion is very well possible in a protected space.

Aesthetics

Heterotopias provide a time-out from everyday life.[22] To achieve this, they interpret concepts of an ideal world.[23] As places for "compensation"[24], they provide a space of illusion which exposes any real space and all the places where human life is separated as fatuous. Or they express an alternative which is "as perfect, as meticulous, as well arranged as ours is messy, ill constructed and jumbled".[25]

To achieve this, the projects presented in the book each mount their own aesthetic framework which integrates users into a characteristic spatial experience. It includes a generous amount of available space as well as special views of adjacent urban spaces.

Beyond that, the projects also express specific topics. For instance, the SESC was designed as a sophisticated building shell. The project incorporated the concrete structure of a previous building. Generous openings intentionally frame sections of opposite façades or the neighbouring urban silhouette. When passing through the object, a series of different 'cityscapes' unfolds. Simultaneously, a collage is formed, combining usually unconnected uses such as dance, sports and libraries. Everything is completed by the rooftop swimming pool, which evokes the appearance of a cruise ship.

In a similar way, the other projects also express their own aesthetical agendas:

- The traffic structure Minhocão undulates through the city. Raised above the hectic urban level, the route remains free from usage. From here, the urban arrangement can be rediscovered as a rocky landscape.
- The cultural centre CCSP is an elongated 'ship' anchored at the edge of the Rio Itororó river valley. Its uses are distributed to various 'decks' and interconnected by steel gangways and staircases. The rooftop level can be used as a sun deck and garden.
- The buildings of SESC and Praça das Artes appear like unfinished building shells. This appearance emphasises the ornate facades of adjacent buildings. As a large, walk-in sculpture, they provide unexpected visual and route connections. Besides, they enable crossing through the mostly closed-off sites of Centro Novo. When exploring the inside of the block, a usually concealed arrangement unfolds.
- The Galeria do Rock combines psychedelic and surrealist design elements. Ceilings and facade surfaces are articulated and perforated in a fluent manner.

Heterotopia as workshop

Each of the projects presented has components of a "realized utopia"[26]. They enable the users to try out their own ways of being together and change their relationship to their environment.

- The Minhocão overpass attempts to invert the hierarchy between private vehicle traffic and pedestrians.
- Viewed from the Mirante, the motorway below turns into a scenic canyon.
- At CCSP, the homeless relax next to tourists.
- On the SESC's mezzanine floor, street children show middle-class intellectuals how to play in the wading pool.

As 'spaces of otherness', they react to existing societal circumstances and at the same time make it possible to question these relations.[27] Thus, they can also be understood as 'workshops' to establish alternative practices.[28]

Outlook

It is remarkable that São Paulo's urban society creates its own replacements for missing or unusable public spaces. This emphasises that functioning spaces on squares, streets and in parks are indispensable. The hope is that experience gathered in these projects can contribute to reviving São Paulo's public sphere.

19	**Centro Novo**	
	(S. 38, p. 38)	
a		Edifício Copan
b		Edifício Itália
c		Edifício Conde Silvio Penteado
d		Edifício Louvre
e		Conjunto Zarvos e Amboss
f		Galeria Metrópole
g		Edifícios Esther e Arthur Nogueira
h		Galeria Itapetininga
i		Galeria Califórnia
j		Galeria Lousã
k		Galeria das Artes
l		Galeria 7 de Abril
m		Galeria Ipê
n		Galeria Nova Barão
o		SESC 24 de Maio
p		Galeria Guatapará
q		Galeria Predio Ita
r		Galeria Apolo
s		Galeria Presidente
t		‚Grandes Galerias' Galeria do Rock
u		Galeria Olido
v		Praça das Artes

2
PROJEKTE
PROJECTS

GALERIA METRÓPOLE

RAUM UND GESTALT

Die Galeria Metrópole liegt in einem stark frequentierten Teil des Centro Novo. Das Projekt nimmt ein etwa 5.000qm großes Eckgrundstück zwischen der Avenida São Luís und der Praça Dom José Gaspar ein. Städtebaulich ergänzt das Ensemble einen von drei Straßenzügen eingefassten Bestandsblock zwischen der Rua 7 de Abril, der Avenida São Luís und der Avenida Ipiranga. Zusätzlich akzentuiert ein baulicher Hochpunkt den Übergang zur Praça Dom José Gaspar. Das offene Erdgeschoss der Galerie erlaubt das Abkürzen von Wegen. Von hier aus gut erreichbar sind: die Praça da República, die Praça Roosevelt, das Viaduto Nove de Julho und die Bibliothek Mário de Andrade. Das Projekt wird zwischen 1959 und 1964 realisiert.[1]

Das Gebäudeensemble besteht aus einem Punkthochhaus, einer u-förmigen Brandwandbebauung sowie einer mehrgeschossigen Galerie, die einen Lichthof einfasst. Der Hof verbindet alle Ebenen einschließlich Untergeschoss. Die zentral platzierte Baumgruppe dient als ‚Lichtfänger' und erleichtert über alle Geschosse hinweg die Orientierung.

Alle Galerieebenen sind durch zwei Rolltreppen-Einheiten zu erreichen. Zwischen den Gebäudeeinheiten sind großzügige Loggien eingefügt. Von hier aus eröffnen sich jeweils unterschiedliche Blickbeziehungen zu den umgebenden Stadträumen. Eine begrünte Dachterrasse bildet den Abschluß der Galerieebenen. Die Terrasse öffnet sich zur Praça Dom José Gaspar und zur Rua Basílio da Gama.

Die Galerie kann im Erdgeschoss über drei unterschiedliche Zugänge betreten werden. Der nördliche Zugang von der Rua Basílio da Gama führt durch die Galerie auf die Praça Dom José Gaspar.[2] Entlang dieser Achse liegt eine der beiden Rolltreppen-Einheiten.

Hochhaus und Gewerbeflächen bilden jeweils abgeschlossene Einheiten. Dagegen sind alle übrigen Flächen öffentlich zugänglich.[3]

NUTZUNG UND NUTZERGRUPPEN

Das Projekt verknüpft abgeschlossene Flächen für Dienstleistung und Gewerbe mit großzügigen Bewegungsflächen. Wichtiges Bindeglied und Orientierungselement ist der zentrale Lichthof, der alle Galerieebenen miteinander verbindet.

Die Gliederung des Gebäudes durch wichtige Laufwege führt innerhalb des Flächenangebotes zu Lagevorteilen. Entsprechend haben sich unterschiedliche Nutzungsschwerpunkte etabliert:

- Nutzungen mit Außenbezug: In Bereichen mit Durchgangsverkehr und in der Nähe zur vertikalen Erschließung befinden sich überwiegend Restaurants und Cafés. Die meisten Angebote liegen in Richtung Avenida São Luís oder zum Lichthof. Hochpreisige Angebote bieten zusätzlich einen freien Ausblick zur Praça Dom José Gaspar.

- Alt-Nutzungen: Über das Gebäude verteilt, finden sich verschiedene Altmieter als Dienstleistungs- und Serviceanbieter. Dazu gehören Schneidereien, Modefachgeschäfte, Reisebüros und Friseure sowie kleinere Einzelhandelsunternehmen, Buchläden und ein Weinfachhandel. Im Untergeschoss sind in den weniger gut belichteten Bereichen zwei Kinosäle angeordnet.

- Nutzungen mit besonderer Adresse: Im obersten Geschoss haben sich Unternehmen der Kreativbranche eingemietet. Dazu gehören Architekturbüros, Design-Studios, Modeateliers sowie Werbeagenturen. Diese Mieter sind nicht abhängig von Laufkundschaft. Zu ihnen gehören die ‚Entdecker' der Galerie.

1 Atrium als Mittelpunkt
Atrium as focal point

[1] Ferroni (2008): S. 89
[2] Ferroni (2008): S. 162
[3] Die Verknüpfung von Stadtraum und Gebäude und die Einbindung von Fußgängerverbindungen ist ein wiederkehrendes Motiv in späteren Entwürfen von Salvador Candia; Ferroni (2008): S. 89

Sie haben besonders zur Erneuerung des Images der Galerie als Ort der Kreativwirtschaft beigetragen. Neben der außergewöhnlichen Lage ist ihnen auch die niedrige Miete in den Obergeschossen wichtig. Mit dem Imagewechsel der Galerie werden diese Nutzer inzwischen schrittweise durch zahlungskräftigere Mieter ersetzt, die die inzwischen etablierte Adresse zu Marketingzwecken nutzen.

Die Galerie hat wöchentlich an sechs Tagen geöffnet, davon an zwei Tagen bis Mitternacht. Über den Tagesverlauf ändern sich die Nutzungsschwerpunkte. Zwischen 11:00 und 15:00 Uhr nehmen Anwohner und Angestellte aus der Nachbarschaft das gastronomische Angebot in Anspruch. Die Lage und das Angebot an Cafés und Restaurants sind auf diese Nachfrage abgestimmt. Gegen Abend verlagert sich der Fußgängerstrom eher in Richtung Praça Dom José Gaspar. In den oberen Geschossen finden Lesungen und Ausstellungen statt.

Bei Bedarf können sich die Laden- und Gewerbeeinheiten auf die davorliegenden Galerieflächen ausweiten. Restaurants und Cafés nutzen diese Möglichkeit um zusätzliche Sitzplätze anzubieten. Darüber hinaus werden die Flächen von Betreibern und Arbeitnehmern zum Besprechen, zum Telefonieren oder zum Ausruhen genutzt. Verbindungstreppen und Sitzmauern entlang des Dachgartens bieten zusätzlich informelle Angebote zum Verweilen.

Ähnlich heterogen wie die Nutzungen ist auch der Kundenkreis der Galerie. Viele Geschäfte verfügen über langjährige Stammkunden, die zum Teil lange Wege auf sich nehmen. Vereinzelt besuchen auch Architektur-Touristen die Galerie.

Zur Kontrolle der Zugänge im Gebäude sind Sicherheitsleute im Schichtbetrieb verantwortlich. Von einem zentral gelegenen Tresen aus können sie gleichzeitig alle Zugänge beobachten. Zusätzlich finden regelmäßig Kontrollgänge durch die Galerie statt.

Die Gewerbeeinheiten in den öffentlich zugänglichen Geschossen sowie die Büroeinheiten im Turmbau sind im Besitz von rund zehn Eigentümern. Infrastruktur, Erschließungsflächen und die Kinosäle gehören zum Gemeinschaftseigentum. Die Kosten für Instandhaltungsarbeiten, Reparaturen sowie für bauliche Veränderungen werden zwischen den Eigentümern aufgeteilt. Die Organisation übernimmt eine gemeinsam beauftragte Gebäudeverwaltung.

KONZEPT

Grundlage für das Projekt bildet die Zusammenlegung von benachbarten Grundstücksparzellen. Für die geplante Querbarkeit des Erdgeschosses ist die Integration des Zugangs von der Rua Basílio da Gama besonders wichtig.[4]

Der Entwurf zur Galeria Metrópole kombiniert die Wettbewerbsbeiträge der Architekten Salvador Candia und Gian Carlo Gasperini. Deren Entwürfe wurden unabhängig voneinander in einem 1959 durchgeführten Wettbewerb ausgezeichnet.[5] Der danach gemeinsam entwickelte Entwurf übernimmt Elemente beider Wettbewerbsbeiträge. Dazu gehören die orthogonale Grundform, die geöffneten Fassadenflächen sowie die filigranen Stützen.

Die angrenzenden Platz- und Straßenräume zwischen der Praça Dom José Gaspar und der Rua Basílio da Gama werden durch einen Durchgang mit dem Galeriebereich verbunden. Im dreiseitig umbauten rückwärtigen Teil ist eine an den Bestand angepasste Gebäudehöhe vorgesehen. Dagegen wird die Blockkante zwischen der Praça Dom José Gaspar und der Avenida São Luís durch einen Hochpunkt betont. Die Idee des offenen Galeriegartens ist während der Kooperationsphase der Architekten entstanden.[6] Ursprünglich sollte der Bereich überdacht werden.[7]

ENTWICKLUNG

Das Projekt ist zunächst als hochpreisige Einkaufsgalerie für ein exklusives Publikum konzipiert. Allerdings wird bereits zur Eröffnung der Umbruch des Centro Novos und ein damit einhergehender Imagewandel spürbar. Im Zuge des innerstädtischen Baubooms steigt die Verkehrs- und Immissionsbelastung. Gleichzeitig verlagert sich der Investitionsschwerpunkt nach Südwesten zur Avenida Paulista. Entsprechend wandern schrittweise Investoren und mit ihnen wohlhabende Mieter, Dienstleister und Gewerbetreibende ab.

An den 1960er Jahren wird die entstehende Nachfrage-Lücke zunächst durch Künstler, Musiker und Schriftsteller ausgefüllt. In direkter Nachbarschaft zur Stadtbibliothek gelegen, entwickelt sich die Galerie zu einem gern besuchten Szene-Treffpunkt mit einer eigenen Mischung aus Läden, Restaurants, Cafés, Nachtclubs und Bars. Das Gebäude taucht in zeitgenössischen Büchern, Filmen und Liedern auf.

2	Lageplan / Site plan
	1:2000

[4] Ferroni (2008): S. 162 f.
[5] Ferroni (2008): S. 161; Ferroni, Shundi Iwamizu (2013): S. 149 f.
[6] Ferroni, Shundi Iwamizu (2013): S. 150
[7] Ferroni (2008): S. 164

3	Offenes Treppenhaus Open staircase
8	Ferroni, Shundi Iwamizu (2013): S. 150
9	Ferroni, Shundi Iwamizu (2013): S. 150

Mit der Machtübernahme durch das Militär beginnt 1964 jedoch eine Kampagne gegen die Galerie und ihre Nutzungen. Sukzessive verändert sich die Belegung hin zu niedrigpreisigen Dienstleistungen und Geschäften. Ab den 1970er Jahren entsteht eine Mischung aus Reisebüros, Bekleidungsgeschäften, Reinigungen und Änderungsschneidereien, ergänzt um Restaurants und Cafés in unterschiedlichen Preisklassen. Ab 2000, zeitgleich zur Wiederentdeckung des Stadtteils Centro Novo, beziehen erste Mieter aus dem Bereich Kreativwirtschaft die Gewerberäume im oberen Galeriegeschoss. Inzwischen ist die Galeria Metrópole fast wieder eine ‚In-Adresse'.

REZEPTION

Das Gebäude wird nicht als exklusive und hochpreisige Einkaufsgalerie wahrgenommen. Trotzdem ist das ursprüngliche Entwurfskonzept gut ablesbar. Damit wird ein Galeriebesuch zu einer Zeitreise in die Spätmoderne der 1950er-Jahre.

Zu den besonders frequentierten Nutzungen gehören Restaurants und Cafés zur Mittagszeit. Der Kundenstamm setzt sich zusammen aus Angestellten und Bewohnern aus der Nachbarschaft. Dagegen wird das Gebäude nachmittags weniger stark frequentiert. Touristen entdecken die Galerie eher zufällig oder auf Empfehlung von Einheimischen. Aufgrund der Nähe zu den Tanz- und Musikveranstaltungen an der Praça Dom José Gaspar wird das gastronomische Angebot auch gerne abends in Anspruch genommen.

Von den Nutzern hervorgehoben werden die offene Disposition des Gebäudes als Zwischenraum zwischen Innen und Außen, sowie die Blickbeziehungen zur Praça Dom José Gaspar. Wind und Schatten sorgen für ein angenehmes Klima. Die großzügig geschnittene Galeriefläche und offene Bauweise des Gebäudes stellen zudem eine gute Belichtung und Belüftung sicher.[8]

Die weit auskragenden offenen Terrassen und Balkone verschränken das Gebäude in alle Richtungen mit dem Stadtraum.[9] Der innenliegende Garten greift den grüngeprägten Eindruck der Praça Dom José Gaspar auf.

KONFLIKTE UND KÜNFTIGE ENTWICKLUNG

Das Betreten und Nutzen der Galerie wird Wohnungslosen nicht untersagt, solange die auf dem Privatgelände geltenden Regeln beachtet werden. Am Übergang zur Rua Basílio da Gama halten sich oft Wohnungslose auf. Entsprechend wird die Möglichkeit der Abkürzung zur U-Bahn Station República von vielen Besuchern nicht genutzt. Das gilt insbesondere zur Abendzeit. Der Galerieeingang wird nachts als Schlafplatz genutzt. Entsprechend hat das Sicherheitspersonal die Anweisung den Eingang zur Öffnungszeit der Galerie zu räumen.

Einige Mieter wünschen sich einen besseren Pflegezustand sowie mehr Instandhaltungsmaßnahmen. Die Gebäudeverwaltung beauftragt regelmäßig Instandsetzungs- und Renovierungsarbeiten. Der für das Gebäude bestehende Denkmalschutz macht die Beschaffung von geeigneten Materialien aufwändig. Teilweise sind dazu kostenintensive Importe notwendig. Entsprechend sind umfangreichere Arbeiten nur langfristig umsetzbar.

Viele der Befragten wünschen sich künftig eine stärkere Belebung der Galerie, insbesondere außerhalb der Mittagspausen und an den Wochenenden. Wünschenswert ist auch, dass die Galerie nachts zur Durchquerung offen bleibt. Dazu sind zusätzliche Sicherheitsmaßnahmen sowie eine Verbesserung der Beleuchtung notwendig.

4 **Schnitt Süd-Nord**
  South-north section
  1:1000

5 **Punkthochhaus**
  Solitary high-rise

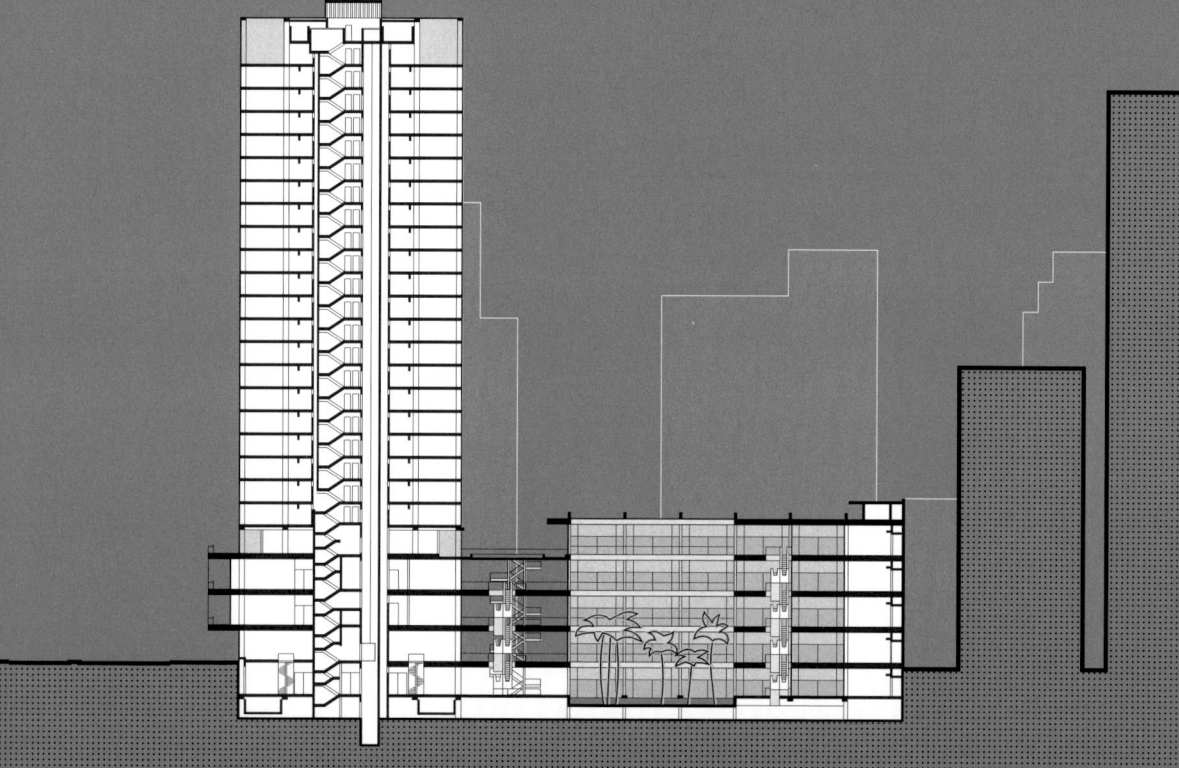

GALERIA METRÓPOLE

SPACE AND FORM

The Galeria Metrópole is located in a highly frequented part of the Centro Novo quarter. The project occupies a corner property of about 5,000sqm between Avenida São Luís and Praça Dom José Gaspar.

The ensemble complements an existing block bordered by three residential streets between Rua 7 de Abril, Avenida São Luís and Avenida Ipiranga. The open ground floor of the gallery cuts walking time to important destinations. Praça da República, Praça Roosevelt, Viaduto Nove de Julho as well as the Mário de Andrade library can be reached easily from here. In addition, the transition to Praça Dom José Gaspar is accentuated by a high-rise building. The project was realised between 1959 and 1964.[1]

The ensemble consists of a square-plan highrise building, a U-shaped structure as well as a multi-storey gallery enclosing a central atrium. The cluster of trees in the atrium serves as a 'light catcher' and facilitates orientation across the floors.

All gallery levels can be reached by two escalator units. Between the building blocks, generous openings allow visual relations to the surrounding urban spaces. A green roof terrace forms at the end of the gallery levels. The terrace opens up towards Praça Dom José Gaspar and Rua Basílio da Gama.

The gallery can be entered on the ground floor via three different entrances. The northern entrance from Rua Basílio da Gama leads through the gallery onto Praça Dom José Gaspar.[2] One of the two escalator units is located on this axis. The only enclosed spaces are the commercial units and the square-plan high-rise. All other areas are accessible to the public.[3]

USE AND USER GROUPS

The project connects closed area units for services and commerce with generous movement areas. The central atrium serves as an important link and orientation element connecting all gallery levels. A similar task is performed by the various lookout points into adjacent urban spaces.

The location of the building in relation to important pedestrian routes leads to advantages within the area. Accordingly, different main uses have become established in the spaces:

- Uses with relation to the surrounding: Areas with transit traffic close to vertical access points are predominantly occupied by restaurants and cafés. The largest number of establishments are located in the direction of Avenida São Luís or connected to the atrium. Upscale establishments also feature an unobstructed view of Praça Dom José Gaspar.

- Legacy uses: Various legacy tenants as service providers are distributed throughout the building. Among them are tailors, boutiques, travel agencies, hairdressers as well as smaller retail companies, book shops and a specialised wine vendor. Areas of the basement floor which receive less light contain two cinemas.

- Uses with a particular address: The top floor is leased to creative industry companies. Those include architecture offices, design and fashion studios as well as advertising agencies. These tenants do not rely on walk-in business. Among them are the 'revitalisers' of the gallery. They particularly contributed to the modernisation of the gallery's image as a creative industry site. Besides the extraordinary location, they are attracted to the low rent of the upper floors.

6　Dachgeschoss der Galerie
　　Gallery top floor

[1]　Ferroni (2008): p. 89
[2]　Ferroni (2008): p. 162
[3]　The connection of urban space and building as well as the incorporation of pedestrian routes is a recurrent theme in later designs by Salvador Candia; Ferroni (2008): p. 89

7 Grundriss EG
Floor plan GF
1:1000

8 Grundriss 2. OG
Floor plan 2F
1:1000

9 Grundriss DG
Floor plan TF
1:1000

---

4 Ferroni (2008): p. 162 f.
5 Ferroni (2008): p. 161;
   Ferroni, Shundi Iwamizu (2013):
   p. 149 f.
6 Ferroni, Shundi Iwamizu (2013):
   p. 150
7 Ferroni (2008): p. 164

- In connection with the image change of the gallery, these tenants are gradually being replaced by more solvent ones who use the address, which has become well-established at this point, for marketing purposes.

The gallery is open six days a week, two of them until midnight. Its main uses change throughout the day. Between 11 a.m. and 3 p.m., residents and staff from the neighbourhood frequent the gastronomic facilities. The location and the range of cafés and restaurants are tailored to this demand. Towards nighttime, the stream of pedestrians shifts towards Praça Dom José Gaspar. On the upper floors, literary readings and exhibitions take place.

If required, shop and commerce units can extend to the gallery areas in front. Restaurants and cafés take advantage of this opportunity to offer additional seating. Beyond that, operators and employees use the areas for discussions, phone calls or relaxation. Seating is mostly associated with commercial use. The connecting stairs and sitting walls along the rooftop garden provide informal places to linger and sit down.

Uses and clientele of the gallery are heterogeneous. Many businesses have long-term patrons, some of whom travel long distances to get to the gallery. Sporadically, architecture tourists also visit the gallery.

Security staff working in shifts is in charge of building access and security. Their central location is a counter which facilitates monitoring the three access points at once. In addition, there are regular patrols of the gallery.

The commercial units on the publicly accessible floors as well as the office units in the tower building are held by a total of ten owners. Infrastructure, open areas and cinemas are common property. The costs for maintenance work, repairs as well as reconstruction are divided up between the owners. This is organised by a joint-commissioned building management agency.

CONCEPT

The basis of the project was formed by a consolidation of neighbouring properties. For the planned open passage through the ground floor the integration of an access point from Rua Basílio da Gama was particularly important.[4]

The design for Galeria Metrópole combined the competition entries of architects Salvador Candia and Gian Carlo Gasperini. Their designs, independent of each other, received awards in a competition held in 1959.[5] The subsequent joint design incorporated elements of the two competition entries. Those include the orthogonal layout, the open facade areas and the delicate supporting elements.

The adjacent square and street spaces between Praça Dom José Gaspar and Rua Basílio da Gama are connected to the gallery area by a passage. The rear portion, which is bordered by buildings on three sides, envisaged a building height adjusted to the existing buildings. In contrast, the edge of the block between Praça Dom José Gaspar and Avenida São Luís is emphasised with an elevation.

The idea of the gallery garden emerged during the cooperation phase.[6] Originally, the area was supposed to be canopied as well.[7]

DEVELOPMENT

The project was originally intended as an upscale shopping gallery for an exclusive audience. However, changes in Centro Novo, which involved the image of the location, was already tangible at the grand opening. Over the course of the inner-city construction boom, traffic and immission load increased. At the same time, the focus of investments shifted to the southwest to Avenida Paulista. Gradually, investors and solvent tenants, services providers and tradespeople migrated.

The resulting gap in demand was initially filled by artists, musicians and writers starting in the 1960s. The gallery next to the municipal library transformed into a well-frequented scene spot with a unique mix of shops, restaurants, cafés, night clubs and bars. The gallery appears in contemporary books, films and songs.

With the military's rise to power in 1964, however, a campaign was launched against the gallery and its uses. Gradually, the occupancy changed towards low-priced service providers and shops. The 1970s gave rise to a mixture of travel agencies, clothing shops, dry cleaners and tailors. Over time, restaurants of various price segments opened in the gallery.

From 2000, contemporaneously to the rediscovery of the Centro Novo quarter, the first tenants from the creative industry moved into the commercial spaces of the upper gallery floor. Today, the Galeria Metrópole has almost become the hip place it once was.

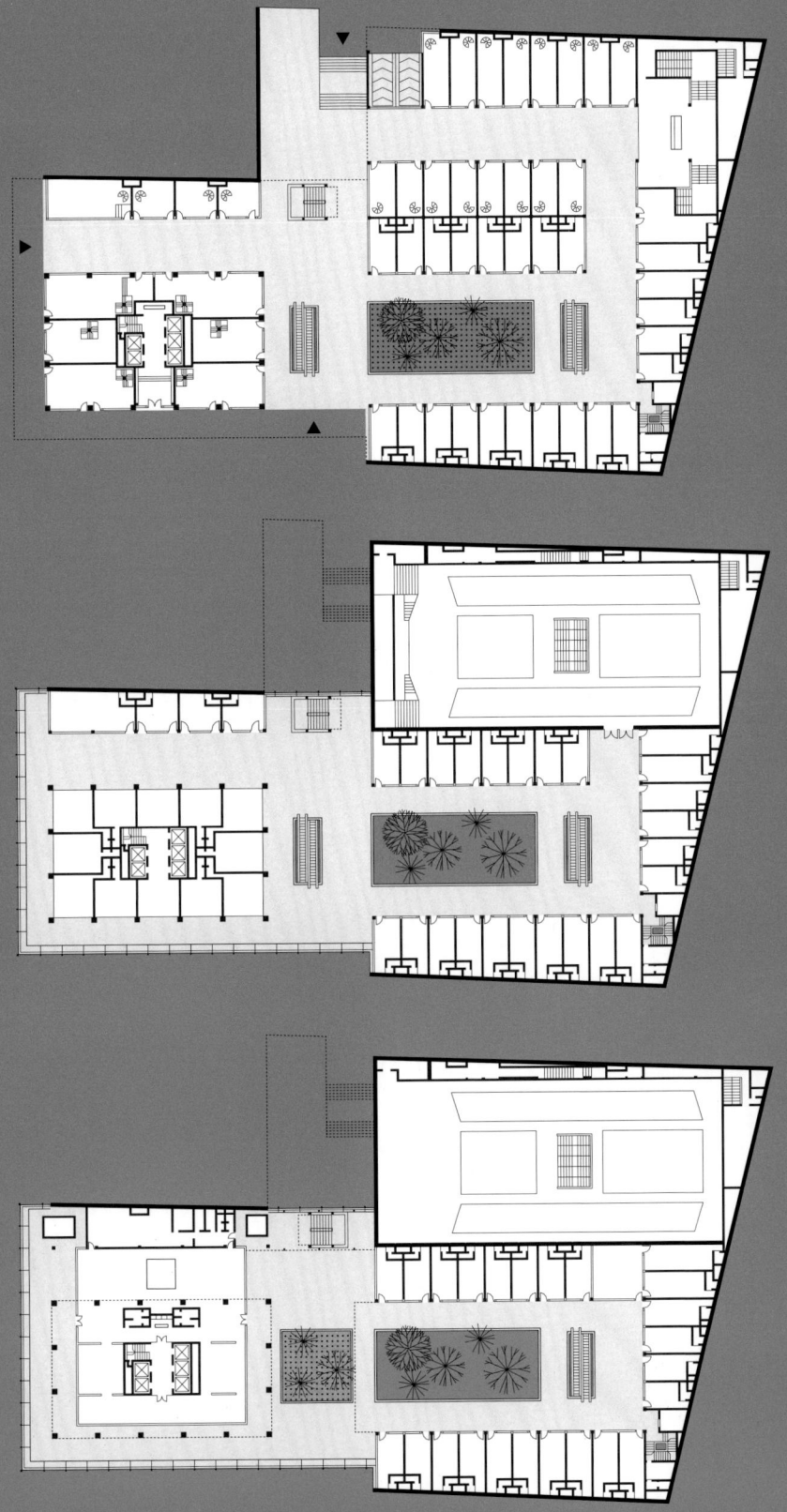

RECEPTION

The building is not perceived as an exclusive and upscale shopping gallery. Still, the original design concept is clearly discernible. This turns a visit to the gallery into a journey to the late-Modern era of the 1950s.

Its destinations are the gastronomic facilities with partially long-term owners as well as its vicinity to the dance and music events at Praça Dom José Gaspar. Uses with the greatest frequency of visitors include restaurants and cafés during lunch hours. Their customer base is composed of staff and residents from the neighbourhood. In the afternoon, the building is less frequented. Tourists mostly discover the gallery by accident or based on recommendations by locals.

Those surveyed emphasised the open disposition of the building as an intermediate space between indoors and outdoors as well as the visual relation to Praça Dom José Gaspar. Breeze and shade generate a pleasant climate. The generously designed gallery area and the open architecture of the building also ensure sufficient light and ventilation.[8]

The pronounced protrusions of the open terraces and balconies interlace the building with the urban space in all directions.[9] The inner garden picks up on the verdant character of Praça Dom José Gaspar.

CONFLICTS AND FUTURE DEVELOPMENT

Homeless people are not prohibited from entering and using the gallery as long as the house rules of the private property are observed. Homeless people are often found at the transition to Rua Basílio da Gama. As a consequence, many visitors do not use the shortcut to the underground station República. This particularly applies during evening hours. The gallery entrance is used as a sleeping place at night. Accordingly, security staff are instructed to clear the entrance by the opening time of the gallery.

Some tenants would prefer an improved state of care as well as more maintenance measures. The building management agency regularly commissions maintenance as well as renovation work. The listed status of the building makes obtaining suitable materials rather laborious. At times, cost-intensive imports are necessary. As a result, comprehensive works can only be implemented over the long term.

Many of those surveyed would like a livelier gallery atmosphere in the future, particularly outside of lunch hours and on the weekends. There is also a desire for the gallery remaining open at night as a passage. This requires security measures as well as an improvement in terms of lighting.

10 Terrassen und Stadtraum
   Terraces und urban context

[8] Ferroni, Shundi Iwamizu (2013): p. 150

[9] Ferroni, Shundi Iwamizu (2013): p. 150

GALERIA DO ROCK

RAUM UND GESTALT

Die Galeria do Rock liegt im Stadtteil Centro Novo. Das Gebäude belegt eine rund 140m tiefe Parzelle zwischen dem Largo do Paissandú und der Rua 24 de Maio. Während der Geschäftszeiten ermöglicht die Passage ein Abkürzen zwischen Platz und Straße. Erkennungszeichen der Galerie ist eine konkav geschwungene Fassade. Das Motiv unterstreicht den Charakter des Gebäudes als Passage und betont jeweils die Eingänge. Das inzwischen unter Denkmalschutz stehende Gebäude illustriert die für das Centro Novo charakteristische Typologie der Galeriebauten.

Das Projekt wurde 1962 unter dem Namen ‚Grandes Galerias' eröffnet.[1] Mit der schrittweisen Stagnation des Centro Novo verschiebt sich der Fokus der Galerie ab den 1980er Jahren hin zu Angeboten rund um den Bereich Pop-, Rock- und Independent-Musik. Der Namenswechsel von ‚Grandes Galerias' zur ‚Galeria do Rock' im Jahr 1994 berücksichtigt diese Schwerpunktverschiebung.[2]

Auf sieben Etagen, einschließlich Dachgeschoss, bietet das Gebäude Platz für 450 Geschäfte und Dienstleister, rund 1.200 Beschäftigte und etwa 200 unterschiedliche Unternehmen. Dazu gehören Fachgeschäfte für Tonträger und Instrumente, Anbieter von Fan-Artikeln und Fan-Outfits, Dienstleistungen im Bereich Körperschmuck sowie Hersteller von T-Shirts und Postern.

KONZEPT

Ab den 1950er Jahren fördert die Planungsverwaltung São Paulos verstärkt innerstädtische Galerie-Projekte, die das Netz an öffentlichen Straßen und Plätzen um Passagen ergänzen.[3] Die Förderung zielt darauf ab entlang vielbefahrener Straßen fußgängerfreundliche Alternativen zu entwickeln.

Die Architekten Ermanno Siffredi und Maria Bardelli[4] greifen bei ihrem Entwurf zur Grandes Galerias diese Vorgaben auf.

Das Gebäude ist als mehrgeschossige Passage konzipiert. Die Laden- und Dienstleistungsflächen sind in zwei langgestreckten Riegelbauten entlang der Parzellenränder gebündelt. Sie werden einhüftig über eine großzügig dimensionierte, offene Galerie-Straße erschlossen. Verkaufsflächen und Passage werden durch eine geschwungene Glasfassade getrennt. Eine Abfolge aus Schaufenstern und Eingängen gliedert den langgestreckten Innenraum des Gebäudes.

Die beiden unteren Geschossebenen schließen beide an das Straßenniveau an, um die besonders gut frequentierten Nutzflächen zu verdoppeln. Die Rampensteigungen werden dazu über eine große Öffnung aneinander vorbeigeführt. Die Architekten Siffredi und Bardelli nutzen eine ähnliche Erschließung auch bei der Galerie Centro Comercial Presidente und der Galeria 7 de Abril.[5]

Die darüberliegenden Ebenen der Galerie sind über eine durchgehende Wendeltreppe sowie Aufzüge angebunden. Jede Geschossebene ist mit unterschiedlichen ovalen Lichtöffnungen versehen. Damit entstehen über alle Geschosse hinweg unterschiedliche Sichtbeziehungen.

Die übereinanderliegenden Galerie-Straßen bleiben beidseitig am Übergang zum Stadtraum offen und weichen gegenüber der Gebäudeflucht konkav zurück. Die über alle Geschosse hinweg nach innen geschwungene Öffnung rahmt als großzügiger Stadtbalkon die umgebende Stadtszenerie.[6] Gleichzeitig wirkt sie als auffällige Geste in den Stadtraum hinein. Besonders charakteristisch für das Gebäude ist der Wechsel zwischen Flanieren und Beobachten. Wind, Wetter und Tageszeit bleiben im Inneren des Gebäudes spürbar.

---

1 **Offene Galerie**
Open gallery
Largo do Paissandú

[1] Ferroni (2008): S. 89
[2] Aleixo (2005): S. 228
[3] Ferroni (2008): S. 87
[4] Aleixo (2005): S. 214
[5] Lobato (2009): S. 117
[6] Aleixo (2005): S. 223

Das sehr tiefe Gebäude wird durch eine Kombination aus Tages- und Kunstlicht beleuchtet. Neben den großzügigen Lichtöffnungen und den beiden konkaven Gebäudeabschlüssen sind alle Deckenflächen mit Lichtspots versehen.[7]

NUTZUNG UND NUTZERGRUPPEN

Zwischen 1962 und 1972, kurz nach der Eröffnung etablieren sich in den beiden ebenerdig erreichbaren Ebenen Schneider-Ateliers. Die darüberliegenden Geschosse sind weniger gut angeschlossen und werden durch Anwaltskanzleien und Zahnärzte belegt. Anfang der 1990er Jahre verändert sich der Schwerpunkt der Galerie. Schrittweise konzentriert sich das Angebot auf den Bereich rund um Rock-, Pop- und Independent-Musik. Imbiss-Angebote sowie eine öffentlich zugängliche Dachterrasse ergänzen dieses Angebot. In den beiden unteren Galerie-Geschossen nutzen Mode- und Musikgeschäfte die höhere Besucherfrequenz. Entsprechend erzielen diese Flächen auch die höchsten Kauf- und Mietpreise. Dagegen werden die Flächen in den oberen Stockwerken auch durch Dienstleister, Designer und Künstler belegt.

An Wochentagen besuchen rund 25.000 Besucher die Galerie. Samstags steigt diese Zahl auf bis zu 40.000 Personen an. Die besondere Schwerpunktsetzung und die prägnante Architektursprache machen das Gebäude zu einem beliebten Treffpunkt. Die Besucher setzen sich zusammen aus Musikern, Fans, Hipstern, Selbstdarstellern, Touristen und Passanten. Sie eint ein gemeinsames Interesse an bestimmten Musikstilen und dem damit verbundenen Lebensgefühl.

Das Gebäude wirkt einladend, ohne die Besucher durch Konsumangebote zu bedrängen. Durch die Reihung der Geschäfte, bleiben die Passagen unverstellt und gut einsehbar. Zusätzlich ergeben sich vielfältige Blickbeziehungen in den angrenzenden Stadtraum und über die Galeriegeschosse hinweg. Entsprechend nutzen die Besucher die Galerie mehr als Straßenraum und weniger als Einkaufszentrum.

Der offene Charakter der Galerie wird durch besondere Angebote ergänzt. Dazu gehören Konzerte, Modenschauen, Lesungen, Kurse, Nachhilfeangebote sowie künstlerische Events. Als Veranstaltungsort wird vorwiegend das Dachgeschoss genutzt. Die Organisation dieser Aktivitäten übernimmt der Kulturverein ‚Instituto Cultural Galeria do Rock´, der von den Gebäudeeigentümern betrieben wird.

Entscheidungen, die das Gebäude betreffen, werden von den Teilhabern gemeinsam getroffen. Dazu haben sich die Ladeninhaber zu einer Kooperation organisiert. Ihr Vorsitz wird in einem zweijährlichen Turnus neu gewählt. Zwischen 1980 und 2002 wird das Gebäude schrittweise saniert und modernisiert. Die entsprechenden Kosten übernehmen anteilig die Ladenbesitzer.

REZEPTION UND KONFLIKTE

Die Galerie ist ein wichtiger Treffpunkt für die alternative Musikszene São Paulos. Entsprechend betonen die meisten Befragten die Vielfalt der Besucher als besonderes Merkmal. Anbieter und Besucher können sich entfalten und werden möglichst wenig eingeschränkt. Die Bandbreite der Musikstile bleibt auf Rock, Pop und Independent beschränkt - Punk gilt inzwischen als zu aggressiv.

Über die Jahre hinweg hat sich die Atmosphäre der Galerie rund um den Schwerpunkt alternative Musikszene kaum verändert. Das Angebot konzentriert sich auf den Verkauf von Tonträgern, ergänzt durch Dienstleistungen wie Piercings und Tattoos. Aktuell verschiebt sich der Fokus der Galerie allerdings schrittweise in Richtung Fan-Ausstattung und -Accessoires. Mittelfristig wird befürchtet, dass das Alleinstellungsmerkmal Musik in den Hintergrund tritt und lediglich als historischer Rahmen den Verkauf von Modeartikeln aufwertet.

Viele der Befragten betonen die besonderen Eigenarten des Gebäudes und die lange Geschichte als Anziehungspunkt für Rock- und Pop-Kultur. Beide Merkmale werden als schützenswert eingestuft. Darüber hinaus ist die Galeria do Rock oft mit der Biografie der Nutzer verbunden - als Ort, der bei der Suche nach einer eigenen Identität einen Beitrag geleistet hat.

Viele der Befragten verbinden die einladende Geste des Gebäudes mit der offenen Haltung der Inhaber. In einem freundlichen Rahmen, umgeben von einem offenen, jungen Publikum spielen Kleiderordnung, Herkunft, Hautfarbe oder Einkommen keine Rolle. Der Ort richtet sich besonders an Menschen mit individuellem Geschmack und Ausdruckswunsch, schließt dabei aber andere Besucher nicht aus. In der Galeria do Rock spielen Herkunft und Einkommensklasse keine Rolle.

2   **Lageplan**
    Site plan
    1:2000

7   Aleixo (2005): S. 229

Zum Angebot der Galerie gehören ein differenziertes Produkt-Sortiment sowie dazu passende Dienstleistungen und Veranstaltungen. Gleichzeitig verbinden die Befragten den Ort mit jeweils eigenen Eindrücken und Erlebnissen. Entsprechend unterschiedliche Gründe gibt es für einen Galeriebesuch: ein neuer Haarschnitt, Events wie das Lollapalooza oder ein rasches Update zum Thema Tattoo-Art.

Über die Jahre hinweg haben sich Gebäude- und Geschäftsstruktur schrittweise verändert. Dazu gehören u.a. die Sanierung von Geschäften, der Umbau von Aufzügen und Treppenanlagen, sowie der Einbau eines Sprinklersystems. Inzwischen hat sich dadurch die Anzahl der Geschäfte in der Galerie erhöht. Vereinzelt gibt es allerdings weiterhin Kritik am Gebäudezustand. Aktuell besteht der Wunsch die Treppenanlagen zu modernisieren.

Bis in die späten 1970er Jahre ist die Galerie auch nachts geöffnet. Aufgrund der steigenden Kriminalitätsrate in der Innenstadt bleibt der Durchgang inzwischen außerhalb der Öffnungszeiten geschlossen.

In den 90er Jahren waren Ladengeschäfte und Drogenhandel miteinander verschränkt. Unterschiedliche Sicherheitsmaßnahmen, die Modernisierung des Gebäudes sowie ein schrittweiser Wechsel der Eigentümer haben dazu beigetragen illegale Aktivitäten erfolgreich zurück zu drängen.

Seit 1993 investieren die Betreiber verstärkt in das Sicherheitskonzept des Gebäudes. Inzwischen bietet die Galerie ein deutlich höheres Maß an Sicherheit für die Besucher. Sie wird dazu durch einen Sicherheitsdienst überwacht.

Für einige der Befragten wird der offene Charakter des Gebäudes durch die Präsenz des Sicherheitsdienstes eingeschränkt. Generell wünschen sich Betreiber und Sicherheitspersonal keine starke Überwachung, sehen aber aufgrund der aktuellen Sicherheitslage keine Alternative. Wohnungslose können die Galerieflächen nutzen, sind aber nur eingeschränkt willkommen. Verwehrt wird ihnen lediglich der Zutritt zur Dachterrasse, die privat bewirtschaftet wird.

3   **Blickbeziehungen**
    Visual relations

GALERIA DO ROCK

SPACE AND FORM

The Galeria do Rock is located in the Centro Novo quarter. The building occupies a parcel of 140m in depth between the Largo do Paissandú and Rua 24 de Maio. During business hours, the passage facilitates short cuts between the square and the street. The gallery's identifying feature is a concave facade. This motif underlines the character of the building as a passage and emphasises the entrances. The building, which has been listed at this point, illustrates a characteristic typology for Centro Novo's gallery buildings.

The project was inaugurated in 1962 bearing the name 'Grandes Galerias'.[1] Following the gradual stagnation of Centro Novo from the 1980s, the focus of the gallery shifted towards offers surrounding pop, rock and independent music. The name change from 'Grandes Galerias' to 'Galeria do Rock' in 1994 reflected this change in direction.[2]

On seven floors including the rooftop terrace the building provides space for 450 shops and service providers, roughly 1,200 employees and approximately 200 different businesses. This includes specialised shops for sound recording media and instruments, retailers of fan articles and band merchandise, tattoo and piercing services as well as manufacturers of t-shirts and posters.

CONCEPT

From the 1950s, São Paulo's planning authority increasingly promoted inner-city gallery projects to add passages to the grid of public streets and squares.[3] This promotion aimed at developing pedestrian-friendly alternatives along streets with intense traffic. Architects Ermanno Siffredi and Maria Bardelli[4] addressed these requirements in their design for the Grandes Galerias.

The building was designed as a multi-storey passage. Shop and service areas are arranged in two elongated building elements along the edges of the parcel. A generously dimensioned, open gallery street provides access to the retailers. Sales areas and passages are divided by a curved glass facade. The elongated inner space of the building is structured by its sequence of shop windows and entrances.

Its two lower floor levels both connect to the street level to double the especially well-frequented useful areas. This is done by directing the ramp inclinations past each other through a large opening. The architects Siffredi and Bardelli also used a similar arrangement for the galleries Centro Comercial Presidente and Galeria 7 de Abril.[5]

The upper floors of the gallery are connected via a continuous spiral staircase as well as elevators. Each floor level features varying oval light openings, creating visual relations across all floors.

The stacked gallery streets remain open at the transition to the urban space on both ends and recede from the building line in a concave manner. This opening curved inwards across all floors creates an eye-catching gesture towards the urban space. Inside the building, it articulates generous urban balconies, framing the surrounding city scenery.[6] One particular characteristic of the building is the alternation of strolling and observing. Wind, weather and time of day remain perceivable within the building.

The deep building is illuminated by a combination of daylight and artificial light. In addition to the generous light openings and the two concave building sides, all ceilings are equipped with spotlights.[7]

4 Eingangssituation
  Entrance

5 Übergangsraum
  Transition area
  (S. 64 / p. 64)

[1] Ferroni (2013): p. 89
[2] Aleixo (2005): p. 228
[3] Ferroni (2008): p. 87
[4] Aleixo (2005): p. 214
[5] Lobato (2009): p. 117
[6] Aleixo (2005): p. 223
[7] Aleixo (2015): p. 229

USE AND USER GROUPS

Between 1962 and 1972, shortly after the opening, tailoring studios became established on the two levels accessible via the ground floor. Less well connected, the floors above are used by law firms and dentists. In the early 1990s, the focus of the gallery changed. Gradually, the range shifted to the segment around rock, pop and independent music. Fast food shops and a publicly accessible rooftop terrace complete the facilities. On the two lower gallery floors, fashion and music shops take advantage of the increased visitor footfall. Accordingly, these areas achieve the highest sales as well as rental prices. In contrast, the shops on the upper floors are used by service providers, designers and artists.

On weekdays, roughly 25,000 visitors frequent the gallery. On Saturdays, this number rises to up to 40,000. Its particular emphasis and expressive architectural language make the building an attractive meeting point. Visitors include musicians, fans, hipsters, show-offs, tourists and passersby. What unites them is a mutual interest in certain music styles and their associated attitudes to life.

The building has an inviting effect without hassling visitors with offers to consume. Thanks to the arrangement of shops, passages remain unobstructed and easy to overlook. In addition, there is a variety of visual relations to the adjacent urban space and across the gallery floors. Accordingly, visitors use the gallery more as a street space and less as a shopping centre.

This open character is reinforced with a series of offers of a less consumerist nature. This includes events such as concerts, fashion shows, literary readings, classes, tutoring services as well as artistic events. The top floor is mainly used as a venue for these events, which are organised by the 'Instituto Cultural Galeria do Rock', a cultural association founded and operated by the building owners.

Decisions regarding the building are made jointly by the members of the ownership. To this end, shop owners have organised themselves in a cooperation. Their chair rotates every two years. Between 1980 and 2002, the building was renovated and modernised gradually with the costs distributed between the shop owners.

RECEPTION AND CONFLICTS

The gallery is an important meeting point for São Paulo's alternative music scene. Accordingly, most of those surveyed stress the diversity of visitors as a particular characteristic. Tenants and visitors can be freely creative and are restricted as little as possible. The range of music styles, however, remains limited to rock, pop and independent - punk has been deemed too aggressive at this point.

The atmosphere surrounding the focal point of the alternative music scene has changed little over the years. In the most recent years, however, some users noticed that the thematic emphasis of the gallery has been shifting constantly. Where it used to be on the sale of sound recording media, it has shifted towards fan merchandise and accessories. Another core area is the sale of piercings, tattoos and shoes. In the medium term some fear that the emphasis on music will recede further to the background and will only serve to upgrade the sale of fashion items as a historical framework. There is a worry about the commercial focus progressively moving towards tourism.

The development of the gallery into a point of attraction for rock and pop culture is a reminiscence distinguishing the place for many of those surveyed. It is closely tied with the spatial peculiarities of the building and its stand-alone architectural expression. Both features are classified as worthy of protection. Beyond that, the Galeria do Rock is often connected to the biography of its users, as a place making a contribution in the search of people's own identities.

Many of those surveyed associate the inviting gesture of the building with the open attitude of the owners. In a friendly context, surrounded by an open-minded, young audience, dress codes, origin, skin colour or income do not matter. The place particularly addresses people with individual tastes and desires for expression, yet it does not exclude other visitors. In the Galeria do Rock, origin and income bracket do not play any important role: everyone is welcome here.

The gallery offers a differentiated range of products as well as associated services and events. At the same time, those surveyed connect the place to their own impressions and experiences. Reasons for visiting are correspondingly diverse - a new haircut, events such as Lollapalooza or a quick update regarding tattoo art.

6   Grundriss EG / Floor plan GF   1:1000

7   Grundriss 1. OG / Floor plan 1F   1:1000

8   Schnitt Nord-Süd / North-south section   1:1000

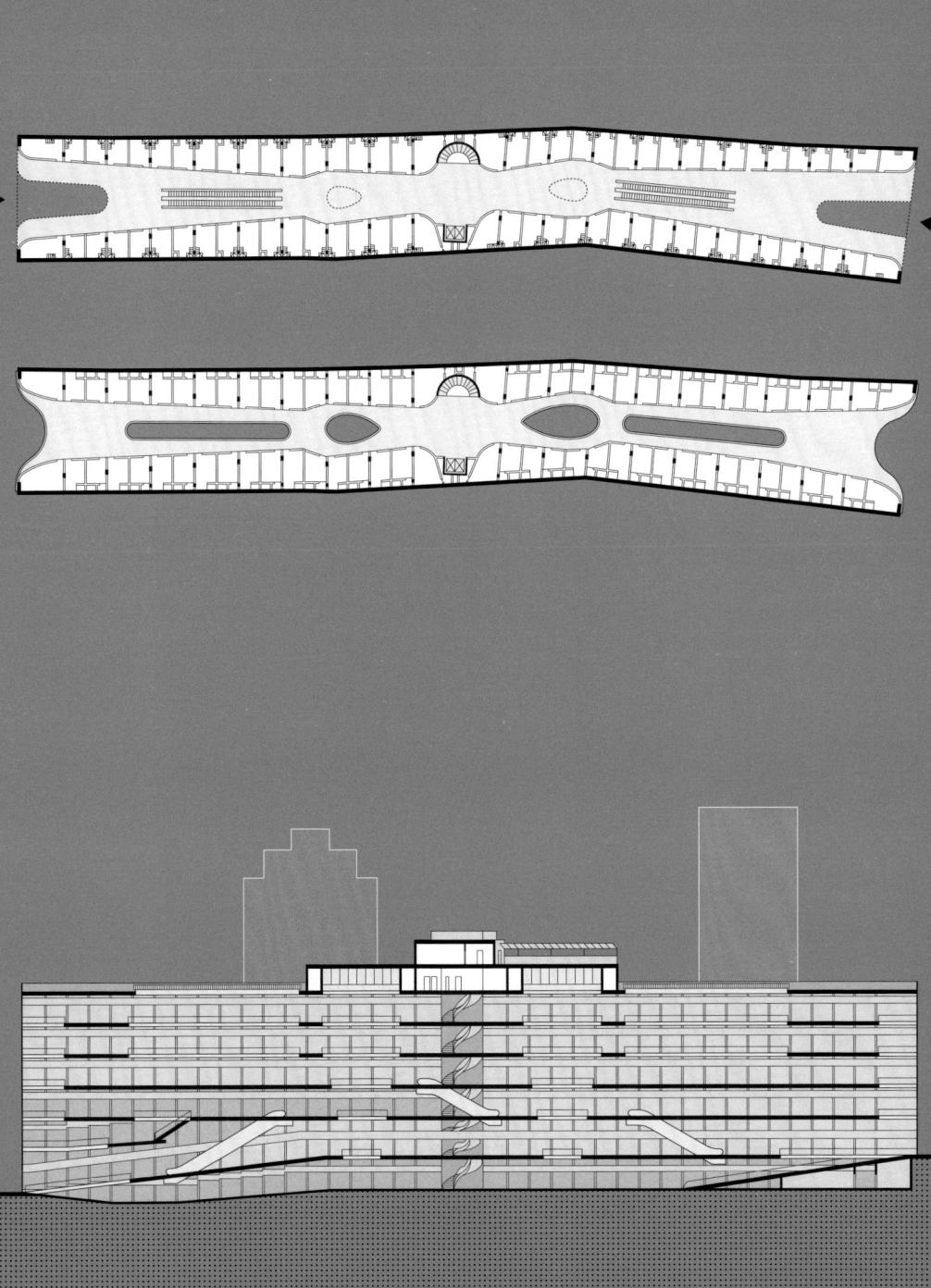

Over the years, building and business structure have changed gradually. This involves, among other things, the renovation of shops, the remodelling of elevators and staircases as well as the installation of a sprinkler system. At this point, these measures have led to an increase in the number of shops in the gallery. Still, there is sporadic criticism regarding the state of the building - among other things, there is the wish to have the staircases modernised.

Until the late 1970s, the gallery remained open at night as well. However, due to the rising crime rate in the inner city, the gallery nowadays remains closed outside of opening hours. In the 1990s, there was a link between shop business and drug dealing. Various security measures, the modernisation of the building as well as a gradual change in owners have contributed to a successful pushback against illegal activities.

Since 1993, the operators have been making more investments in the building's security concept. In the meantime, the gallery offers a significantly higher degree of safety for visitors, due to surveillance by a security agency, whose staff intervenes as required.

For some of those surveyed, the open character of the building is encumbered by the presence of security staff. In general, operators as well as security staff are not intent on intense surveillance, yet they see no alternative in the face of the current safety situation. Homeless people can use the gallery areas, but are only welcome to a certain extent. They are not permitted access to the rooftop terrace, which is not jointly managed.

9 **Blick**
   View
   Largo do Paissandú

10	**Galerieebenen** Gallery floors
11	**Ausblick** View

Rua Vinte e Quatro de Maio

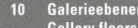

GALERIA NOVA BARÃO

RAUM UND GESTALT

Die Galeria Nova Barão befindet sich im Centro Novo. Sie verbindet die Rua Barão de Itapetininga mit der Rua 7 de Abril - zwei wichtigen Fußgängerverbindungen zwischen dem Anhangabaú-Tal und der Praça da República.[1] In Sichtweite zum Theatro Municipal ermöglicht die Passage eine zusätzliche Querung durch den Baublock. Beidseitig durch Geschäfte und Dienstleistungsangebote eingefasst, zieht sie eine hohe Frequenz an Fußgängern und Laufkundschaft an.

Das Grundstück der Galerie teilt den Gebäudeblock über eine Tiefe von rund 150m. Die Grundstücksbreite beträgt durchschnittlich nur etwa 22m. Die Passage wird entsprechend beidseitig jeweils durch einen 5 bis 11m tiefen Baukörper eingefasst.

In Richtung Rua Barão de Itapetininga befinden sich in den Obergeschossen Wohnungen, in Richtung Rua 7 de Abril hingegen Büroräume. Die Ladeneinheiten im Erdgeschoss und im ersten Obergeschoss werden durch einen Mix aus Einzelhändlern und Dienstleistern belegt. Zwei offene, langgestreckte Laubengänge fassen die beiden Bauteile im ersten Geschoss zusammen. Sie sind jeweils über Rolltreppen erreichbar und über vier Brücken miteinander verbunden. Zwei der Brücken rahmen jeweils den Eingang zur Passage. Die beiden anderen Brücken gliedern die Passage in drei Abschnitte von unterschiedlicher Länge. Das im Bewegungsraum verwendete Kleinsteinpflaster greift den Pflasterbelag der anschließenden Straßenräume auf. Die mittig liegende Platzfläche wird durch Straßenmobiliar und ein Wasserspiel betont. Diese Elemente gehören nicht zum ursprünglichen Entwurf.[2] Das Grundstück der Galerie fällt von Nordost nach Südwest um etwa 5m ab. Zwischen ansteigendem Bodenniveau und Galeriehöhe wird durch die Deckenhöhe der Gewerbeeinheiten vermittelt.

Die Ladeneinheiten sind 4,5m breit, und je nach Lage bis zu 6m hoch. Dagegen besitzen die darüberliegenden Regelgeschosse eine einheitliche Geschosshöhe. Die Gebäuderiegel bestehen durchschnittlich aus sieben Geschossen. Im Bereich der Aufweitung verspringen sie jeweils um ein Geschoss nach oben. Der südliche Gebäudeteil wird im Bereich der Galerieaufweitung mit vier zusätzlichen Geschossen betont.

Die Besucher der Galerie kommen größtenteils aus São Paulos Zentrum. Viele Passanten nutzen die Passage als bequeme Abkürzung. Für manche Besucher bietet der Aufenthalt in der Passage auch die Gelegenheit, sich auszuruhen und zu entspannen. Um Spezialgeschäfte aufzusuchen, werden teilweise auch längere Anreisewege in Kauf genommen. Aktuell nimmt die Zahl der jüngeren Besucher zu.

Die Angebote der Galerie reagieren jeweils auf die Umgebungsbedingungen. An den Übergängen zu den angrenzenden Straßen nutzen Schnellimbisse das höhere Aufkommen an Laufkundschaft. Entlang der ruhigeren Laubengänge reihen sich rund 20 ‚Sebos' (second-hand book stores), mit jeweils eigenen Schwerpunkten im Bereich gebrauchter Bücher und Tonträger. Ihr Sortiment richtet sich an eine bestimmte Stammkundschaft. Dazwischen liegen Bekleidungs- und Schmuckgeschäfte, Friseursalons, Optiker sowie ein Geschäft für vegane Lebensmittel.

Die Galerie öffnet täglich zwischen 7:00 und 19:30 Uhr. Nachts und an Sonntagen bleibt sie geschlossen. Der Durchgang ist dann auf Mieter und Eigentümer beschränkt. Der Zugang zu den oberen Wohn- und Bürogeschossen ist vom Durchgang im Erdgeschoss sowie von den Galerien aus möglich. Im Erdgeschoss werden die Aufgänge jeweils von einem Portier eingesehen. Zusätzlich sind Sicherheitskräfte in Zivilkleidung im Einsatz.

1   Eingang
    Entrance
    Rua Barão de Itapetininga

[1] Rupf (2015): S. 197 f.
[2] Rupf (2015): S. 208

ENTSTEHUNG

Die Galeria Nova Barão befindet sich in der Nähe der Einkaufsstraßen Rua Marconi und Rua Conselheiro Crispiniano. Entsprechend wird sie nach der Eröffnung zunächst als neue ‚Rua'[3] beworben. Der offene Zugang soll den Eindruck vermitteln, dass die Passage nahtlos die Struktur der umliegenden Straßenräume ergänzt.[4]

Das Projekt wird von der Entwicklungsgesellschaft Alfredo Mathias initiiert und 1962 eröffnet.[5] Als Kooperationspartner erarbeiten die Architekten Ermanno Siffredi und Maria Bardelli den Entwurf. In gleicher Kooperation entwickelt das Unternehmen weitere Galerie-Projekte im Stadtteil Centro Novo.[6] Alfredo Mathias übernimmt zusätzlich Grundstückserwerb und einen Teil der Vorfinanzierung.

Noch vor Baubeginn werden zur Restfinanzierung Wohn- und Gewerbeeinheiten beworben und verkauft. Für die Gewerbe-, Wohn- oder Büroeinheiten sind vor Baubeginn zwischen 50 - 60% des Kaufpreises zu zahlen.[7] Die Gewerbeeinheiten verkaufen sich bereits innerhalb eines Tages, die übrigen Gebäudeteile innerhalb von nur 3 Tagen.[8]

Heute verteilen sich die etwa 200 Wohn- und rund 130 Gewerbeeinheiten der Galerie auf annähernd 100 Eigentümer. Ein großer Teil der Einheiten werden inzwischen weitervermietet. Die Mietpreise orientieren sich am Marktwert, unterscheiden sich aber innerhalb des Gebäudekomplexes.

Für Instandsetzung und bauliche Veränderungen ihrer Einheiten sind Eigentümer und Mieter selbst verantwortlich. Gebäudesicherheit, Straßenmobiliar sowie Instandhaltung und Reparatur gemeinsam genutzter Gebäudebereiche liegt dagegen in der Verantwortung einer Gebäudeverwaltung, die die Interessen aller Eigentümer vertritt. Allerdings verzögert die hohe Anzahl der Eigentümer die Umsetzung von Änderungs- und Reparaturvorhaben.

Passanten und Nutzer nehmen die Galerie als Fortsetzung der umgebenden Einkaufsstraßen wahr. Dabei orientiert sich die Geschäftsstruktur an bestimmten Trends. Bis Mitte der 2000er Jahre liegt der Schwerpunkt bei Friseursalons und Schmuckgeschäften. Seit 2007 verschiebt er sich auf den Verkauf von gebrauchten Medien.

Für Laufkundschaft ist die Galerie ein Durchgangsort. Dagegen richten sich ihre spezialisierten Geschäfte an einen ausgewählten Kundenkreis. Dabei profitieren die einzelnen Ladeninhaber voneinander. Sie schätzen die besondere Atmosphäre des Ortes und pflegen ein nachbarschaftliches Verhältnis untereinander. Gemeinsames Ziel von Eignern und Mietern ist, die Galerie als Ort mit einer einladenden und offenen Atmosphäre zu erhalten.

2 **Lageplan**
Site plan
1:2000

3 Aleixo (2005): S. 240
4 Segurança Imobiliária S.A. (1962): S. 2
5 Machado (2008): S. 113
6 Ferroni (2008): S. 89
7 Segurança Imobiliária S.A. (1962): S. 2
8 Rupf (2015): S. 194

3 Blick von der Galeriebrücke
View from the gallery bridge

4 Schnitt Süd-Nord
South-north section
1:1000

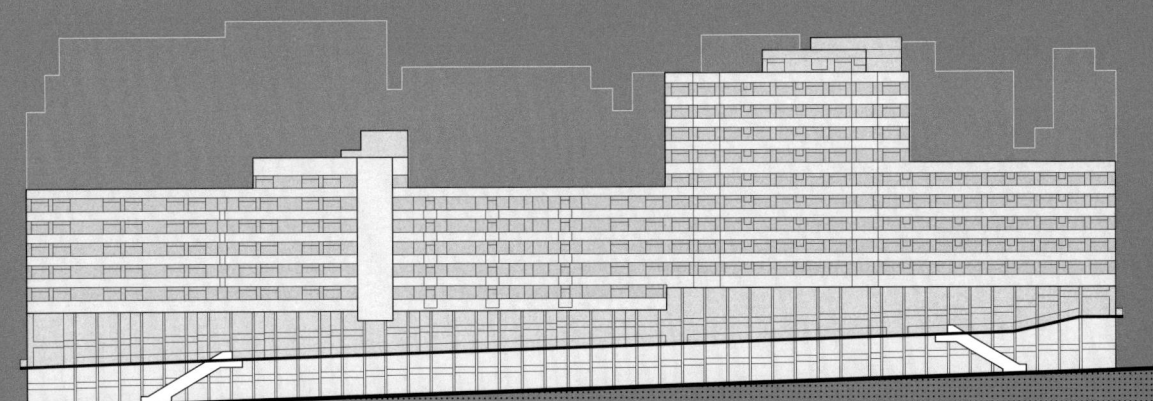

KONFLIKTE UND KÜNFTIGE ENTWICKLUNG

Die kleinteilige Eigentümerstruktur der Galerie bietet Vor- und Nachteile. Die Mieter sind untereinander vernetzt. Entsprechend können sie gemeinsam Lösungen finden und dabei flexibler reagieren, als es die regulierten Verfahrenswege in einem Shopping Center zulassen. Gleichzeitig erschwert die kleinteilige Nutzerstruktur aber auch die Entscheidungsfindung. Veränderungen verzögern sich und lassen sich nur schrittweise umsetzen.

Zudem sind die Mieter in ihren Mitspracherechten eingeschränkt. Beispielsweise will ein Teil der Betreiber während und nach den Öffnungszeiten öffentlich zugängliche Flächen für Veranstaltungen und Konzerte nutzen. Eine Zeitlang wurden die Verbindungsbrücken zwischen den Laubengängen von den angrenzenden Cafés und Bars bespielt. Inzwischen hat aber die Gebäudeverwaltung diese Nutzungen untersagt.

Ein weiterer Konflikt betrifft das ‚Selbstverständnis' der Galerie. Das Projekt ist ursprünglich als offene Passage konzipiert, die sich nahtlos in die umgebende Stadtstruktur einfügt.[9] Dadurch lässt sich nicht verhindern, dass bestimmte Bereiche als Schlaf- oder Abstellplatz zweckentfremdet werden. Inzwischen wird die Passage daher durch ein Rolltor eingefasst und nachts abgeschlossen.[10] Zusätzlich weisen Hinweisschilder darauf hin, dass die Passage ein Privatgrundstück quert. Diese Veränderungen werden von einigen Befragten bedauert.

Aktuell wird anhand von Studien geprüft, ob die Passage überdacht werden kann. Einige der Befragten erwarten eine weitere Spezialisierung der Galerie. Als Vorbild wird auf die Galeria do Rock verwiesen.

5 Blick
View
Rua 7 de Abril

[9] Segurança Imobiliária S.A. (1962): S. 2
[10] Segurança Imobiliária S.A. (1962) S. 2

6   Grundriss EG
    Floor plan GF
    1:1000

7   Grundriss 1. OG
    Floor plan 1F
    1:1000

8   ‚Platz'
    'Square'
    (S. 82 / p. 82)

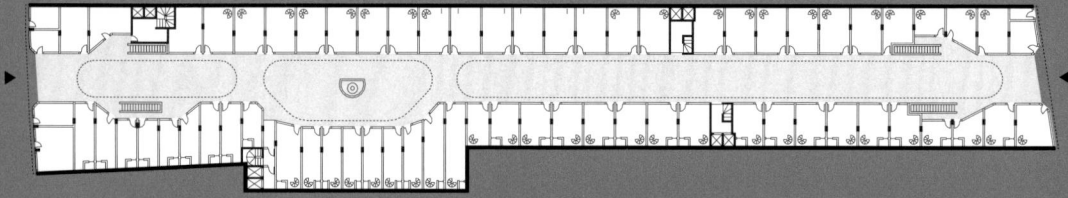

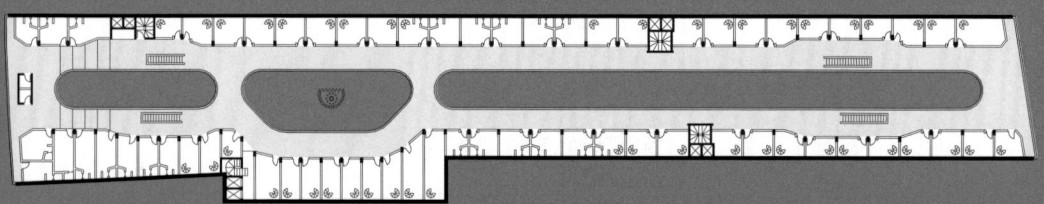

GALERIA NOVA BARÃO

SPACE AND FORM

The Galeria Nova Barão is located in the Centro Novo quarter. It connects Rua Barão de Itapetininga with Rua 7 de Abril - two important pedestrian routes between the Anhangabaú valley and Praça da República.[1] In the range of sight from Theatro Municipal, the passage constitutes an additional crossing point through the block of buildings. Being surrounded on both sides by shops and service establishments, it attracts a high frequency of pedestrians and walk-in customers.

The gallery property divides a block of buildings over a depth of around 150m. Its width averages only 22m. Accordingly, the passage is bordered by a building structure with between 5 and 11m in depth on each side.

Towards Rua Barão de Itapetininga, the upper floors contain residential apartments; towards Rua 7 de Abril, they contain office spaces. The shop units on the ground floor and on the first floor are occupied by a mixture of retailers and service providers. The two structural units are each bordered by an open gallery on the first floor. The gallery sides can be accessed via escalators and are connected by a total of four bridges. Two of those gallery bridges frame the entrances to the passage. The two remaining bridges divide the passage into three sections of different lengths.

The small stone paving used in the movement area corresponds to the paving of the adjacent streets. The central square is emphasised through street furniture and a fountain. This ensemble was not part of the original design.[2]

The gallery property features a slope of about 5m from northeast to southwest. The ceiling height of the commercial units reconciles the ascending ground level with the gallery height. The shop units are 4.5m wide and, according to location, up to 6m high. In contrast, the standard upper floors feature a uniform height. They average about seven floors. Around the enlargement, the building blocks each shift by one floor upwards. The southern building portion is emphasised with four additional floors at the gallery enlargement.

The users of the gallery mainly come from the centre of São Paulo. Many passers-by use the passage as a convenient shortcut. For many visitors, the passage also provides an opportunity to rest and relax. However, some also travel long distances to visit special shops. Currently, the number of younger visitors is increasing.

The services of the gallery react to their surrounding conditions. At the transitions to the adjacent streets, fast food places take advantage of the greater frequency of walk-in customers. On the quieter gallery level, there is an array of about 20 'Sebos' (second-hand book stores), each with their own focus in terms of used books and sound media. Their assortment is each oriented to a dedicated patronage. Between them, there are clothing and jewellery shops, hair salons, opticians as well as a shop for vegan food, among others.

The gallery is open daily between 7 a.m. and 7.30 p.m. At night and on Sundays it remains closed. Access is limited to tenants and owners during those times. Upper floor apartments and offices can be accessed from the passage at ground level as well as from the galleries. The staircases are monitored by one doorman each on the ground floor. The passage itself is monitored by security staff in plain clothes.

[1] Rupf (2015): p. 197 f.
[2] Rupf (2015): p. 208

ORIGIN

The Galeria Nova Barão is located between the surrounding shopping streets such as Rua Marconi and Rua Conselheiro Crispiniano. Accordingly, it is initially marketed as the new 'Rua' after opening.[3] Its open access is intended to communicate that the passage seamlessly fits in with the structure of the surrounding street spaces.[4]

The project was initiated by the development company Alfredo Mathias and inaugurated in 1962.[5] Architects Ermanno Siffredi and Maria Bardelli developed the design as cooperation partners. With the same cooperation team, the company developed further gallery projects in the Centro Novo quarter.[6] Alfredo Mathias also took charge of property acquisition and a share of preliminary financing.

Before the start of construction, residential and commercial units were already advertised and sold to ensure residual financing. For commercial, residential and office units, 50 to 60% of the purchase price had to be paid before the start of construction.[7] All commercial units were sold out in the course of one day; the remaining building parts took only 3 days to sell.[8]

The roughly 200 residential and 130 commercial units of the gallery are distributed over approximately 100 owners. A large portion of the units is sublet at this point. Rental prices are based on the market value but do vary within the building complex.

Owners and tenants are responsible for maintenance and reconstruction measures regarding the units. Building security, street furniture as well as maintenance and repairs to jointly used building areas are taken care of by a building management agency representing all owners. Joint expenses are also included. Due to the large number of owners, modification and repair measures can only be carried out over extended periods of time.

Passersby and users perceive the gallery as a continuation of the surrounding shopping streets. Its shop structure follows certain trends. Until the mid-2000s, the emphasis was on hair salons and jewellery shops. Since 2007, it has shifted to the sale of used media.

The gallery serves as a passageway. However, its specialised shops cater to a particular clientele. The individual shop owners benefit from each other. They value the particular atmosphere and maintain a neighbourly relationship.

The joint aim of owners and tenants is to preserve the gallery as a place with an inviting and open atmosphere.

CONFLICTS AND FUTURE DEVELOPMENT

The fragmented ownership structure of the gallery has advantages as well as disadvantages. Tenants are well-connected among each other. Accordingly, they can find solutions together and react more flexibly than highly regulated procedures a shopping mall would allow. At the same time, the fractured user structure impedes decision-making. Changes are held up and can only be implemented gradually.

Also, tenants are restricted regarding their voice in matters. For example, a share of the music shops would like to use their spaces for events and concerts during and after opening hours. In the past, the connecting bridges between the gallery levels had been used by adjacent cafés and bars. At this point, the building administration has prohibited all events as well as any occupation of the gallery spaces.

Another conflict concerns the gallery's self-image. The project was originally designed as an open passage which seamlessly integrates with the surrounding urban structure.[9] This makes it impossible to prevent gallery and entrance areas from being repurposed for sleeping and depositing things. For this reason, the passage has been fitted with a roller gate at this point and remains closed at night.[10] During the day, signs serve as reminders of the fact that the passage is a private property. Many of those surveyed regret these changes.

Currently, studies are conducted to find out whether it is possible to canopy the passage. Some of those surveyed expect a further specialisation of the gallery. The Galeria do Rock is pointed to as an example.

---

9 **Balkon mit Aussicht / Balcony with a view**
Rua Barão de Itapetininga

3 Aleixo (2005): p. 240
4 Segurança Imobiliária S.A. (1962): p. 2
5 Machado (2008): p. 113
6 Ferroni (2008): p. 89
7 Segurança Imobiliária S.A. (1962): p. 2
8 Rupf (2015): p. 194
9 Segurança Imobiliária S.A. (1962): p. 2
10 Segurança Imobiliária S.A. (1962): p. 2

SESC 24 DE MAIO

RAUM UND GESTALT

Das Kulturzentrum SESC 24 de Maio liegt im Stadtteil Centro Novo an der Straßenkreuzung Rua 24 de Maio und Rua Dom José de Barros. Der Standort befindet sich in der Nähe der Praça da República. Die umgebenden Straßen werden tagsüber, abends und samstags stark durch Einheimische und Touristen genutzt. Entlang der Rua 24 de Maio finden in den Abendstunden regelmäßig Straßenpartys statt.

Das Grundstück liegt gegenüber der Galeria do Rock und dem Centro Comercial Presidente. Direkt südöstlich grenzt die Galeria R. Monteiro an. Das Erdgeschoss des Kulturzentrums ist über zwei Eingänge mit den angrenzenden Straßenräumen verbunden und bietet damit eine Abkürzungsmöglichkeit.

Das Kulturzentrum gehört zu den Einrichtungen des Serviço Social do Comércio (SESC). Die halbstaatliche Organisation entwickelt und betreibt Zentren mit den Schwerpunkten Kultur, Bildung, Freizeit und Sport.[1] Die entsprechenden Gebäude sind von Montag bis Samstag geöffnet und größtenteils öffentlich zugänglich. Neben Aufenthaltsmöglichkeiten bieten sie ein breites Spektrum an Veranstaltungen, Kursen, Lesungen und Vorführungen. Finanziert werden die Projekte durch Unternehmen, die einen Teil ihrer Steuerabgaben an die Organisation SESC abführen.

Das Projekt im Centro Novo kombiniert typische Merkmale von SESC-Einrichtungen. Zu dem differenzierten Nutzungsprogramm gehört ein Mix aus Aufenthaltsbereichen, ein Theater, ein Lesesaal und eine Bibliothek, Sportflächen sowie ein Dach-Schwimmbad. Ergänzt wird dieses Programm um ein gastronomisches Angebot aus Cafés und einem Großrestaurant. Diese Nutzungen sind eingebunden in ein Gefüge aus großzügig dimensionierten, frei zugänglichen Aufenthaltsflächen.

KONZEPT

Die Organisation SESC ist in São Paulo mit verschiedenen Einrichtungen vertreten. Das Kulturzentrum 24 de Maio ergänzt das SESC-Angebot im Centro Novo. Das Nutzungsgefüge des Stadtteils ist überwiegend kommerziell geprägt. Das Projekt erweitert dieses Angebot um Kultur- und Freizeit-Nutzungen. Als neuer innerstädtischer Anziehungspunkt soll es die Attraktivität des Centro Novo steigern und die Aufenthaltsdauer von Besuchern, Bewohnern und Touristen in der Innenstadt verlängern.

Entsprechend wird das Projekt zusätzlich durch die Stadtverwaltung unterstützt. Die seit 1997 bestehende ‚Operação Urbana Centro' zielt auf die Aufwertung des Stadtzentrums ab und sieht dazu finanzielle Anreize für Investoren vor. Gefördert wird der Umbau von Bestandsbauten für kulturelle oder bildungsorientierte Nutzungen.

Die Festsetzung soll den Trading-Down-Prozess der Innenstadt umkehren und die Vielfalt an innerstädtischen Nutzungen und Akteuren bereichern.[2] Sie sieht vor bestimmte Nutzungen bei der Berechnung der Grundflächenzahl (GRZ) auszunehmen.[3] Dazu gehören Kinosäle, Konferenzräume, Auditorien, Museen, Kitas, Räume mit Bildungs- und Kulturangeboten im Allgemeinen sowie Erdgeschossflächen, die zur öffentlichen Nutzung bestimmt sind. Damit wird eine höhere bauliche Ausnutzung des Grundstücks möglich.

Auf dem Grundstück des Kulturzentrums befindet sich ursprünglich das Kaufhaus Mesbla. Auf Grundlage der ‚Operação Urbana Centro' integriert der Gebäudeentwurf den Rohbau des Kaufhauses. Der Entwurf wird von Paulo Mendes da Rocha und dem Büro MMBB Arquitetos entwickelt. Planung und Bau beanspruchen einen Zeitraum von rund 15 Jahren.[4]

---

1 Dachschwimmbad
Pool at the rooftop

[1] Lepik, Bader (2014): S. 359
[2] Operação Urbana Centro (Lei 12.349 de 6 de Junho de 1997 do Município de São Paulo)
[3] Operação Urbana Centro (Lei 12.349 de 6 de Junho de 1997 do Município de São Paulo)
[4] Serapião (2018): S. 273

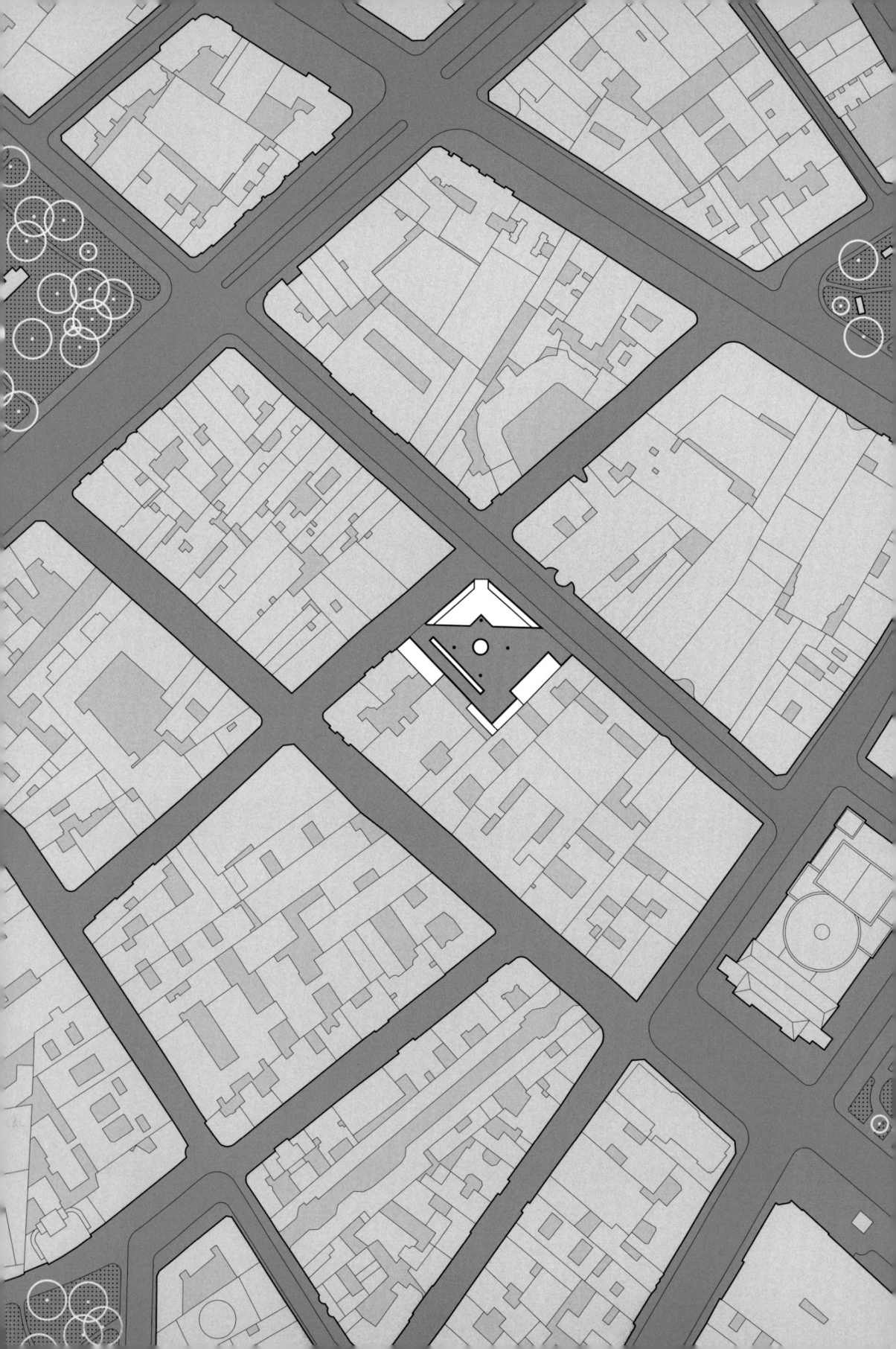

Der Ursprungsbau besitzt einen U-förmigen Lichthof. In diesem Bereich werden neue, durchgehende Stützen ergänzt, die die Zusatzlast der Aufstockung aufnehmen.[5] Zusätzlich zum Umbau der bestehenden Etagen wird das Gebäude aufgestockt. Mit dem Umbau erhöht sich die nutzbare Geschossfläche von 13.000qm auf rund 27.900qm.[6]

Durch den Erhalt des Bestands-Rohbaus ist die Disposition der Innenräume stark vorgeprägt. Für das Projekt wird eine südlich an das Grundstück angrenzende Parzelle mit erworben. In diesem Gebäudeteil sind Lager, Not-Treppenhäuser, Leitungen sowie sanitäre Einrichtungen untergebracht.[7] Das Auslagern der Nebenräume und Aufzugsschächte ermöglicht es, die Hauptflächen von Einbauten freizuhalten und eine offene Raumdisposition zu sichern.

Der Konzept greift Motive der umgebenden Galeriebauten auf. Das Erdgeschoss öffnet sich an zwei Seiten zu den angrenzenden Straßenräumen. Es knüpft dabei bewusst an die offenen Erdgeschossbereiche der benachbarten Galeriebauten an.

Das Gebäude stellt ein großzügiges und frei zugängliches Angebot an Bewegungs-, Aufenthalts- und Funktionsflächen bereit, das sich über alle Etagen erstreckt.[8] Alle Geschosse sind über Aufzüge zu erreichen. Als vertikale ‚Promenade' ist zusätzlich eine doppelläufige Erschließungsrampe vorgesehen. Anfangs- und Endpunkt dieser ‚Promenade' führen jeweils zu nutzungsoffenen Flächen[9], die unterschiedlich möbliert sind. Die Möbelserien werden für das Projekt entwickelt.

Der Entwurf inszeniert über großzügige Fenster und Balkone die umgebenden Stadträume. Lage und Zuschnitt von Rampe und innerer Erschließung rahmen Ausschnitte der Stadtsilhouette sowie ausgewählte Fassadenabschnitte. Entlang der Rampe sind Einblicke in das angrenzende Bürogebäude möglich.[10] Sichtbeziehungen bestehen u.a. zum Innenraum des Centro Comercial Presidente sowie zur Dachterrasse der Galeria do Rock.

NUTZUNG UND NUTZERGRUPPEN

Das SESC umfasst insgesamt 14 Etagen mit einem breitgefächerten Nutzungsmix. Als neuer innerstädtischer Anziehungspunkt formulieren Programm und Bespielung ein Angebot, das sich an unterschiedliche Alters- und Einkommensgruppen richtet. Im Gebäude begegnen sich Anrainer, Angestellte, Bewohner aus anderen Stadtteilen, Wohnungslose und Touristen. Zur Zeit wird das Gebäude täglich von etwa 10.000 Personen in Anspruch genommen.

Grob unterscheiden lassen sich Flächen für kulturelle Nutzungen, Sportflächen, gastronomische Angebote sowie ein kleiner Teil an privatwirtschaftlich genutzter Flächen.[11] Sie sind eingebettet in jeweils großzügige Raumabschnitte, die unbelegt bleiben und frei genutzt werden können. Die Abschnitte unterscheiden sich durch ihre Sonnenexpositionen, durch ihre Lage im Gebäude sowie durch die jeweiligen Ausblicke zum umgebenden Stadtgefüge.

Das Angebot an Kultur-Nutzungen umfasst ein Theater, Ausstellungsräume, Workshopräume, Gruppenräume und eine Bibliothek. Zu den Sportnutzungen zählen der Pool auf der Dachfläche sowie weitere Sport-, Fitness- und Kinderspielbereiche. Zusätzlich in das Nutzungsgefüge eingeflochten sind ein Buffetrestaurant, ein Café, eine privat betriebene Zahnarztpraxis sowie der Managementbereich des Gebäudes.

Kurse in den Bereichen Sport, Fitness und Tanz stehen ganztägig zur Verfügung, um eine hohe Inanspruchnahme zu gewährleisten. Das Mittagsangebot des Restaurants zieht zusätzlich eine Vielzahl von Besuchern an, insbesondere auch Angestellte aus der Umgebung des SESC. Ganztägig werden die Aufenthaltsbereiche zum Sitzen, Liegen, Ausruhen, Lesen, Spielen und Diskutieren in Anspruch genommen. Diese Nutzungen finden in einem belebten Rahmen statt - es gibt ein ständiges Kommen und Gehen. Dagegen wird der Zugang zum Pool kurz nach der Eröffnung aufgrund der sehr starken Nachfrage eingeschränkt. Inzwischen steht der Schwimmbereich nur noch SESC-Mitgliedern zur Verfügung.

EINSCHÄTZUNG

Für viele Nutzer ist das SESC ein besonderer und außergewöhnlicher Ort. Besonders beliebt sind die offenen, unbespielten Flächen. In der 11. Etage ist der Gebäuderand durch ein flaches Wasserbassin eingefasst. Ursprünglich als Distanzfläche zur Absturzsicherung gedacht, wird sie inzwischen als Plansche und zum Abkühlen genutzt. Initiiert wurde diese Nutzung durch Kinder. Sie nutzen die Fläche zum Spielen und Toben. Inzwischen wird die Fläche auch von Erwachsenen genutzt. Eine besondere Erfahrung ist es, im Wasser stehend, auf die umgebende Stadtsilhouette zu schauen.

Das Angebot an Räumen und Nutzungen werden von den Befragten grundsätzlich positiv bewertet. Im Kontrast zum lebhaften und hektischen Alltag bietet das Gebäude einen ruhigen und kontemplativen ‚Zufluchtsort'.

2	**Lageplan** **Site plan** 1:2000
3	**Dachschwimmbad** **Pool at the rooftop** (S. 90 / p. 90)
5	Serapião (2018): S. 273
6	Serapião (2018): S. 276
7	Ausnahme bilden die zwei, in einem Zusatzschacht untergebrachten Aufzüge.
8	mit Ausnahme des Dachgeschosses
9	Serapião (2018): S. 273
10	Serapião (2018): S. 276; Mungioli (2017): S. 62
11	Mungioli (2017): S. 62

Die Befragten verbringen einen Teil ihrer Freizeit im Gebäude und nutzen die unterschiedlichen Angebote zum Üben, zum Lernen, zur Unterhaltung oder zum Entspannen.

Die meisten Angebote des SESC richten sich an eine breite Öffentlichkeit. Zum Gebäudekonzept gehört eine einheitlich gestaltete Möbelfamilie, deren Elemente unterschiedliche Nutzungen wie Sitzen, Liegen, Einzelarbeiten oder Austausch ermöglichen. Allerdings dürfen die Möbel nicht frei verstellt werden.

Exklusiv werden SESC-Mitgliedern zusätzlich Nutzungsprogramme zur Verfügung gestellt, u.a. hier der Poolbereich und die dazugehörige Dachterrasse. Vereinzelt werden zusätzliche Nutzungen wie beispielsweise Ballsportplätze vermisst. Nicht alle Anwohner können sich die Preise im Großrestaurant leisten. Sie bringen stattdessen ihr Essen mit.

Für das Gebäude besteht kein besonderes Sicherheitskonzept. Allerdings werden die öffentlich zugänglichen Bereiche durch Sicherheitspersonal überwacht. Viele der Befragten fühlen sich im Gebäude deutlich sicherer als in den umgebenden Stadträumen. Familien schätzen das Angebot, um ihren Kindern Sport und Spiel in einer sicheren Umgebung zu ermöglichen. Betont wird auch der gepflegte Zustand des Gebäudes.

Inzwischen wird auch eine Aufwertung des umgebenden Quartiers sichtbar. Zu den positiven Veränderungen gehören neu eröffnete Restaurants sowie eine sich wandelnde Zusammensetzung von Geschäften. Entsprechend verändert sich auch die Zusammensetzung der Besucher, die sich in diesem Teil des Centro Novo aufhalten.

4 **Grundriss EG**
Floor plan GF
1:1000

5 **Grundriss 2. OG**
Floor plan 2F
1:1000

6 **Grundriss 11. OG**
Floor plan 11F
1:1000

7 **Grundriss DG**
Floor plan TF
1:1000

8 **Zugang**
Accessibility
(S. 94 / p. 94)

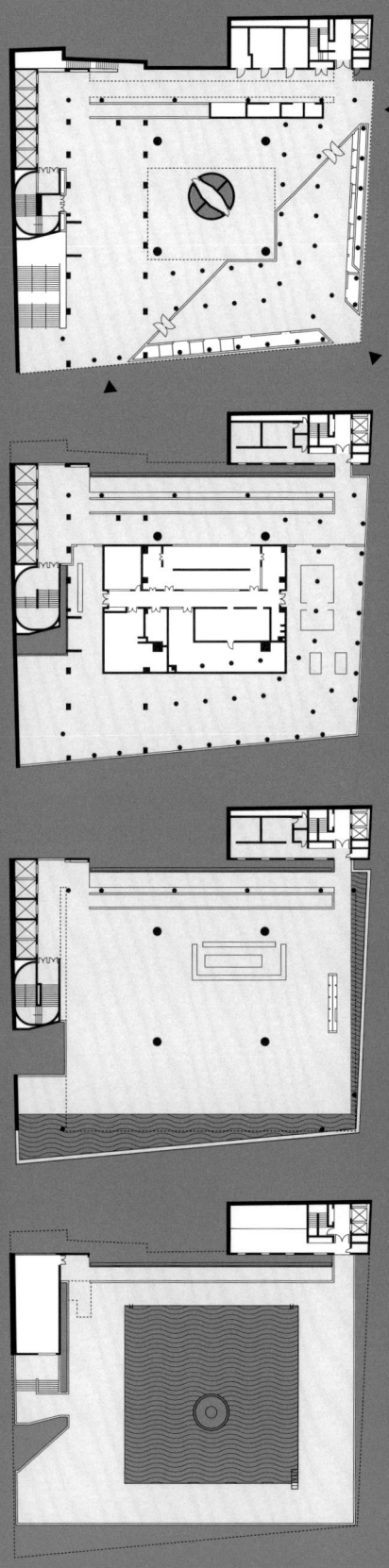

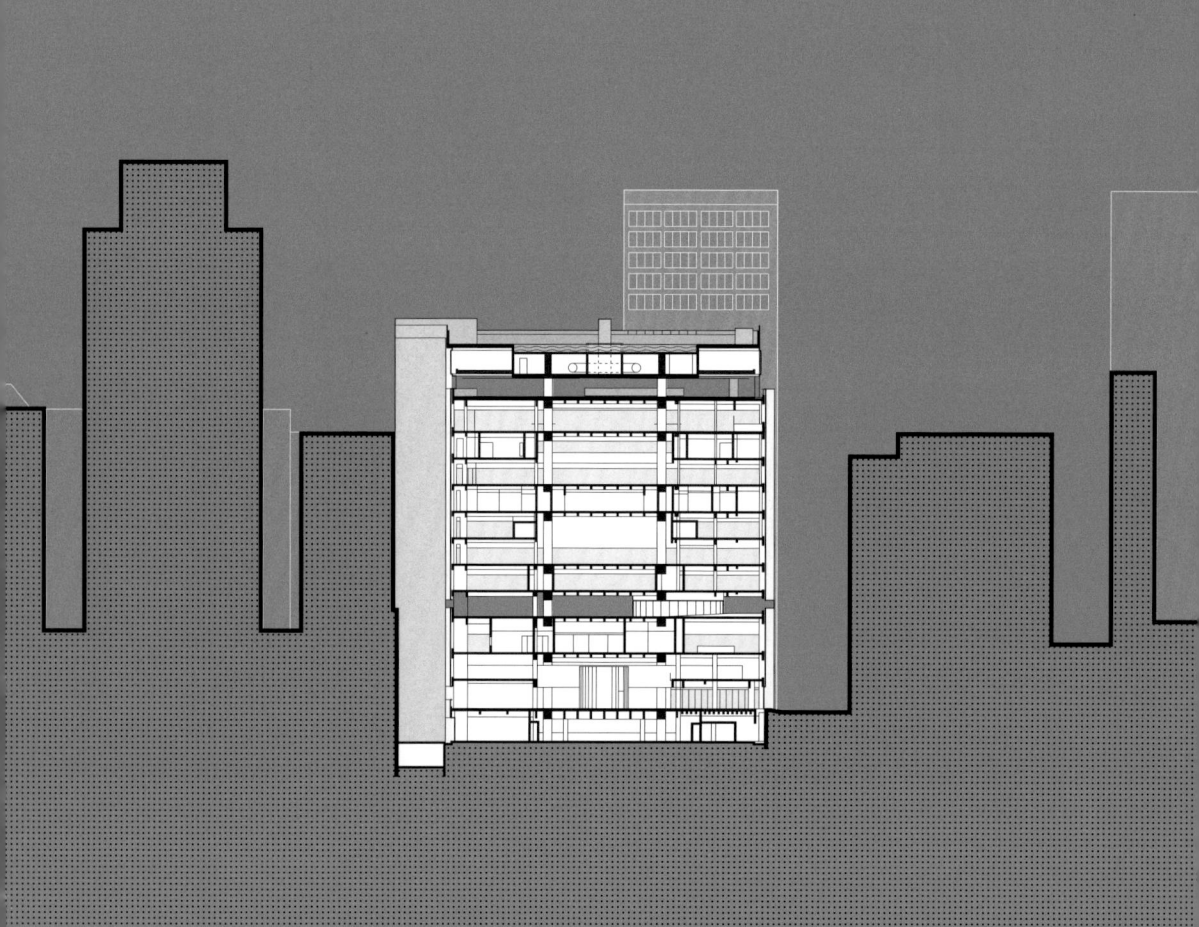

SESC 24 DE MAIO

SPACE AND FORM

The cultural centre SESC 24 de Maio is located in the Centro Novo quarter at the intersection of Rua 24 de Maio and Rua Dom José de Barros. Its location is near Praça da República. Surrounding streets are heavily used by locals and tourists alike during the day, in the evening and on Saturdays. Along Rua 24 de Maio, street parties regularly take place in the evening hours.

The property faces the Galeria do Rock and the Centro Comercial Presidente. To the southeast, it is directly bordered by the Galeria R. Monteiro. The ground floor of the cultural centre is connected to the adjacent street spaces via two entrances and therefore provides an additional shortcut.

The cultural centre is one of the facilities of the abbreviation SESC denotes: the parastatal organisation Serviço Social do Comércio (SESC). The semi-governmental organisation develops and operates facilities centres with a focus on culture, education, leisure and sport.[1] Its centres are open Monday through Saturday and publicly accessible for the most part. They provide various facilities for lingering, a wide range of ad-hoc events as well as programme-based classes, practice units, literary readings and performances. The centres are funded through companies which pay a portion of their taxes to the SESC organisation.

The project in Centro Novo combines typical features of SESC establishments. Its differentiated use programme includes a mix of areas for lingering, a theatre, a reading room and a library, sports areas as well as a rooftop swimming pool. This concept is completed by gastronomic facilities such as cafés and a large restaurant. These uses are integrated into a structure of generously-dimensioned, freely accessible spaces for lingering.

CONCEPT

The SESC organisation is present in most quarters of São Paulo with at least one establishment. The cultural centre 24 de Maio supplements the SESC presence in Centro Novo. The district has a predominantly commercial character. The project enhances this spectrum with cultural and leisure uses. As a new inner-city attraction, it increases the attractiveness of Centro Novo and encourages visitors, residents and tourists to spend more time in the city centre.

Accordingly, the project is supported by the city administration. The 'Operação Urbana Centro', which has been in place since 1997, aims to upgrade São Paulo's city centre and provides financial incentives for investors. It promotes the reconfiguration of existing buildings for cultural or education-based uses.[2] The regulation is designed to reverse the trading-down process of the city centre and to increase the diversity of inner-city uses and stakeholders. It provides for certain uses to be excluded from the calculation of the floor area ratio.[3] This includes cinemas, conference rooms, auditoriums, museums, childcare facilities, rooms with educational and cultural programmes in general as well as ground floors intended for public use. This allows for a higher degree of structural utilisation of the property.

The property originally housed the Mesbla department store. Based on the 'Operação Urbana Centro', the building design integrates the shell of the department stores'. The design was developed by Paulo Mendes da Rocha and the office MMBB Arquitetos. Planning and construction took a period of roughly 15 years to complete.[4]

The original building has a U-shaped atrium. In this area, new continuous columns were added to carry the additional load of the raising.[5]

9 **Schnitt Ost-West**
East-west section
1:1000

10 **Stadtpanorama**
City panorama
(S. 98 / p. 98)

[1] Lepik, Bader (2014): p. 359
[2] Operação Urbana Centro (Lei 12.349 de 6 de Junho de 1997 do Município de São Paulo)
[3] Operação Urbana Centro (Lei 12.349 de 6 de Junho de 1997 do Município de São Paulo)
[4] Serapião (2018): p. 273
[5] Serapião (2018): p. 273

11	**Planschbecken** **Wading pool** Stadtsilhouette Cityscape
6	Serapião (2018): p. 276
7	The exception being its two elevators, which are located in an additional shaft.
8	Except for the top floor
9	Serapião (2018): p. 273
10	Serapião (2018): p. 276; Mungioli (2017): p. 62
11	Mungioli (2017): p. 62

In addition to the conversion of the existing floors, the building is being raised. Through the conversion, the usable floor space increased from 13,000sqm to roughly 27,900sqm.[6]

Due to the preservation of the existing building shell, the disposition of the interior spaces is strongly predetermined. For the project, a neighbouring parcel to the south was also purchased. This building portion houses storages, emergency staircases, piping as well as sanitary facilities.[7] Shifting ancillary rooms and elevator shafts this way facilitates keeping the main areas free from installations and ensuring an open disposition of space.

The concept picks up on themes of the surrounding gallery buildings. The ground floor opens up to the adjacent street spaces on two sides. This way, it intentionally connects the open ground floors of the neighbouring galleries. The building offers a generous and free range of movement, lingering and functional areas across all floors.[8]

All floors can be accessed via elevators. A two-way access ramp is intended as an additional vertical 'promenade'. The starting and end points of this 'promenade' each are open-to-use areas[9] equipped with various types of seating furniture.

The design showcases the surrounding urban spaces via generous windows and balconies. Ramp and circulation frame particular urban spaces or facade parts. From the ramp, it is possible to see inside the neighbouring office building.[10] Other vistas include the interior of the Centro Comercial Presidente and the roof terrace of the Galeria do Rock.

USES

The SESC features a total of 14 floors with a wide range of uses. As a new inner-city point of attraction, programme and utilisation form an offer for various age and income groups. Inside the building, residents, employees, visitors from other parts of the city, homeless people and tourists cross paths. Currently, the building is used by around 10,000 persons per day.

A distinction can be made between cultural uses, sports uses and areas for lingering and relaxation.[11] The first group includes a theatre, exhibition spaces, workshop spaces, group spaces and a library. Sports uses include the swimming pool on the rooftop as well as further sports, fitness and children's play areas.

The gastronomic facilities include a buffet restaurant and a café. The combination of uses also incorporates a private dentist as well as the building's management.

Room sections which remain unoccupied and can be used freely are situated in between. As 'indoor plazas', their varying features promote and support prolonged stays in the building. The areas are distinguished by their exposure to sunlight, their location within the building and the respective views of the surrounding urban structure.

Sports, fitness and dance classes are available all day to ensure a high degree of utilisation. The lunch menu of the restaurant attracts an additional crowd, among others, employees from the vicinity of the SESC.

The lounge areas are used for sitting, reclining, relaxing, reading, playing and discussing throughout the day. These uses take place in a busy atmosphere - there is a continual coming and going. Shortly after the opening, due to the massive demand, access to the pool facilities was strongly restricted. At this point, the swimming area is only accessible to SESC members.

EVALUATION

For many users, the SESC 24 de Maio is a special and extraordinary place. Its open, unoccupied areas and the pool on the top floor are very popular. On the 11th floor, the building edge is bordered with a shallow water basin. This area was originally intended as a safety barrier.

However, in a departure from that, it is now used as a wading pool. This use was initiated by children. They use the space for playing, romping and cooling off. Adults have also taken to using the space at this point. It is a particular experience to stand in the water and look out onto the surrounding urban silhouette.

Persons surveyed fundamentally rated the facilities and the spatial characteristic of the cultural centre positively. In contrast to the bustle and rush of everyday life, the building provides a calm and contemplative 'refuge'. Accordingly, those surveyed spend a part of their free time in the building, taking advantage of the spaces for practising, studying, relaxing or meeting up.

Most facilities of the SESC are geared to a wide section of the public. The building concept includes a uniform-design furniture range whose individual parts enable different uses such as sitting, reclining, individual work or exchange.

If furniture is rearranged, staff will urge users to restore the original arrangement. However, the furniture must not be moved freely.

Exclusive use programmes are provided to SESC members, however, among other things the pool area and the associated rooftop terrace. Sporadically, users wanted additional facilities such as ball game courts. Not all residents of the quarter can afford the prices at the large restaurant. Instead, they bring their own food.

There is no particular security concept for the building. However, publicly accessible spaces are monitored by security staff. Users rate the associated atmosphere differently. Many of those surveyed felt much safer inside the building than in the streets surrounding it. The well-tended state of the building was emphasised. Families appreciate the facilities which enable them to provide their kids with sports and play activities in a safe environment.

Emphasis was placed on the fact that marginalised populations are welcome here and do not have to face prejudice.

By now, a gradual valorisation of the quarter can be noticed. Positive effects of this change include new restaurants as well as a changing composition of businesses. Accordingly, the mixture of visitors spending time in this part of Centro Novo is also changing.

12 **Rahmung historische Fassade**
Framing a historical facade

13 **Blickbeziehungen**
Visual relationships
(S. 104 / p. 104)

14 **Blickbeziehungen**
Visual relationships
(S. 104 / p. 104)

15 **Vertikale Promenade**
Vertical promenade
(S. 105 / p. 105)

PRAÇA DAS ARTES

RAUM UND GESTALT

Das Gebäude Praça das Artes befindet sich am Rand des Stadtteils Centro Novo in São Paulo, am Übergang zur Altstadt zwischen den beiden historisch bedeutsamen Brücken Viaduto do Chá und dem Viaduto Santa Ifigênia. Der Stadtteil ist gekennzeichnet durch eine sehr heterogene Bebauung. Die Nähe zum Stadtkern und der Bauboom der 1950er Jahre haben zu einer kleinteilig parzellierten Stadtlandschaft geführt: Wohn-, Büro-, Dienstleistungs- und gewerbliche Nutzungen mischen sich hier in Gebäudeeinheiten zwischen zwei und 30 Geschossen.

Typisch für die Baublocks des Centro Novo sind Grundstücksparzellen, die dreiseitig eingefasst und nur von einer Straßenseite aus zu erschließen sind. Innerhalb dieses Gefüges nimmt die Gebäudekomposition der Praça das Artes eine t-förmig zugeschnittene Grundfläche in Anspruch. Das Grundstück ist durch das Zusammenlegen ursprünglich überbauter Parzellen entstanden und öffnet sich zu drei Seiten: in Richtung Anhangabaú-Tal, zur Rua Formosa sowie zur nordwestlich parallel verlaufenden Rua Conselheiro Crispiniano. In Richtung Nord schließt es direkt an die Avenida São João an, einer wichtigen Verbindung zwischen Altstadtkern und Centro Novo.

Das Grundstück verbindet die angrenzenden Straßen mit dem Talraum Anhangabaú. Es bleibt dazu im Erdgeschoss nahezu vollständig unbebaut. Lediglich entlang der Grundstücksgrenzen liegen jeweils schmal ausgebildete Gebäuderiegel, in denen Eingänge und Zulieferung untergebracht sind. Ab dem ersten Obergeschoss sind diese Riegel durch zwei Brückenbauten miteinander verbunden. Zusätzlich sind drei Bestandsbauten in das Projekt integriert: das ‚Conservatório Dramático e Musical', das ‚Cinema Cairo' und die ‚Music Library'.[1]

Die Gebäudekomposition reagiert auf die Eigenschaften der jeweils angrenzenden Bebauung. Sie vermittelt zwischen der Hochhausbebauung entlang des Anhangabaú-Tals und der Bebauung des Centro Novo. Die beiden Brückenbauten teilen das Grundstück in drei Teilbereiche:

- Im Nordwesten entsteht durch die hohe Nachbarbebauung und dem die Grundstücksgrenze begleitenden Riegel ein Eingangshof.
- Richtung Nordost schließt die überdachte Öffnung zur Avenida São João an. Hier liegt der Haupteingang zu allen Gebäudeteilen.
- Hinter der Gebäudebrücke in Richtung Südosten öffnet sich der Raum zum tiefer liegenden Anhangabaú-Tal.

Auf der Freifläche sind Angebote zum Sitzen und Verweilen verteilt. Dazu gehören Sitzstufen in Richtung Anhangabaú, Bänke unterhalb der überdachten Flächen sowie eine fest installierte Bar einschließlich Tresen. Die Flächen werden tagsüber stark in Anspruch genommen - nicht nur von den Nutzern des Gebäudekomplexes, sondern auch von Passanten und Wohnungslosen.

NUTZUNG UND NUTZERGRUPPEN

Das Projekt Praça das Artes ergänzt das Theatro Municipal de São Paulo, eine etwa 150m entfernt liegende Kultureinrichtung. Dazu verfügt das Gebäude über rund 28.500qm Nutzfläche.[2] Das Raumprogramm umfasst eine Tanz- und Musikschule mit Kurs- und Unterrichtsräumen, Räume für Künstlergruppen, ein historisches Konservatorium für Theater und Musik, Ausstellungsbereiche sowie Säle für Aufführungen und Events.[3] Als Trägerorganisation verantwortet die Secretaria Municipal de Cultura der Stadt São Paulo[4] die Nutzungen im Gebäude.

---

1   **Blick Anhangabaú-Tal**
    View into Anhangabaú valley

1   Nosek (2013): S. 8
2   Fanucci, Ferraz (2016): S. 29
3   Fanucci, Ferraz, Cartum (2013): S. 36
4   Fanucci, Ferraz (2016): S. 31

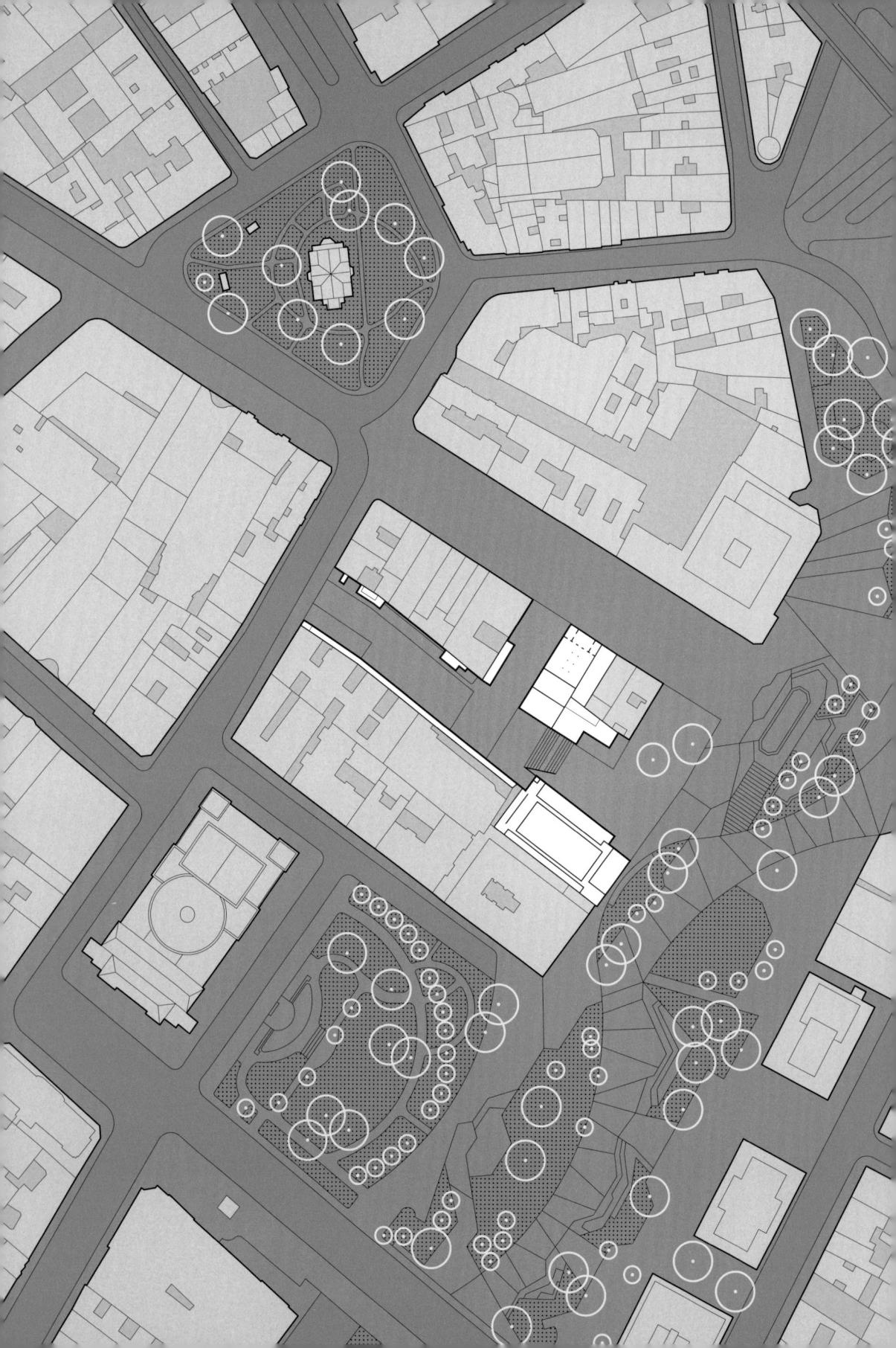

Die Veranstaltungen und Ausstellungen werden durch das Instituto Odeon und die Fundação Theatro Municipal organisiert und kuratiert.[5]

Der Gebäudekomplex ist introvertiert ausgebildet. Auch die EG-Bereiche zeigen sich überwiegend geschlossen. Entsprechend lassen sich von außen die Nutzungen nur schwer erkennen. Zudem wird der Gebäudezugang im Foyerbereich kontrolliert. Zugelassen sind nur Schüler, Lehrpersonal sowie eingeladene Besucher.

Tagsüber wird die Freifläche durch Passanten, Touristen und Wohnungslose in Anspruch genommen. Die Flächen sind offen und laden zum Aufenthalt ein. Dabei bieten die überdachten Bereiche Schutz vor Witterung ohne in einen kommerziellen Kontext eingebunden zu sein. Freiflächen und Gebäudezugang werden ganztägig durch Sicherheitspersonal überwacht, im Kontrast zu den oft ungesicherten innerstädtischen Platzräumen. Viele Nutzer verbinden damit eine besondere Qualität. Nachts wird das Grundstück abgeschlossen. Die Tore sind tagsüber unsichtbar im Boden versenkt oder verdeckt.

Zu den Schwerpunktnutzungen der Freifläche gehören:

- Eingang: Der Durchgang zur Avenida São João dient als Haupteingang.
- Warten: Vor dem Haupteingang sammeln sich Eltern zum Abholen ihrer Kinder nach dem Unterricht.
- Querung: Die Freifläche wird als Abkürzung genutzt.
- Mischung: Die Flächen dienen als Treffpunkt und als Erholungsort. Die Nutzergruppe ist gemischt - sie umfasst Schüler, Anwohner und Angestellte aus der Nachbarschaft sowie Passanten, Touristen und Wohnungslose.
- Stadtbühne: Der Übergangsbereich zum Anhangabaú-Tal ist geprägt durch einen topographischen Sprung sowie eine breite Treppenanlage. Der Bereich dient als Treffpunkt sowie Aufführungs- und Aufenthaltsort. Die Nutzung als öffentliche Bühne wird allerdings durch das Sicherheitspersonal eingeschränkt.

Zeitweise bespielt der Betreiber die Freifläche selbst. Programmabhängig und saisonal werden dazu Veranstaltungen vom Gebäudeinneren nach draußen ausgeweitet. Für die Flächen am Übergang zum Anhangabaú-Tal ist ein gastronomisches Angebot vorgesehen. Die Umsetzung steht allerdings noch aus.

KONZEPT UND ABWEICHUNGEN

Auftraggeber des Projekts ist die Kulturabteilung der Stadtverwaltung São Paulos (Secretaria Municipal de Cultura). Der Entwurf wird ab 2006 durch das Büro Brasil Arquitetura von den Architekten Francisco Fanucci, Marcelo Ferraz mit Luciana Dornellas und Marcos Cartum entwickelt.[6] Bis 2012 erfolgt die Fertigstellung und Inbetriebnahme von Teilbereichen des Gebäudekomplexes. Zur Einweihung im Jahr 2019 wird die Freifläche zum Anhangabaú-Tal hin geöffnet.

Nicht alle Vorschläge des Entwurfskonzepts werden umgesetzt. Die ursprüngliche Planung integriert ein zusätzliches Nachbargrundstück. Zudem sind Erdgeschoss-Nutzungen mit Bezug zu den Freiflächen vorgesehen. Dazu gehören ein Restaurant, ein Café sowie Geschäfte für Musik- und Tanzbedarf. Diese Ideen werden jedoch vom Auftraggeber nicht weiter verfolgt. Die Umsetzung eines zweiten Verbindungsbaus zur Avenida São João steht noch aus. Der Gebäudeteil nimmt vorwiegend Klassenräume und ein Auditorium auf.

REZEPTION

Ein Großteil der Befragten begrüßt die Durchlässigkeit des Areals. Die neue Öffnung zum Anhangabaú-Tal schafft einen Treffpunkt und trägt dazu bei, die Attraktivität des Stadtteils Centro Novo zu steigern. Zudem bieten die neu gewonnenen Freiflächen zusätzliche Nutzungs- und Entfaltungsangebote in der Innenstadt.

Dagegen wird der Eindruck des stark introvertierten Gebäudekomplexes unterschiedlich beurteilt. Baukörper und die dazugehörigen Freiflächen wirken auf einige der Befragten abweisend. Die Architektursprache vermittle einen einschüchternden und verschlossenen Charakter. Zudem bleiben die Nutzungen im Gebäude verborgen. Gebäudenutzung und Freiraum sind kaum miteinander verknüpft. Durch den fehlenden Kontakt zum Geschehen im Gebäude ist für Besucher unklar, ob sie am Ort erwünscht sind. Diese Wirkung wird durch Tore und Sicherheitspersonal verstärkt.

Gelobt wird der Freiraum als zusätzliches Angebot an die Stadtgesellschaft. Die Flächen werden als sicherer Rückzugsraum wahrgenommen. Besonders Passanten und Touristen nutzen die Fläche gerne als sicheren Ort innerhalb der oft als unsicher wahrgenommenen Stadträume des Centro Novo. Ein Teil der Befragten sieht die geschützten Flächen als wichtigen Beitrag zur Attraktivitätssteigerung der Innenstadt. Dazu sei eine ausreichende Überwachung notwendig.

2   Lageplan
    Site plan
    1:2000

3   Übergang Anhangabaú-Tal
    Anhangabaú valley transition
    (S. 110 / p. 110)

5   Theatro Municipal (2019):
    www.theatromunicipal.org.br;
    Instituto Odeon (2019):
    www.institutoodeon.org.br

6   Fanucci, Ferraz (2016): S. 31

Diese Wirkung wird vor allem mit dem allgegenwärtigen Sicherheitspersonal verbunden. Ein Teil der Befragten betont allerdings die ausgrenzende Wirkung, die von der Überwachung ausgeht.

Einige Befragten fordern mehr Angebote zur Aneignung sowie eine größere Vielfalt bei den Nutzungsmöglichkeiten. Nutzer, die selbst die Flächen bespielen wollen, berichten von bürokratischen Hürden sowie von Einschränkungen durch das Sicherheitspersonal.

AUSDRUCK

Das Projekt Praça das Artes wird auf zwei unterschiedliche Arten wahrgenommen: Einerseits öffnet sich das Projekt zu den umliegenden Stadträumen mit großzügig zugeschnittenen Freiflächen. Andererseits werden die Flächen kontrolliert und außerhalb des Öffungszeiten durch Tor- und Zaunanlagen geschlossen. Damit entsteht Unsicherheit im Umgang mit dem Raumangebot. In Kombination mit der nüchternen Gestaltsprache von Bauvolumen und Fassaden wirkt das Projekt auf manche Besucher einschüchternd und abweisend.

ENTWICKLUNG

Grundsätzlich wünschen sich Nutzer und Besucher der Praça das Artes eine stärkere Belebung des Freiraums durch unterschiedliche Nutzungen. Für eine längere Aufenthaltsdauer wäre eine Ergänzung der Ausstattung hilfreich.

Uneinigkeit herrscht dazu, welche Nutzergruppen die Flächen künftig belegen sollen und ob die Sicherheitsvorkehrungen verstärkt oder abgeschwächt werden sollen. Ein Teil der Befragten bezieht sich dabei auf die aktuelle Sicherheitslage des Centro Novos und lehnt eine stärkere Öffnung der Freiflächen und Mischung der Nutzergruppen ab. Dagegen fordert eine andere Gruppe mehr Möglichkeiten zur Mitwirkung und weniger Einschränkungen.

4 **Bezug Anhangabaú-Tal**
Link Anhangabaú valley
Rua Conselheiro Crispiniano

5　Grundriss EG
　　Floor plan GF
　　1:1000

6　Grundriss 2. OG
　　Floor plan 2F
　　1:1000

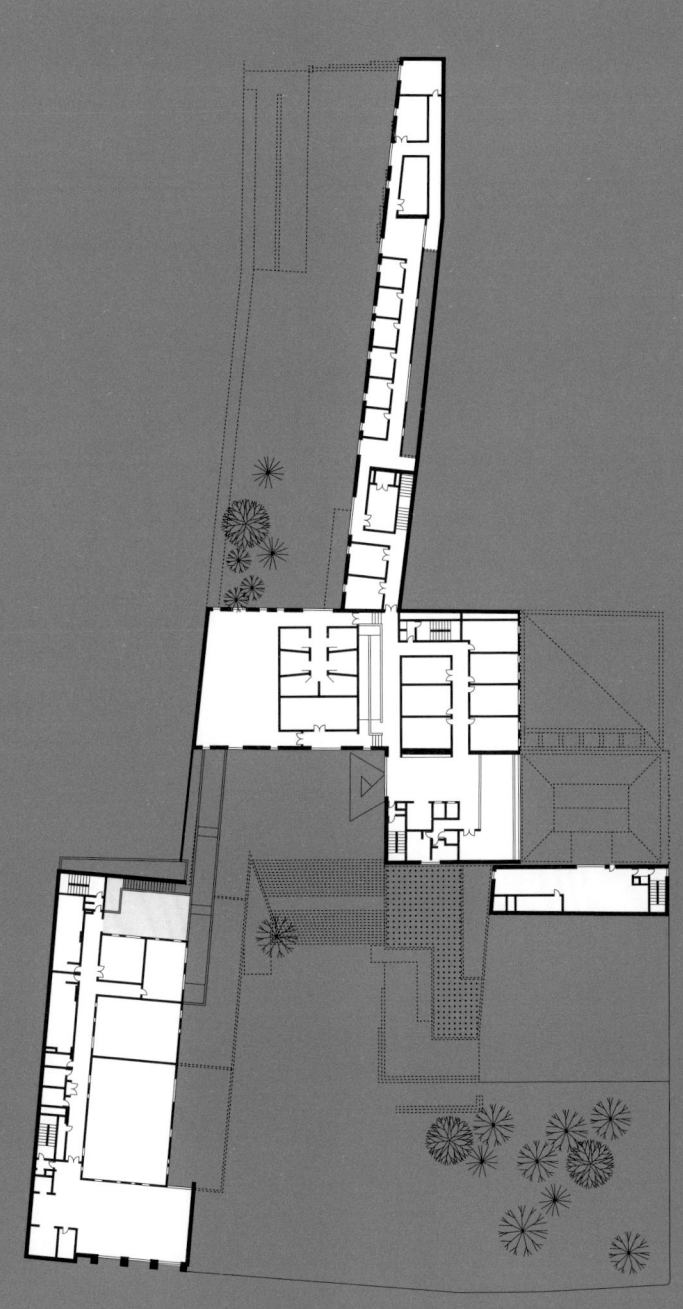

PRAÇA DAS ARTES

SPACE AND FORM

The cultural complex Praça das Artes is located at the edge of the densely-built Centro Novo quarter, at the transition to the old city centre between the historically significant bridges Viaduto do Chá and Viaduto Santa Ifigênia. The Centro Novo quarter is characterised by morphologically and functionally highly heterogeneous development. Its proximity to the city centre and the construction boom of the 1950s led to an urban cityscape parcelled out into small sections. Residential, office, service and commercial uses are combined here, in construction units between two and 30 floors.

Plots that are bordered on three sides and only accessible via one side facing the street are typical for construction blocks in Centro Novo. In contrast, the building composition of Praça das Artes occupies a T-shaped plot. This plot is the result of a consolidation of parcels originally covered with buildings, opening up on three sides: towards the Anhangabaú valley, towards Rua Formosa and towards Rua Conselheiro Crispiniano, which runs parallel to the northwest. To the north, it directly connects to Avenida São João, an important link between the old city centre and Centro Novo. A section of this street has been closed to vehicle traffic at this point.

The property connects the adjacent streets to the Anhangabaú valley area. To this end, its ground floor remains nearly undeveloped. Only the borders of the plot are lined with narrow building blocks containing entrances and arrival areas. From the first floor, these blocks are connected via two bridge constructions. In addition, three existing buildings were integrated into the project. They include the 'Conservatório Dramático e Musical', the 'Cinema Cairo' and the 'Music Library'.[1]

The formation of the construction volume reacts to the respective adjacent granulation of the urban texture. It arbitrates between the high-rises along the Anhangabaú valley and the development of Centro Novo. The two bridge structures of Praça das Artes divide the open space up into three parts:

- To the northwest, the neighbouring tall buildings and the narrow building at the plot border create an entrance courtyard.
- To the northeast, the canopied opening connects to Avenida São João. It contains the main entrance to all parts of the building.
- Behind the bridge to the southeast, the space opens up to the Anhangabaú valley below.

The open area contains facilities for sitting and lingering distributed throughout. Those include sitting steps facing the Anhangabaú valley, benches underneath the canopied areas as well as a permanent bar including a counter. The facilities are well-frequented during the day - not only by users of the building complex, but also by passersby as well as homeless people.

USE AND USER GROUPS

The Praça das Artes project supplements the Theatro Municipal de São Paulo, a cultural institution located approximately 150m from the site. The building's floor space measures roughly 28,500sqm.[2] The room programme includes a dance and music school with rooms for classes and practice, rooms for artist groups, a historical conservatory for theatre and music, exhibition spaces as well as halls for performances and events.[3] The responsible body, the Secretaria Municipal de Cultura of São Paulo[4], is in charge of the uses of the building.

7 Passage und Gebäudebrücke
   Passage and building bridge

[1] Nosek (2013): p. 8
[2] Fanucci, Ferraz (2016): p. 29
[3] Fanucci, Ferraz, Cartum (2013): p. 36
[4] Fanucci, Ferraz (2016): p. 31

8 Sitzgelegenheiten
  Seating arrangements

9 Schnitt Ost-West
  East-west section
  1:1000

Events and exhibitions are organised and curated by the Instituto Odeon and the Fundação Theatro Municipal.[5]

The building complex is designed in an introverted way. The ground floor spaces are also enclosed for the most part. Accordingly, it is difficult to recognise the uses from the outside. Also, access to the building is controlled in the foyer area. The only persons admitted are students, teaching staff as well as invited visitors.

During the day, the property is used by passers-by, tourists and residents of the street. The areas are open and invite people to stay around. Canopied areas provide protection from the weather without being tied to a commercial context. Also, open spaces and building access are monitored by security staff all day. This type of surveillance is quite the contrast to the often unsecured public spaces of the city centre - a special quality for many users. At night, the property is locked with gates. During the day, these gates are lowered into the ground or moved to the side. This way, they remain invisible.

The main uses of the open spaces are the following:

- Entrance: The passage to Avenida São João serves as the main entrance.
- Waiting: In front of the main entrance, parents gather to pick up their children after classes.
- Crossing: The open space is used as a shortcut between various destinations.
- Miscellaneous: The areas are used by groups of students for exercises. At the same time, the space serves as a meeting point and a place for recreation. Its user group is diverse - it includes residents and staff from the neighbourhood as well as passers-by, tourists and homeless people.
- City stage: The transition area to the Anhangabaú valley is characterised by a topographical leap as well as a wide stairway. At the transition to the square, the area is especially emphasised. This area serves as a meeting point as well as a place for performances and lingering. A possible use as a stage, however, is limited by security staff surveillance.

Occasionally, the operator itself uses the open spaces. Depending on programming and season, events from inside the building spills over to the open areas.

Gastronomic facilities were intended for the areas at the transition to the Anhangabaú valley. However, they have yet to be realised.

DESIGN AND DEVIATIONS

The contracting entity for the project is the cultural department of São Paulo's municipal administration (Secretaria Municipal de Cultura). The design was developed from 2006 by the office of Brasil Arquitetura and their architects Francisco Fanucci, Marcelo Ferraz with Luciana Dornellas and Marcos Cartum.[6] Until 2012, parts of the building complex were completed and commissioned. For the inauguration in 2019, the passage between the inner open space of the construction block and the Anhangabaú valley was opened.

Not all suggestions of the design concept were realised. The original plans incorporated an additional neighbouring property. Also intended were ground-floor uses related to the open spaces, including a restaurant, a café and shops for music and dance equipment. However, the contracting entity is no longer pursuing these ideas. The realisation of a second connecting structure to Avenida São João is still pending. This building element will mainly house classrooms and an auditorium.

RECEPTION

The majority of the people surveyed welcomed the permeability of the property. The new opening towards the Anhangabaú valley creates a meeting point and contributes to increasing the appeal of the Centro Novo quarter. Also, the newly obtained areas promise additional possibilities for use and development in the city centre.

In contrast, the impression of the strongly introverted building complex received mixed judgement. The structure and its associated open spaces were perceived as unwelcoming by some of the people surveyed. They assigned an intimidating and withdrawn character to the architectural language. Also, the uses inside the building remained concealed. Open spaces and building uses are hardly connected at all.

The lack of contact to everything taking place inside the building makes it unclear whether or not visitors are welcome to the place. This impression is reinforced by the gates and the security staff.

---

[5] Theatro Municipal (2019): www.theatromunicipal.org.br; Instituto Odeon (2019): www.institutoodeon.org.br

[6] Fanucci, Ferraz (2016): p. 31

10 Schnitt West-Ost
West-east section
1:1000

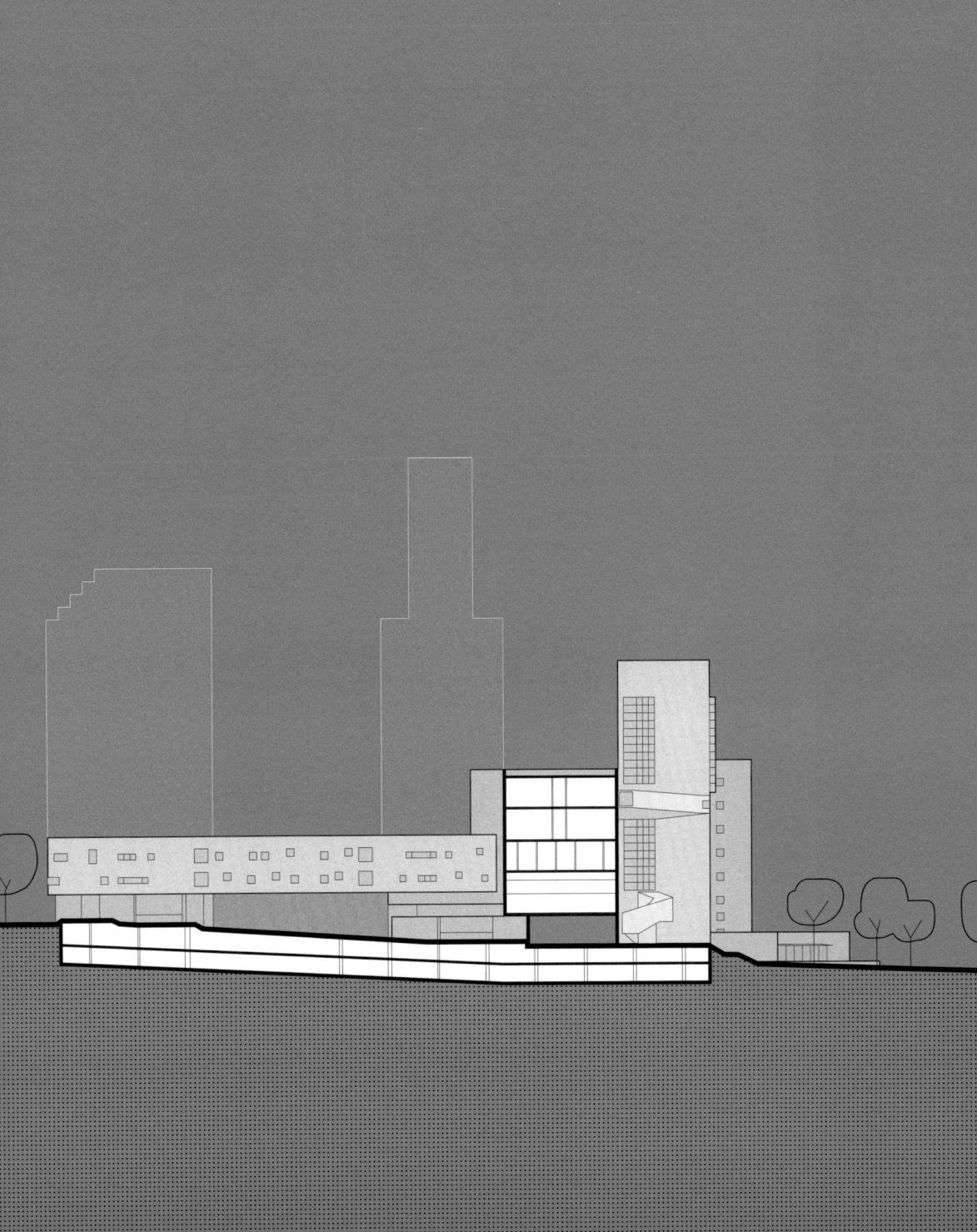

The generous amount of open space was lauded as an additional offer to the urban public. The spaces are perceived as a safe location to retreat to. Users include families with children, visitors, tourists as well as homeless people. Especially passers-by and tourists like to use the area as a safe haven in the urban spaces of Centro Novo, which are often perceived as unsafe. One part of those surveyed saw the protected spaces as an important contribution to increasing the appeal of the city centre. Most notably, the omnipresent security staff contributed to this impression. Another part of those surveyed, however, also emphasised the excluding and limiting effect of the surveillance measures.

Those surveyed requested for a greater variety of possible uses. Users wanting to take advantage of the space themselves reported bureaucratic hurdles as well as limitations by security staff.

EXPRESSION

The Praça das Artes project presents itself in two different ways: On the one hand, the project connects to the adjacent urban spaces with generously designed open areas. On the other hand, the areas are controlled by security staff and are closed off by gates and fences outside of opening hours. This creates uncertainty for many users in connection with the available space. Combined with the matter-of-fact design language of structures and facades, the project has an intimidating and unwelcoming effect on some visitors.

DEVELOPMENT

Fundamentally, users and visitors of Praça das Artes wish for more excitement in the open spaces by means of more diverse uses. Enhancing the facility would help extend stays in the space.

Opinions were divided regarding the user groups which were to occupy the spaces in the future and regarding whether to reinforce or to reduce security measures. One part of those surveyed referenced the current security situation in Centro Novo and opposed any further opening up and diversification of the open spaces. In contrast, another group demanded more opportunities for participation and fewer limitations.

11 Blick Anhangabaú-Tal
   View Anhangabaú valley
   Rua Conselheiro Crispiniano

MASP UND MIRANTE

RAUM UND GESTALT

Das São Paulo Museum of Art (MASP) liegt im nördlichen Drittel der Avenida Paulista am Schnittpunkt zum Anhangabaú-Tal. Das Museumsgebäude setzt sich zusammen aus einem Sockelbau unterhalb der Straßenebene und einer aufgeständerten, zweiseitig verglasten Ausstellungshalle. Dazwischen liegt eine großzügige ‚Stadtloggia', die den Blick freigibt zum Talraum.

Das MASP inszeniert die räumliche Beziehung zwischen Avenida Paulista und dem südlich liegenden Anhangabaú-Tal. Die entsprechende Verknüpfung zwischen Stadt- und Landschaftsraum besteht allerdings schon seit 1916. Bereits der Vorgängerbau Belvedere Trianon inszeniert diesen Ausblick.

Ab 1891 entwickelt sich die Avenida Paulista rasch zu einer beliebten Wohnstraße des wohlhabenden Bürgertums. Der rund 2,8km lange Straßenraum wird beidseitig begleitet durch freistehende Villenbauten. Die offene Bauweise kontrastiert bewusst die geschlossene Blockrandbebauung der Kernstadt.[1]

Der Grundstücksentwickler Joaquim Eugênio de Lima formuliert dazu eigene städtebauliche Regeln: Zwischen den Gebäuden muss ein Abstand von mindestens 10m bestehen; zur Avenida ist zusätzlich ein Grünstreifen von mindestens 2m Breite einzuhalten.

An der Schnittstelle zwischen Avenida Paulista und dem Anhangabaú-Tal entsteht bis 1916 das Belvedere Trianon, eine Terrassenanlage mit Restaurants und Bars. Der Ort steigt rasch zu einem bürgerlichen Treffpunkt auf. Bis Ende der 1920er Jahre bleibt es ein beliebtes Ausflugsziel. Dann verliert die Anlage an Exklusivität, u.a. aufgrund des stetigen Anstiegs an Wochenend-Touristen.[2]

Ab den 1930er Jahren wird das Anhangabaú-Tal zu einer Schnellstraße umgebaut.[3]

Die dort verlaufende Avenida Nove de Julho verbindet das alte Stadtzentrum São Paulos mit dem Südwesten der Stadt. Die Avenida ist Teil des übergeordneten Y-Plans[4] des Stadtplaners Prestes Maia. Sie unterquert über eine Länge von 450m das Belvedere, die Avenida Paulista und den südlich angrenzenden Park Trianon.

Als sichtbares Zeichen der Modernisierung São Paulos wird die Tunneleinfahrt unterhalb des Belvederes besonders inszeniert. Die beiden Zufahrtsrampen zur Schnellstraße fassen den Tunnelmund symmetrisch ein. Die bogenförmig geführten Stützwände werden jeweils durch ein Wasser- und Lichtspiel inszeniert. Der Tunneleingang selbst erhält als Aufbau eine Aussichtsloggia sowie einen schlanken Turmaufsatz.

Über den Zeitraum der Umsetzung hinweg werden Abbildungen und Fotografien des Ensembles unter dem Namen Mirante veröffentlicht. Das Motiv illustriert stellvertretend den laufenden Umbau- und Modernisierungsprozess São Paulos. Sichtbar wird, dass künftig der motorisierte Individualverkehr in den Mittelpunkt der Stadtentwicklung gerückt wird. Neben einer Inszenierung des Orts berücksichtigt die Anlage aber auch die Perspektive des Fußgängers und räumt ihm mit der Loggia eine bevorzugte Stellung ein. Das ist kein Einzelfall, denn Prestes Maias Entwürfe verknüpfen oft Verkehrsbauwerke mit neuen öffentlichen Räumen.[5]

---

1 **Blick**
   View
   MASP und Mirante
   MASP and Mirante

[1] Rolnik (2008): S. 13
[2] Batista (2015): www.acervo.estadao.com.br
[3] Prestes Maia (1930): S. 97
[4] Plano de Avenidas; Prestes Maia (1930): S. 111
[5] vgl. Kapitel Überblick: Prestes Maias Plano de Avenidas

Ab den 1950er Jahren verändert sich die Bebauung entlang der Avenida Paulista. Teilweise unter Beibehaltung der freistehende Bauweise werden die zweigeschossigen Villenbauten schrittweise durch schlanke Hochhaustürme ersetzt. Gleichzeitig verlagert sich das Handels- und Finanzzentrum São Paulos aus dem historischen Stadtzentrum an die Avenida Paulista.[6] Der neue Nutzungsschwerpunkt, das großzügige Straßenprofil und eine extravagante Randbebauung machen die Straße zum repräsentativen Mittelpunkt der Stadt.

Im Zuge dieses Umbaus wird 1951 das Belvedere Trianon abgerissen. Auf der Fläche entsteht zwischen 1957 und 1968 das São Paulo Museum of Art (MASP).[7] Durch die Überbauung rückt das Observatorium Mirante in den Hintergrund. Bezugslos liegt es nun auf der Rückseite des neuen Museumsbaus, auf halber Höhe zwischen Avenida Paulista und der Schnellstraße Nove de Julho; zu Fuß lediglich über steile Zufahrten erreichbar. Insgesamt ist dabei ein Höhenunterschied von etwa 30m zu überwinden.

Der Turmaufsatz des Mirante weicht in den 1970er Jahren einer neuen Autobrücke.[8] Ungünstig gelegen und schwer erreichbar, gerät das Bauwerk in Vergessenheit. Erst 2015 wird es als Café Mirante Nove de Julho wieder eröffnet. Impulsgeber dazu ist Facundo Guerra, dessen Unternehmen Grupo Vegas sich auf die Revitalisierung ungenutzter Orte spezialisiert hat. Mit einer Kombination aus gastronomischer Nutzung und Veranstaltungsort überzeugt Guerra die Stadt, der Anlage und Grundstück gehören. Dabei wird er unterstützt von Immobilieninvestoren, die nahe gelegene Grundstücke aufwerten wollen.

Nach etwa vierjährigen Verhandlungen mit Stadt und Investoren erhält Guerra die Genehmigung den Ort mit eigenen Mitteln zu sanieren. Zusätzlich gefördert wird das Projekt durch eine Befreiung von der Grundsteuer (IPTU). Das Projekt ist ein erster Präzedenzfall für die privatwirtschaftliche Nutzung eines ursprünglich öffentlichen Raumes.[9]

Umbau und Sanierung des Mirante übernimmt das Architekturbüro MM18 Arquitetura. Der Entwurf berücksichtigt die Auflagen des Denkmalschutzes. Frei zugänglich bleiben die großzügige Zugangstreppe sowie die sanitären Anlagen. Die Fläche wird als Café-Bar und für Konzertveranstaltungen genutzt.[10]

Als zweiter Betreiber steigt 2016 der Geschäftsmann und Clubbesitzer José Victor Oliva ein.

Nach dem Abbruch der Zusammenarbeit übernimmt Oliva den Pachtvertrag[11] und verändert die Ausrichtung des Café Mirante. Dabei verlagert sich der Schwerpunkt vom Party- und Barbetrieb auf Kulturevents mit Konzerten und Filmabenden. Ziel ist ein breiteres Publikum zu erreichen. Der Ort wird auch als Marketingplattform sowie für private Veranstaltungen genutzt. Als Kulturort und Treffpunkt zieht er die junge Mittel- und Oberschicht São Paulos an. Der Cafébetrieb erwirtschaftet die Betriebskosten, wirft aber keinen Profit ab.

MASP

1947 stellt der italienische Galerist und Kunstkritiker Pietro Maria Bardi seine Sammlung an zeitgenössischen Kunstwerken in Rio de Janeiro aus. Nach dem Besuch der Ausstellung wird Bardi vom Medienunternehmer Francisco Chateaubriand eingeladen bei der Entwicklung eines brasilianischen Kunstmuseums mitzuwirken. Die Konzeption der Ausstellung übernimmt Lina Bo Bardi, die Frau Pietro Maria Bardis. Bereits im gleichen Jahr findet eine erste Ausstellung in São Paulo statt. Als Ausstellungsort dient die große Halle des Verlagsgebäudes von Chateaubriand.

Als Alternative zu diesem improvisierten Ausstellungsort stellt Lina Bo Bardi 1957 Ideen für einen Museumsbau vor, der auf dem Grundstück des Belvedere Trianons entstehen soll.[12] Die Fläche ist im Besitz der Stadt - eine Schenkung des Ingenieurs Joaquim Eugênio de Lima, der als Bauunternehmer die Avenida Paulista entwickelte. De Lima verband mit seiner Schenkung die Auflage, dass der Blick vom Park Trianon über die Avenida Paulista auf das Anhangabaú-Tal unverstellt bleiben muss.[13]

Bo Bardis Entwurf berücksichtigt diese Anforderungen.[14] Im Anschluss an die Avenida Paulista soll eine frei zugängliche Platzfläche entstehen, die sich über eine Aussichtsterrasse zum Anhangabaú-Tal öffnet[15]. Das Museum ist dazu als zweigeteiltes Gebäude konzipiert. Die Ausstellungshalle schwebt acht Meter über dem Straßenniveau. Ergänzend liegt unter der Platzfläche ein Sockelbau. Die beiden Gebäudeteile sind über eine Freitreppe miteinander verbunden.

Die Entwurfsskizzen Bo Bardis konzentrieren sich zunächst auf den Platzraum und die darüber liegende Ausstellungshalle. Ihre Zeichnungen illustrieren Bespielungsmöglichkeiten, wie Open-Air-Ausstellungen, Performances, Kundgebungen sowie niedrigschwellige Angebote wie Zirkus-Aufführungen oder Stadtfeste.[16]

2 **Lageplan**
   Site plan
   1:2000

3 **MASP Stadtrahmen**
   MASP city frame
   (S. 128 / p. 128)

6 Riodel (2010): S. 84
7 Caffey, Campagnol (2015-2): S. 3
8 Viaduto Professor Bernardino Tranchesi
9 Ribeiro (2016): www.passeiosbaratosemsp.com.br
10 Ribeiro (2016): www.passeiosbaratosemsp.com.br
11 Diniz (2019): www.folha.uol.com.br
12 Caffey, Campagnol (2015-1): S. 1 f.
13 Fernández Galiano (2015): S. 46
14 Unter Berücksichtigung dieser Bedingungen bewilligt die Stadt die Errichtung des Museum; Caffey, Campagnol (2015-2): S. 3
15 Klanten, Borges (2016): S. 320
16 Ferraz (1994): S. 100

4   **Grundriss 2.OG**
    Floor plan 2F
    1:1000

5   **Blick**
    View
    (S. 132 / p. 132)
    Treppenanlage zum Café Mirante
    Stairs to Café Mirante

17 Oliveira (2014): S. 61
18 Caffey, Campagnol (2015-2): S. 3
19 Fernández Galiano (2015): S. 56
20 Bo Bardi, Ferraz (2018): S. 110

Der Platz gehört zu wenigen offen-zugänglichen Flächen entlang der sonst dicht bebauten Avenida Paulista. Zum Talraum hin wird er durch eine umlaufende Sitzkante abgegrenzt. Beidseitig durch ein längliches Wasserbecken eingefasst, bildet sie zur Avenida Paulista eine Stufe aus.

Die Ausstellungshalle überspannt eine Fläche von 70 x 29m und wird lediglich auf vier Betonstützen abgesetzt.[17] Sie lässt sich ausschließlich über die Treppe im südöstlichen Teil des Platzes erschließen. Die Hängekonstruktion ermöglicht eine stützenfreie Ausstellungsfläche. Entsprechend können die Ausstellungsobjekte frei angeordnet werden. Die Tragkonstruktion in Spannbetonweise wird vom Ingenieur José Carlos de Figueiredo Ferraz entwickelt.[18] Um die Stützen vor Wassereintritt zu schützen erhalten sie Anfang der 1990er Jahre einen roten Anstrich.[19]

Der untere Gebäudeteil ist in den Hang eingebettet. Hier befinden sich zusätzliche Ausstellungsflächen, ein Café, der Museumsshop, Veranstaltungsräume für Lesungen, Seminare, Workshops sowie die Räume der Museumsverwaltung. Der untere Bauteil orientiert sich zum Talraum und bestimmt den Zuschnitt der darüberliegenden Platzfläche. Trotz einer umlaufenden Einfassung durch Fensterbänder wirkt er eher geschlossen und introvertiert.

NUTZUNG UND NUTZERGRUPPEN

Genutzt wird die Platzfläche[20] als Freizeit- und Pausenort, als Bühne für Darbietungen, als Verkaufsfläche und als Wohnort. Zu den Nutzern gehören tagsüber Museumsbesucher, Touristen, Straßenverkäufer und Künstler, Polizisten und Sicherheitsleute sowie Museumsangestellte. Tageweise kommen Standverkäufer und Promoter hinzu. Die Platzfläche wird gerne als Start- und/oder Endpunkt für Kundgebungen genutzt.

Touristen queren die Fläche meist bis zur Platzkante entlang des Talraums. Die Stadtsilhouette bietet ein beliebtes Fotomotiv für Schnappschüsse und für Fotoshootings. Der rückwärtige Teil der Platzfläche wird gerne von Kleingruppen wie Jugendlichen oder Fahrradkurieren genutzt. Mittags wird die Fläche auch von den Angestellten der umliegenden Büros während ihrer Arbeitspausen in Anspruch genommen.

Bei sehr populären Ausstellungen im MASP entsteht unter dem Galeriebau eine lange Schlange. Straßenverkäufer bieten den Wartenden unterschiedliche Waren und Dienstleistungen an. Die Schwelle zur Avenida Paulista wird oft von Straßenkünstlern genutzt.

Im Laufe des Nachmittags nimmt die Frequenz an Touristen und Museumsbesuchern ab. Die Platzfläche wird dafür häufiger durch Polizeistreifen und Sicherheitspersonal observiert. Die Präsenz von Sicherheitskräften und Verkäufern orientiert sich an den Öffnungszeiten des Museums. Abends nutzen meist Jugendliche die Flächen zum Musikhören und Tanzen. Etwas später wird der rückwärtige Teil zu einem großen Schlafplatz. Der Museumsbau bietet zusätzlich Witterungsschutz.

REZEPTION UND KONFLIKTE

Bo Bardis Konzept sieht ursprünglich eine offene und bespielbare Platzfläche vor. Als besonderer Raum in der Stadt soll er Alltag, Kunst und politisches Engagement miteinander verbinden. Aufgrund von Veränderungen im Sozialgefüge der Stadt ist der Platz inzwischen auch ein wichtiger Aufenthalts- und Ruheort für Wohnungslose geworden.

Entsprechend wird die Qualität der Platzfläche unterschiedlich eingeschätzt. Für einen Teil der Befragten bildet der Platz einen wichtigen Gegenpol zur stark kommerziell geprägten Avenida Paulista. Hervorgehoben wird die heterogene Mischung aus Passanten, Touristen, Museumsbesuchern, Straßenverkäufern, Künstlern und Wohnungslosen. Für die Befragten zeichnet gerade das Nebeneinander unterschiedlicher Sozialgruppen den Ort besonders aus. Der großzügige Flächenzuschnitt und die hervorgehobene stadträumliche Lage bieten dazu eine geeignete Bühne. Dabei trägt die Aussicht zum Talraum besonders zur Beliebtheit des Ortes bei.

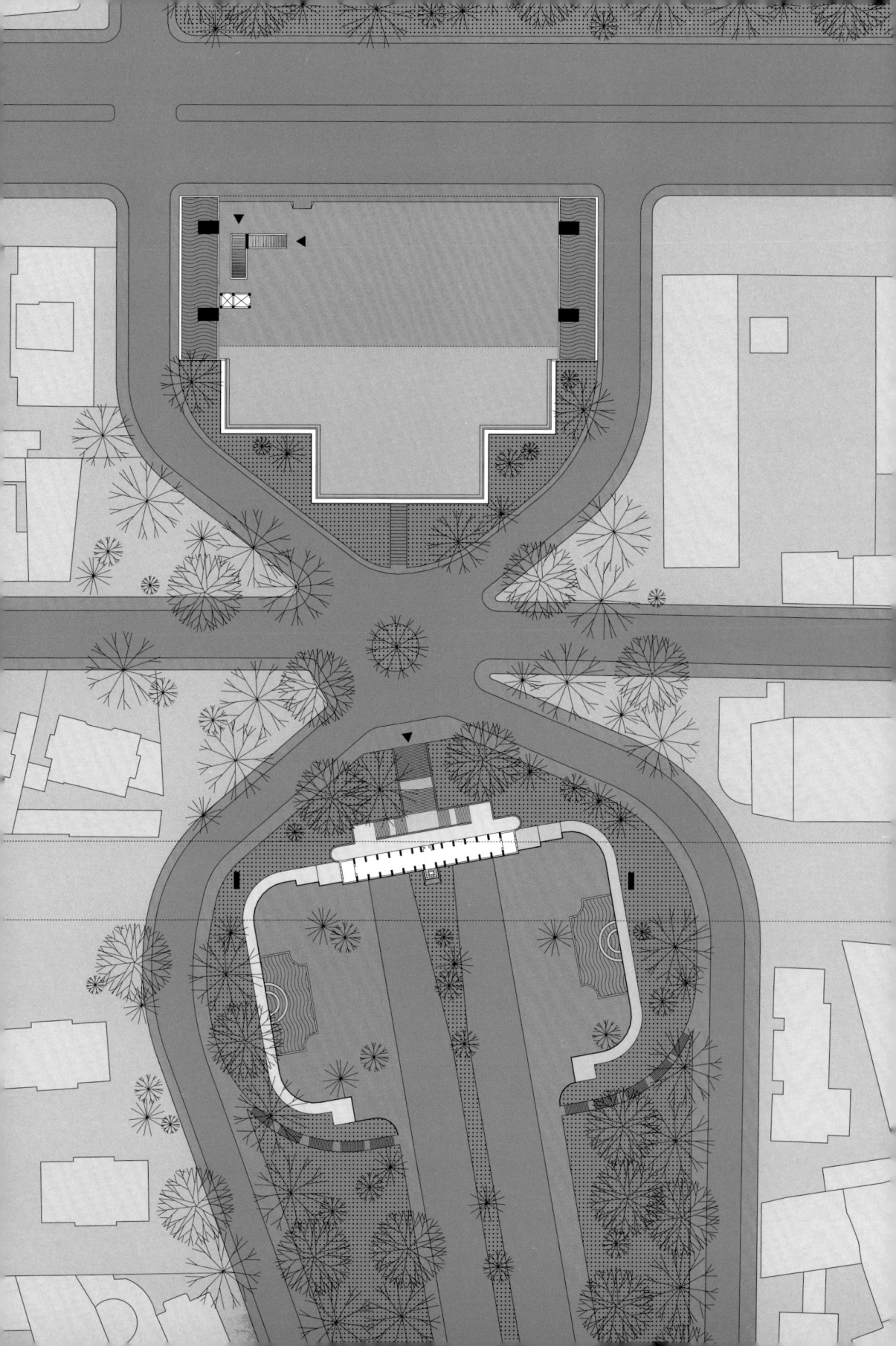

Ein anderer Teil der Befragten empfindet den Platzraum unter dem MASP als unsicher. Der Charakter des Raums wird stark durch informelle Nutzungen beeinflusst. Gefordert wird eine stärkere Unterstützung der Wohnungslosen vor Ort - aber auch eine durchgängige Kontrolle des Raums durch Sicherheitspersonal.

Bo Bardi hat den Eingangsbereich zum MASP als offenen Bereich konzipiert. Auf dem Platz, insbesondere im überdachten Bereich waren entsprechend auch Installationen und Ausstellungen vorgesehen. Dagegen sind heute Bereiche des Platzes abgesperrt.[21] Die Leitung des MASP schätzt die Bespielung einer offenen Fläche als unökonomisch ein.

Diskutiert werden Szenarien, die vorsehen die Fläche einzufrieden und den Zugang zu kontrollieren. Im Gegensatz dazu wollen Stadtverwaltung und Politik die Platzfläche als öffentlichen Raum und Aussichtspunkt erhalten.[22]

Bei Großveranstaltungen auf der Fläche gibt es inzwischen Sicherheitsbedenken hinsichtlich der Tragfähigkeit der Platzkonstruktion. 2019 sieht sich das MASP gezwungen während einer Demonstration den unter der Platzfläche liegenden Gebäudeteil zu schließen. Inzwischen beschränkt das MASP die Anzahl der zulässigen Personen: Auf einer Platzfläche von 10qm sind lediglich 28 Personen akzeptabel. Gruppen über 57 Personen sind nicht erlaubt.[23]

6   **Beziehung**
Relation
(S. 136 / p. 136)
Avenida Paulista und MASP
Avenida Paulista and MASP

[21] Oliveira (2014): S. 7 ff.
[22] Andreoli, Forty (2004): S. 82
[23] Petrov (2019):
www.riotimesonline.com

7 Schnitt Nord-Süd
North-south section
1:1000

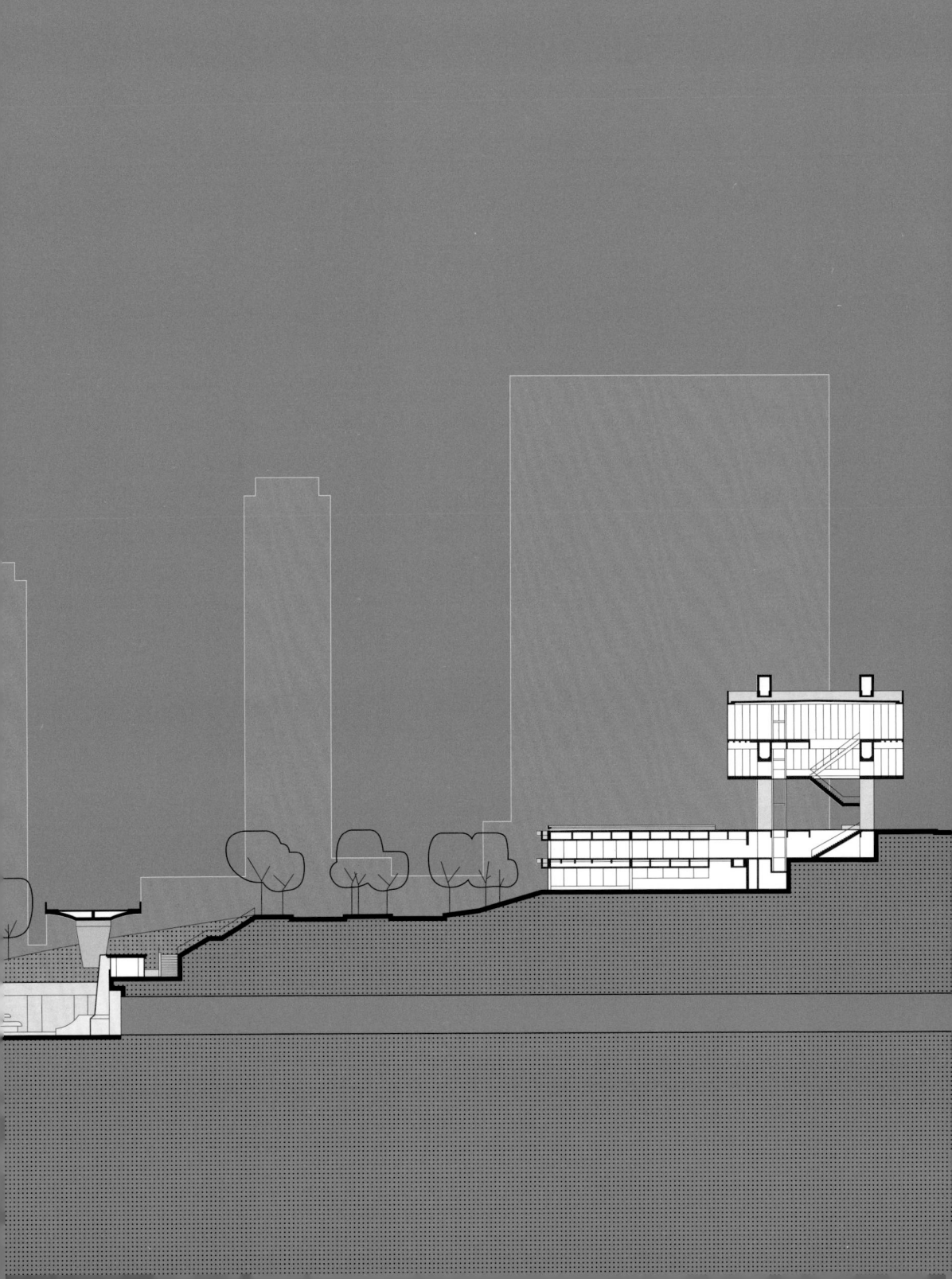

MASP AND MIRANTE

SPACE AND FORM

The São Paulo Museum of Art (MASP) is located in the northern third of Avenida Paulista at the intersection with the Anhangabaú valley. Its building consists of a base construction below street level and a raised exhibition hall with glass panels on two sides. Between the two, a generous 'urban loggia' provides a view to the valley area. The MASP showcases the spatial relationship between Avenida Paulista and the Anhangabaú valley to the south. However, the corresponding connection between urban and landscape space has existed since 1916. The building's precursor, Belvedere Trianon, already staged the same view.

From 1891, Avenida Paulista quickly developed into a popular residential street for the affluent middle class. The street area which spans roughly 2.8km in length is lined by detached mansions on both sides. This open style of construction is an intentional contrast to the tight perimeter block developments of the city core.[1] Property developer Joaquim Eugênio de Lima devised his own urban development rules for this purpose: buildings must be at least 10m apart, and a grass strip of at least 2m width must be left towards the Avenida.

The Belvedere Trianon, a terraced structure facing towards Anhangabaú valley to the north-east, was opened as a special attraction in 1916. Restaurants and bars were located below the terrace. The choice of the name 'Belvedere' (French for beautiful view) was intended to evoke the baroque castle complex in Versailles. It quickly became a middle-class meeting point. Up until the 1920s, it remained a popular destination. Due to progressing urbanisation and the continuous increase in weekend tourists, however, it lost its exclusivity.[2]

From the 1930s, the Anhangabaú valley was converted to a motorway, Avenida Nove de Julho.[3]

The Avenida connects the old city centre of São Paulo with the south-west of the city and is part of the superordinate Y-plan[4] of urban planner Prestes Maia. It crosses under the Belvedere, Avenida Paulista and the Trianon park to the south at a length of 450m.

As a visible sign of São Paulo's modernisation, the tunnel entrance below the Belvedere was showcased in a particular way. The two access ramps to the motorway symmetrically frame the tunnel opening. The arched support walls were accented with a fountain and a light display each. The tunnel entrance itself received an observation loggia and a slender tower structure.

Over the time period of construction, pictures and photographs of the ensemble were published with the name Mirante. The motif stands in as an illustration of the ongoing conversion and modernisation process of São Paulo. It became apparent that in the future, private vehicle traffic would take centre stage in urban development. Besides showcasing the location, the installation also considers the pedestrian perspective, giving it a favourable position through the loggia. This is not an isolated case, since Prestes Maia's designs often combined traffic structures with new, public spaces.[5]

After the great traffic conversion measures, development along Avenida Paulista also changed from the 1950s. Partially preserving the detached mode of construction, the two-storey mansions were gradually replaced with slender high-rise towers. Simultaneously, the trade and financial centre of São Paulo shifted from the historic city centre to Avenida Paulista.[6] The new main use, a generous street profile and an extravagant building development made the street a representative centre of the city.

---

8   Sicherheitskräfte
    Security forces

1   Rolnik (2008): p. 13
2   Batista (2015):
    www.acervo.estadao.com.br
3   Prestes Maia (1930): p. 97
4   Plano de Avenidas,
    Prestes Maia (1930): p. 111
5   cf. chapter Overview:
    Prestes Maia's Plano de Avenidas
6   Riodel (2010): p. 84

9 Überbaute Platzfläche
  Roofed plaza

10 Schnitt Ost-West
   East-west section
   1:1000

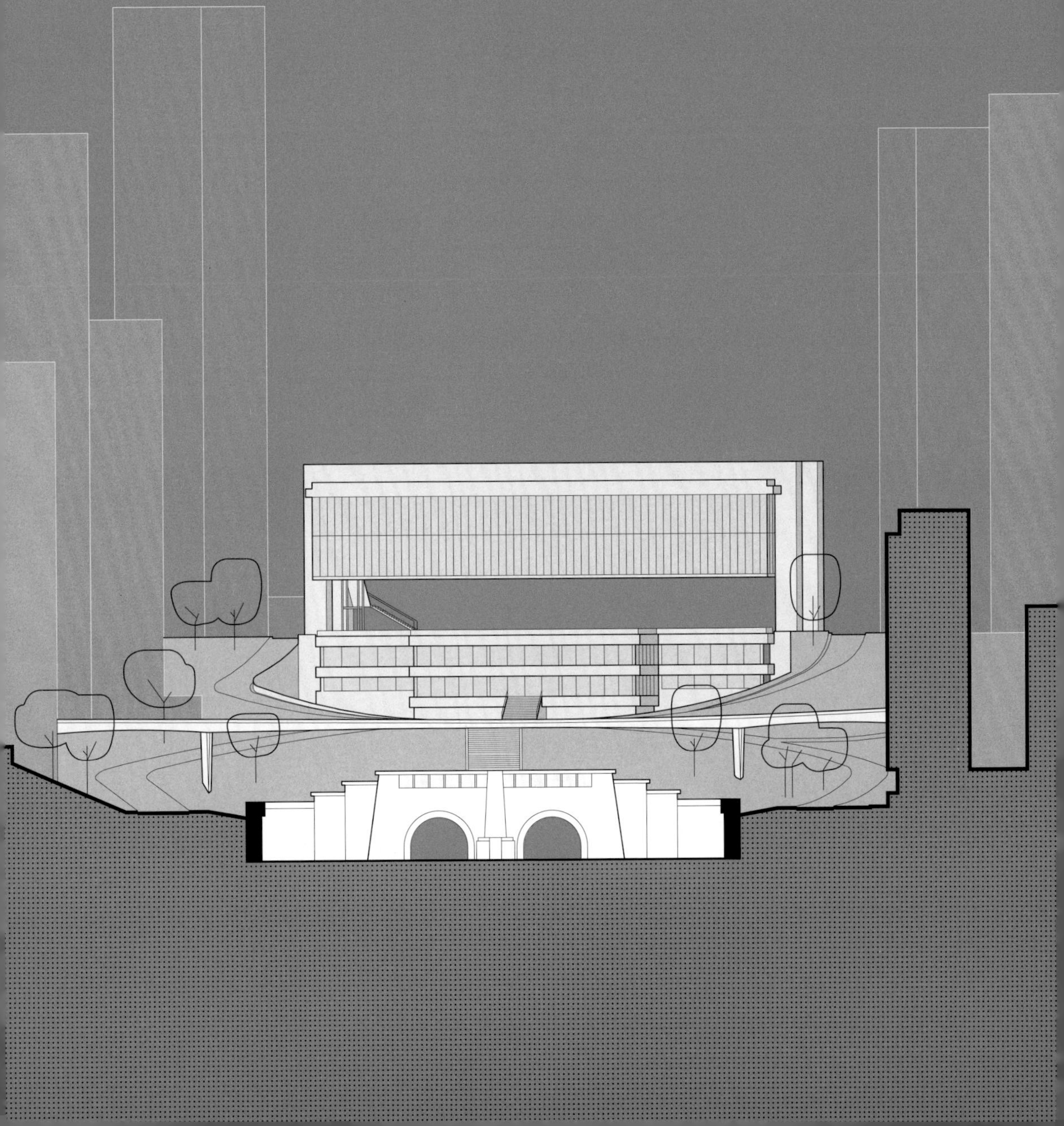

11	'Stadtbalkon' 'Urban balcony' (S. 144 / p. 144)
12	Café Mirante (S. 145 / p. 145)

7	Caffey, Campagnol (2015-2): p. 3
8	Viaduto Professor Bernardino Tranchesi
9	Ribeiro (2016): www.passeiosbaratosemsp.com.br
10	Ribeiro (2016): www.passeiosbaratosemsp.com.br
11	Diniz (2019): www.folha.uol.com.br
12	Caffey, Campagnol (2015-1): p. 1 f.
13	Fernández Galiano (2015) p. 46
14	With consideration to these conditions, the city gave permission for the construction of the museum; Caffey, Campagnol (2015-2): p. 3
15	Klanten, Borges (2016): p. 320
16	Ferraz (1994): p. 100
17	Oliveira (2014): p. 61

In the course of this conversion, the Belvedere Trianon gave way to the pavilion for the first art biennial in São Paulo.

Between 1957 and 1968, the São Paulo Museum of Art was constructed on the premises.[7] The structures above the plot put the Mirante observatory in the background. It became isolated at the back of the new museum complex, halfway between Avenida Paulista and the Nove de Julho motorway - only accessible by foot via steep access ways covering a total elevation of about 30m.

The tower of the Mirante gave way to a new motorway bridge in the 1970s.[8] Its now-unfavourable location and lack of accessibility made people forget about the ensemble. Only in 2015, it was reopened as Café Mirante Nove de Julho. The impulse for this came from businessman Facundo Guerra, whose company Grupo Vegas specialises in revitalising disused sites. With a combination of gastronomic use and event venue, Guerra convinced the city, who owns the site and the plot. His project was supported by real estate investors wanting to upgrade properties nearby.

After around four years of negotiations with the city and investors, Guerra received the permit to refurbish the site with his own means. The project is exempt from property tax (IPTU). At the same time, it is a precedent for private enterprise use of an originally public space.[9] The refurbishment of the Mirante was planned by the architects MM18 Arquitetura. The design factored in listed status constraints. The generous access staircase as well as the sanitary facilities remained freely accessible. The café/bar use was complemented with concert events.[10]

As a second operator, businessman and club owner José Victor Oliva joined the venture in 2016. Once the cooperation ended, Oliva took over the tenancy agreement[11] and changed the direction of Café Mirante. The emphasis shifted from party and bar business to cultural events with concerts and film nights targeting a wider and more family-friendly audience. The location was also used as a marketing platform and for private events. As a cultural site and meeting point, it attracted the young middle and upper classes of São Paulo. The café operation covers its operating costs, but does not yield any profit.

MASP

In 1947, Italian gallery owner and art critic Pietro Maria Bardi exhibited his collection of contemporary art in Rio de Janeiro. Upon visiting his exhibition, media entrepreneur Francisco Chateaubriand invited Bardi to participate in developing a Brazilian art museum. Lina Bo Bardi, Pietro Maria Bardi's wife, was tasked with designing the exhibition. As early as the same year, the first exhibition was held in São Paulo. The large hall of Chateaubriand's publishing building served as the venue.

In 1957, Lina Bo Bardi presented ideas for a museum building on the premises of the Belvedere Trianon as an alternative to this improvised exhibition venue.[12] The plot was owned by the city - a donation of engineer Joaquim Eugênio de Lima, who developed Avenida Paulista as a prime contractor. Lima tied his donation to the constraint that the view from the Trianon park over the Avenida Paulista to the Anhangabaú valley had to remain unobstructed.[13]

Bo Bardi's design factors in this requirement.[14] The museum building is split in two: above street level, an exhibition hall covers the plot at eight metres from the ground; below street level there is an additional base construction. Between the two lies an open, empty space. It connects the Avenida Paulista with the observation terrace facing the Anhangabaú valley.[15] Both sections of the building are only connected via an outside staircase.

Bo Bardi's first design approaches focused on the exhibition hall and the open public space below it. Her drawings in particular illustrated the various possibilities for use.[16] Those included open air exhibitions, performances, rallies as well as low-threshold events like circus performances or city festivals. The area is one of few publicly accessible spaces along the otherwise densely developed Avenida Paulista. Towards the valley, it is demarcated by a bordering edge for sitting. On both sides, it is framed by oblong water basins and towards Avenida Paulista, it forms a step.

The exhibition hall covers a surface of 70 x 29m and rests solely on four concrete supports.[17] It can only be accessed via the staircase to the south-east of the square. The suspended construction facilitates an unsupported exhibition floor. Accordingly, exhibits can be freely arranged in the space and remain accessible from all sides.

The reinforced concrete supporting structure was developed by engineer José Carlos de Figueiredo Ferraz.[18] To protect the supports from water ingress, they received a red coat of paint in the early 1990s.[19]

The lower portion of the building is embedded in the slope. It houses additional exhibition spaces, a café, the museum shop, event spaces for literary readings, seminars and workshops as well as museum administration rooms. This portion is oriented towards the valley and determines the layout of the square above. In spite of its window strip frame, it appears closed-off and introverted.

USE AND USER GROUPS

The square[20] is used as a leisure and break location, as a stage for performances, as a sales space and also as a living space. Daytime users include museum visitors, tourists, street vendors and artists, police and security officers as well as museum staff. On a per-day basis, they are joined by booth vendors and promoters. The square is frequently used as a start and/or end point for demonstrations.

Tourists and passers-by usually cross the square up to the border of the adjacent valley. The urban silhouette is a popular motif for photographs, snapshots and photo shoots. The rear of the square is frequented by small groups of youths and bicycle messengers. At midday, the space is also used by employees from the surrounding offices who spend their breaks there.

The user groups with the highest degree of fluctuation are tourists and museum visitors, whose stays are usually short. With highly popular exhibitions in the MASP, lines of waiting people often go around the gallery building multiple times. Street vendors cater to them with various goods and services. In addition, the border towards Avenida Paulista is often used by street artists.

Over the course of the afternoon, the frequency of tourists and museum visitors declines. The space is then surveilled by police patrols and security staff at shorter intervals. The presence of security staff and vendors is tied to the museum's opening hours. In the evenings, adolescents usually gather in the space to listen to music and to dance. A little later, the rear part becomes a large sleeping space. In case of rain, the suspended museum building provides additional shelter. In the morning hours, the area is cleared again. The exception to this is the area behind the tills, which is somewhat offside of the main routes.

RECEPTION AND CONFLICTS

Bo Bardi's concept originally envisioned an open, multi-use space. As a special space in the city it was supposed to connect urban everyday life, various art forms and political activity. Due to changes in the social structure of the city, the space has also become an important space for homeless people to gather and rest. Accordingly, the quality of the space is assessed varyingly.

Some of those surveyed see the space as an important counterpole to the highly commercially oriented Avenida Paulista. They emphasised the heterogeneous mixture of passers-by, tourists, museum visitors, street vendors, artists and homeless people. For those surveyed, the coexistence of various social groups in particular is what distinguishes the place. The generous layout and the accentuated location in the urban space provide a suitable stage for it. Especially with the view of the valley that contributes to the popularity of the place.

Others of those surveyed perceive the urban area around the MASP as unsafe. The character of the space is strongly influenced by informal uses. They demanded more support for the homeless on site - but also continuous surveillance of the space by security staff.

Bo Bardi designed the entrance to the MASP as an open space. On the square, especially in the covered area, she envisioned corresponding installations and exhibitions. In contrast, parts of the square are closed off today.[21] MASP management sees formal uses of the area to be unprofitable. Correspondingly, there are considerations of privatising and additionally enclosing it. In contrast, the municipal administration and political entities want to preserve the space as a public area and an observation point. They intend to keep it accessible to all parts of the population in the future.[22]

With large events on the premises, security concerns have been raised at this point regarding the capacity of the construction. In 2019, MASP had to close the building portion beneath the square during a demonstration. Nowadays, it is limiting the number of admissible people: on a 10 square-metre surface, only 28 people are acceptable. Groups with more than 57 people are not permitted.[23]

18   Caffey, Campagnol (2015-2): p. 3
19   Fernández Galiano (2015): p. 56
20   Bo Bardi, Ferraz (2018): p. 110
21   Oliveira (2014): p. 7 ff.
22   Andreoli, Forty (2004): p. 82
23   Petrov (2019): www.riotimesonline.com

MINHOCÃO

ENTSTEHUNG

Zwischen 1900 und 1970 steigt die Bevölkerungszahl São Paulos von 240.000[1] auf etwa 2 Millionen an.[2] Zeitgleich mit dem Wachstum von Industrie und Wirtschaft vergrößert sich das Siedlungsgebiet dramatisch. Unter diesem Eindruck sehen Prognosen vor, dass sich die Stadtfläche bis 1980 verdoppelt und bis 2010 Jahren verdreifacht. Im Umgang mit diesen Voraussagen greift die Verwaltung São Paulos auf zwei Planungsansätze zurück. Dazu gehören der Plano de Avenidas (1930) als frühes Gesamtkonzept von Prestes Maia sowie das Programa de Melhoramentos Públicos para a cidade de São Paulo (1950) des US-amerikanischen Stadtplaners Robert Moses.[3]

In den 1930 Jahren entwickelt der brasilianische Architekt und Stadtplaner Prestes Maia für São Paulo ein radiales Straßensystem.[4] Sein Plano de Avenidas greift Aspekte der autogerechten Stadt auf, verknüpft diese aber mit traditionellen Vorstellungen des europäischen Städtebaus. Für Prestes Maia sind Interventionen zum Verkehr immer eingebettet in städtebauliche Maßnahmen, die zugleich Anlass für die Bildung öffentlicher Räume geben. Prestes Maias Planung gibt über einen langen Zeitraum den Rahmen für die Stadtentwicklung São Paulos vor.[5]

Dagegen formuliert der US-amerikanische Stadtplaner Robert Moses in den 1940er Jahren deutlich radikalere Ansätze. Auch seine Planung priorisiert den motorisierten Individualverkehr. Ergänzend schlägt er vor, das Wohnen aus der Innenstadt in die Vorstädte zu verlagern.[6] Leistungsfähige Schnellstraßen verbinden die neu entstehenden Vorstädte mit der Kernstadt. Die dazu notwendigen Trassen überzeichnen die bestehende Stadtstruktur in Form von Hochstraßen, Overfly-Kreuzungen und Zufahrtsschleifen.

Ästhetisch illustrieren die expressiven Verkehrsbauwerke Fortschritt und Individualität.[7]

Das Projekt der Via Elevada Presidente João Goulart (ursprünglich: Via Elevada Presidente Costa e Silva) verbindet beide Planungsansätze. Die aufgeständerte Trasse überbaut in einer Länge von 3,4km die von Prestes Maia geplante Hauptradiale Avenida São João und durchquert den Stadtteil Santa Cecília. Ampellos und kreuzungsfrei ausgebildet, soll sie dem Individualverkehr eine zeitsparende Verbindung in die östlichen Stadtteile ermöglichen.

Das Projekt wird vom Architekten Luiz Carlos Gomes Cardim Sangirardi zwischen 1965-1969 konzipiert. Mit dem neuen Bürgermeister Paulo Maluf rückt es 1969 in den Fokus der Tagespolitik und wird in einer Rekordzeit von 14 Monaten umgesetzt. Bei der Einweihung 1971 erhält die Hochstraße den Namen des amtierenden brasilianischen Präsidenten.[8] Die Bevölkerung nutzt dagegen den Spitznamen ‚Minhocão' (‚großer Regenwurm').

Die Hochstraße Via Elevada Presidente Costa e Silva verbindet die Praça Roosevelt und die Avenida General Olímpio da Silveira mit dem Largo Padre Péricles. Sie führt über die Stadtteile Liberdade und Glicério nach Osten und erreicht dort die Avenida Alcântara Machado als übergeordnete Verbindung, ein weiteres Element des Plano de Avenidas von Prestes Maia.

Unter Berücksichtigung dieser Ansätze wird ab den 1970er Jahren ein aktualisierter Plan für das Straßensystem São Paulos entwickelt, der drei Prämissen verbindet: Die Planung soll alle Stadtteile São Paulos erfassen. Eine Reihe von neu zu erstellenden Schnellstraßen dienen dazu Beeinträchtigungen im Verkehrsnetz zu beseitigen. Im Stadtgefüge werden schnelle und langsame Verkehrsmittel konsequent voneinander getrennt.[9]

---

1 **Hochstraße als Freiraum**
Elevated road accessible as open space

[1] Anelli (2012): S. 3
[2] Leme (2010): S. 515
[3] Artigas (2008): S. 62 ff.
[4] Leme (2010): S. 527
[5] Rolnik (2008): S. 13
[6] Anelli (2012): S. 4; Leme (2010): S. 527
[7] Leme (2010): S. 527
[8] Artur Costa e Silva ist 1964 durch einen Staatsstreich an die Macht gekommen.
[9] Anelli (2012): S. 1 f.

KONZEPT UND ABWEICHUNGEN

Die neugebaute Verkehrstraße wird täglich von etwa 78.000 Fahrzeugen genutzt.[10] Stellenweise unterschreitet das Bauwerk einen Abstand von 5m zu den angrenzenden Gebäuden. Unterhalb des Bauwerks sammeln sich Abgase.[11] Bereits kurz nach der Eröffnung beklagen sich die Anrainer über Lärm und Abgasemissionen sowie über die Häufung von Unfällen.

Da die Zahl der Beschwerden konstant hoch bleibt, wird die Hochstraße bereits ab 1976 täglich zwischen Mitternacht und 05:00 Uhr gesperrt. Der Bau führt zu einer Verringerung der Lebensqualität im Wohngebiet und damit auch zu einem Verfall des Mietniveaus. Ab 1989 schränkt die Stadtverwaltung den Verkehr auf der Hochstraße weiter ein.[12] Dazu wird die tägliche Sperrung auf den Zeitraum zwischen 21.30 bis 06.30 Uhr ausgeweitet. An Sonn- und Feiertagen ist das Befahren vollständig untersagt.

ENTWICKLUNG

Von den Auswirkungen der Hochstraße sind etwa 240.000 Menschen betroffen. Entsprechend rückt die ‚Cicatriz urbana' (‚urbane Narbe') immer wieder in den Mittelpunkt öffentlicher Debatten. 1987 legt der Architekt Pitanga do Amparo erste Pläne zur Umgestaltung vor. Der Vorschlag sieht eine Trennung des Verkehrs auf den zwei Ebenen vor. Der motorisierte Individualverkehr soll künftig nur noch die Grundebene nutzen. Dagegen bleibt die Fahrspur auf dem Bauwerk dem öffentlichen Verkehr vorbehalten. Sie wird eingefasst durch ein beidseitiges Gartenband, in dessen Verlauf Aufenthaltsflächen sowie Einstiegspunkte für den ÖPNV eingefügt werden.[13]

Auf Grundlage einer Bürgerinitiative startet 1990 ein Pilotprojekt, das die Hochstraße zeitweise für Fußgänger und Radfahrer öffnet.[14] Schrittweise erobern damit Anrainer und Touristen den Elevado als neuen Freiraum. 2006 wird ein Ideenwettbewerb für die Nachnutzung der Hochstraße ausgelobt. Das Team bestehend aus José Alves und Juliana Corradini erhält für seinen Beitrag den Städtebaupreis ‚Prêmio Prestes Maia de Urbanismo'.[15] Das Konzept schlägt eine abschnittsweise Überbauung des Elevado vor. Der Entwurf teilt die Hochstraße in mehrere Abschnitte und entwickelt dazu Gebäudetypologien mit Seitengalerien sowie einen öffentlichen Park.[16]

Mit dem Ausblick auf eine umfassende Veränderung engagieren sich ab 2013 interessierte Bürger in dem Verein ‚Parque Minhocão'.

2014 legt der Bürgermeister Fernando Haddad einen Masterplan für São Paulo vor, der einen neuen Umgang mit der Hochstraße vorschlägt. Vorgesehen sind eine schrittweise Einschränkung des Autoverkehrs[17] sowie Maßnahmen zur Verbesserung der Aufenthaltsqualität. Die Veröffentlichung des Masterplans bietet einen Impuls für neue Immobilien-, Tourismus- und Kulturprojekte in den angrenzenden Stadtquartieren. Ab 2015 entstehen an den angrenzenden Brandwänden Wandbilder und vertikale Gärten.[18]

Im Jahr 2019 kündigt der Bürgermeister Bruno Covas an, einen Abschnitt der Hochstraße dauerhaft für den motorisierten Verkehr zu schließen. Der 900 m lange Bereich liegt über den Straßen Rua Amaral Gurgel, Rua da Consolação und Avenida São João. Gleichzeitig soll mit dem Bau eines Teilstücks der Parkanlage begonnen werden, um das Bauwerk vor dem Abriss zu schützen.

Das Projekt basiert auf der Studie des Architekten und Stadtplaners Jaime Lerner. Geplant ist ein linearer Park mit einer parallel verlaufenden Dreiteilung. Die Mitte wird durch eine zentrale Achse für Radfahrer und Fußgänger belegt. An den Außenseiten sorgen Grünflächen und stilisierte Bäume aus Bambusholz für Verschattung. Vorgesehen sind zudem neue Zufahrten für den Radverkehr sowie Treppenanlagen und ein Aufzug. Mit einer Bausumme von etwa 38 Mio. Reais soll das Projekt ab 2020 realisiert werden.[19]

NUTZUNG UND NUTZERGRUPPEN

Die Hochstraße quert einen Teil der Innenstadt São Paulos, der durch eine sehr heterogene Bebauung geprägt ist. Insbesondere die Gebäudehöhen und -breiten variieren stark. Wer die Hochstraße begeht oder befährt, löst sich weitgehend vom übrigen Stadtgefüge, denn zwischen Hochstraße und Stadtebene bestehen nur wenige Verbindungen. Die aufgeständerte Trasse verschwenkt über ihren Verlauf hinweg, steigt und fällt. Dabei bieten die querenden Straßenkorridore und die weiter entfernt liegenden Hochhäuser jeweils unterschiedliche Ausblicke und Orientierungspunkte.

Die Straße hat einen glatten, fugenlosen Asphaltbelag und eignet sich damit gut für unterschiedliche Sport- und Bewegungsarten. Die Seiten und die Mitte des Viaduktes sind durch Leitplanken aus Beton eingefasst und geteilt. Die Aufkantungen werden gerne zum Sitzen, Liegen und zum Bespielen genutzt.

---

2 Lageplan
   Site plan
   1:10000

3 Verbindungen Stadtebene
   Connections to the city level
   (S. 150 / p. 150)

---

[10] Quintella (2019): www.vejasp.abril.com.br
[11] Artigas (2008): S. 68 f.
[12] Folha de São Paulo (1989): S. 1, www.acervo.folha.com.br
[13] Pitanga do Amparo Arquitetura & Arte (1987): www.pitangadoamparo.com.br
[14] Folha de São Paulo (1990): S. 6, www.acervo.folha.com.br
[15] Corradini, Alves (2006): www.vitruvius.com.br
[16] Das Konzept wird nach der Preisverleihung nicht weiterverfolgt.
[17] Batista (2015): www.acervo.estadao.com.br
[18] Die Maßnahmen werden über Ausgleichszahlungen finanziert.
[19] Quintella (2019): www.vejasp.abril.com.br

4   **Schnitt Süd-Nord**
    South-north section
    1:1000

5   **Spur und Stadtlandschaft**
    Track and city scape
    (S. 154 / p. 154)

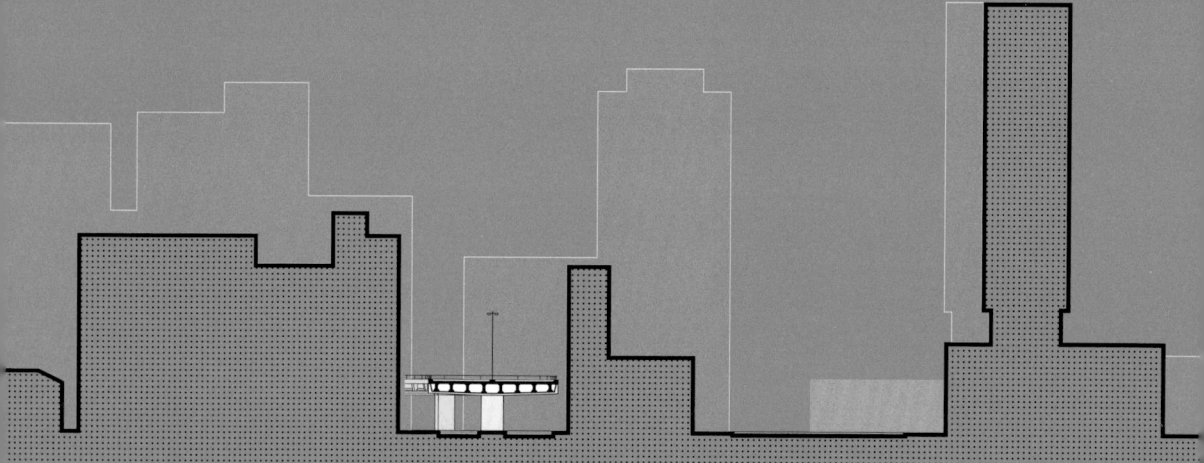

An Wochenenden sowie zwischen 21:30 und Sonnenaufgang lassen sich unterschiedliche Aktivitäten beobachten. Neben Spaziergängern und Joggern bewegen sich viele Nutzer mit dem Fahrrad, Inlineskates und Skateboards. Zu den örtlich gebundenen Nutzungen gehören improvisierte Sport- und Spielflächen, Sonnenbaden und Feiern. Hinzu kommen Fotoshootings sowie der mobile Verkauf von Getränken und Snacks. Saisonal finden zudem organisierte Veranstaltungen wie Tanzabende oder Theateraufführungen[20] statt. Berücksichtigt werden dabei Bereiche mit besonders günstigen Randbedingungen (u.a.: Sonnenstand und Verschattung durch nahe Gebäude, Nähe zu Zufahrten, Sitzmöglichkeit, ...). Auf dem Viadukt hat sich ein sehr spezifischer Begegnungsraum entwickelt, der von unterschiedlichen Sozialgruppen in Anspruch genommen wird.[21]

Die Höhe des Elevado liegt bei durchschnittlich ca. 5,5m. Aus der Stadtebene wirkt der Raum unterhalb des Bauwerks bedrückend und wenig großzügig. Im Kontrast zu den Freizeitaktivitäten mischen sich hier weiterhin Verkehr- und Transitnutzungen. Anwohner unterqueren die Trasse zu den anliegenden Quartieren oder warten an Bushaltestellen. Gleichzeitig nutzen Wohnungslose die überdachte Fläche als Witterungsschutz.

REZEPTION UND KONFLIKTE

Das Bauwerk wird besonders abends und nachts als unbelebter und unsicherer Ort wahrgenommen. Die Trasse und die darunterliegenden Räume wirken sich als stadträumliche Zäsur zudem negativ auf die Umgebung aus. Diese Einschätzung wird auch an den informellen und teilweise illegalen Aktivitäten unter dem Bauwerk festgemacht.

Die Befragten sind über die anstehenden Entwicklungen sowie zu den Optionen zur Transformation der Trasse unterschiedlich gut informiert. Von vielen Befragten wird die Umgestaltung des Elevado zu einer Parkanlage begrüßt. Angesichts der Unterversorgung mit städtischen Freianlagen ergänzt der geplante neue Park die Quartiere um dringend benötigte Flächen. Gleichzeitig steigt damit auch die Attraktivität der Umgebung.

Teilweise wird die Eignung der Trasse als öffentlicher Raum aber auch angezweifelt, schließlich fehlen verschattete und grüne Bereiche. Befürchtet wird auch, dass sich die Nutzungen unterhalb des Bauwerks schrittweise auf die Parkebene verlagern und dort mittelfristig stören. Dagegen stößt eine dauerhafte Schließung der Hochstraße bei einigen der Befragten auch auf Unverständnis. Angesichts der chronischen Überlastung der Verkehrsräume wird damit eine weitere Zuspitzung der Verkehrssituation auf der Stadtebene erwartet.

Einige der befragten Anwohner befürchten, dass eine Aufwertung des Areals vor allem den wirtschaftlichen Interessen der Immobilienwirtschaft dient und die Verdrängung von einkommensschwachen Schichten verstärkt. Stellenweise wird bereits von einem Anstieg der Mieten berichtet.

[20] Einige der Theateraufführungen finden hinter den Fenstern von anliegenden Gebäuden statt. Die Zuschauer befinden sich auf der Straße.

[21] Schröder, Carta, Ferretti, Lino (2017): S. 143

MINHOCÃO

ORIGIN

Between 1900 and 1970, São Paulo's population increased from 240,000[1] to roughly 2 million.[2] Along with industrial and economic growth, the settlement area expanded dramatically. Given this impression, the urban area was projected to double by 1980 and to triple by 2010. To handle these projections, São Paulo's planning authority resorted to two planning approaches. They consist of the Plano de Avenidas (1930) as an early overall concept by Prestes Maia and the Plano de Melhoramentos Públicos para a Cidade de São Paulo (1950) by North American urban planner Robert Moses.[3]

In the 1930s, Brazilian architect and urban planner Prestes Maia developed a radial road network for São Paulo.[4] His Plano de Avenidas factors in aspects of automotive cities, but also connects them to traditional ideas of European urban development.

For Prestes Maia, interventions regarding traffic are always integrated in urban-development measures, which simultaneously motivate the formation of public spaces. Prestes Maia's plan provides the framework for São Paulo's urban development over a long period of time.[5]

In contrast, North American urban planner Robert Moses in the 1940s formulated significantly more radical approaches. He suggested shifting residential uses from the inner city to the suburbs.[6] High-capacity motorways were to connect the newly created suburbs with the city core.

The required routes overlie the existing urban structure in the shape of overpasses, intersection flyovers and access loops. Aesthetically, the expressive traffic structures illustrate progress and individuality.[7] Economically, they prioritise the promotion of private vehicle traffic as a core concern of urban development.[8]

The project of the Via Elevada Presidente João Goulart (originally called Via Elevada Presidente Costa e Silva) connects the two planning approaches. The route is raised over the main radial Avenida São João planned by Prestes Maia, crossing the Santa Cecília quarter at a length of 3.4km. Designed without traffic lights or intersections, it was intended to provide a time-saving connection to the eastern parts of the city for private vehicle traffic.

The concept for the project was created by architect Luiz Carlos Gomes Cardim Sangirardi between 1965 and 1969. Under the new mayor Paulo Maluf, it moved to the centre of the political agenda of the day and was realised in a record time of 14 months. At its inauguration in 1971, the overpass received the name of the Brazilian president in charge.[9] The population, however, uses the nickname 'Minhocão' ('large worm').

The overpass Via Elevada Presidente Costa e Silva connects Praça Roosevelt and Avenida General Olímpio da Silveira with Largo Padre Péricles. It spans the quarters Liberdade and Glicério to the east, where it reaches Avenida Alcântara Machado as a superordinate connection - another element from Prestes Maia's Plano de Avenidas.

From the 1970s, an updated plan for São Paulo's road network was developed which factored in these approaches and connected three propositions: planning was to include all quarters of São Paulo, a series of motorways to be constructed was to remove traffic obstructions from the network, and fast and slow means of transportation were to be separated consistently in the urban fabric.[10]

6	Nutzungsmuster Patterns of use
7	Stadtpromenade City promenade (S. 158 / p. 158)

1	Anelli (2012): p. 3
2	Leme (2010): p. 515
3	Artigas (2008): p. 62 ff.
4	Leme (2010): p. 527
5	Rolnik (2008): p. 13
6	Anelli (2012): p. 4; Leme (2010): p. 527
7	Leme (2010): p. 527
8	Leme (2010): p. 527; Anelli (2012): p. 3
9	Artur Costa e Silva had come to power in 1964 by means of a coup.
10	Anelli (2012): p. 1 f.

DESIGN AND DEVIATIONS

The newly constructed traffic route is used by roughly 78,000 vehicles per day.[11] In places, the structure was located less than 5m away from adjacent buildings and exhaust fumes accumulated below the structure.[12] Shortly after the inauguration, neighbours started complaining about noise and exhaust emissions, as well as numerous accidents.

Since the number of complaints remained consistently high, the overpass was closed to traffic each day between midnight and 5 a.m. as early as 1976. The structure led to a decrease in quality of life in the residential area and thus to a decline in the rent level. From 1989, the municipal administration continued to further restrict traffic on the overpass.[13] The daily closure was extended to the time period between 9.30 p.m. and 6.30 a.m. and driving on the motorway on Sundays and bank holidays was prohibited completely.

DEVELOPMENT

The effects of the overpass impacted roughly 240,000 people, making the 'Cicatriz urbana' (Portuguese for 'urban scar') a hot topic for discussion in the press, planning disciplines and among citizens. In 1987, architect Pitanga do Amparo presented the first designs for remodelling. His suggestion stipulated a separation of traffic over the two levels, with private vehicle traffic restricted to the bottom level. The lane on top of the structure would be reserved for public transport. It was to be bordered by a bilateral garden strip with integrated areas for lingering and access points to public transport vehicles.[14]

In 1990, a pilot project based on a citizens' initiative was started, which opened the overpass to the public intermittently.[15] During the periods without motor traffic, the overpass was gradually discovered and conquered by pedestrians and cyclists. A design competition for subsequent use of the overpass was held in 2006, with the team consisting of José Alves and Juliana Corradini winning the urban development prize 'Prêmio Prestes Maia de Urbanismo' for their contribution.[16] Their concept suggests building on the Elevado in subdivided sections, developing building typologies with lateral galleries as well as a public park on the overpass.[17]

With the perspective of a comprehensive change, interested citizens started getting involved in the association 'Parque Minhocão' in 2013.

In 2014, mayor Fernando Haddad presented a new master plan for São Paulo, which included an approach to handling the overpass. The plan stipulated a gradual limitation of automobile traffic[18], focusing on improvements to the quality of the urban space.

Simultaneously, the publication of the master plan created an impetus for new real estate, tourism and culture projects in adjacent areas of the city. In this context, murals and vertical gardens have been created along the adjacent firewalls since 2015.[19] This demonstrates to neighbours and visitors alike what potential the structure harbours when it is revived with new uses.

In 2019, mayor Bruno Covas announced the permanent closing of one section of the overpass for motor traffic. This 900m stretch is located above the streets Rua Amaral Gurgel, Rua da Consolação and Avenida São João. Simultaneously, construction is supposed to start on a portion of the park to protect the structure from demolition.

The project is based on a study of architect and urban planner Jaime Lerner, which envisages a linear park with a parallel trisection. Its middle is to be occupied by a central axis for cyclists and pedestrians, while green areas and stylised trees made of bamboo timber on the outer lanes provide shade. Other features include new access ramps for bicycle traffic, a staircase as well as an elevator. The project with construction costs of roughly 38 million Reais is scheduled for realisation in 2020.[20]

USE AND USER GROUPS

The overpass traverses a part of São Paulo's inner city, which is characterised by a highly heterogeneous building structure. Particularly, building heights and widths vary widely. Walking or driving on the overpass mostly removes the individual from the remaining urban fabric, since there are only few connections to the ground level. The raised route features many deviations along its path; it ascends and descends. Crossing street corridors with high-rise buildings in the distance each offer different points for viewing and orientation. The particular location, the generous scale, the elevated view, as well as the absence of vehicles create a special experience of space.

Thanks to its smooth, jointless asphalt surface, the road is excellently suited for various sports and activities. The sides and the middle of the viaduct are bordered and divided by concrete barrier elements which are popular for sitting, reclining and other uses.

---

11 Quintella (2019): www.vejasp.abril.com.br
12 Artigas (2008): p. 68 f.
13 Folha de São Paulo (1989): p. 1, www.acervo.folha.com.br
14 Pitanga do Amparo Arquitetura & Arte (1987): www.pitangadoamparo.com.br
15 Folha de São Paulo (1990): p. 6, www.acervo.folha.com.br
16 Corradini, Alves (2006): www.vitruvius.com.br
17 This concept was not pursued after the awards ceremony.
18 Batista (2015): www.acervo.estadao.com.br
19 The measures are funded via offset payments.
20 Quintella (2019): www.vejasp.abril.com.br

8 Schnitt Ost-West
East-west section
1:1000

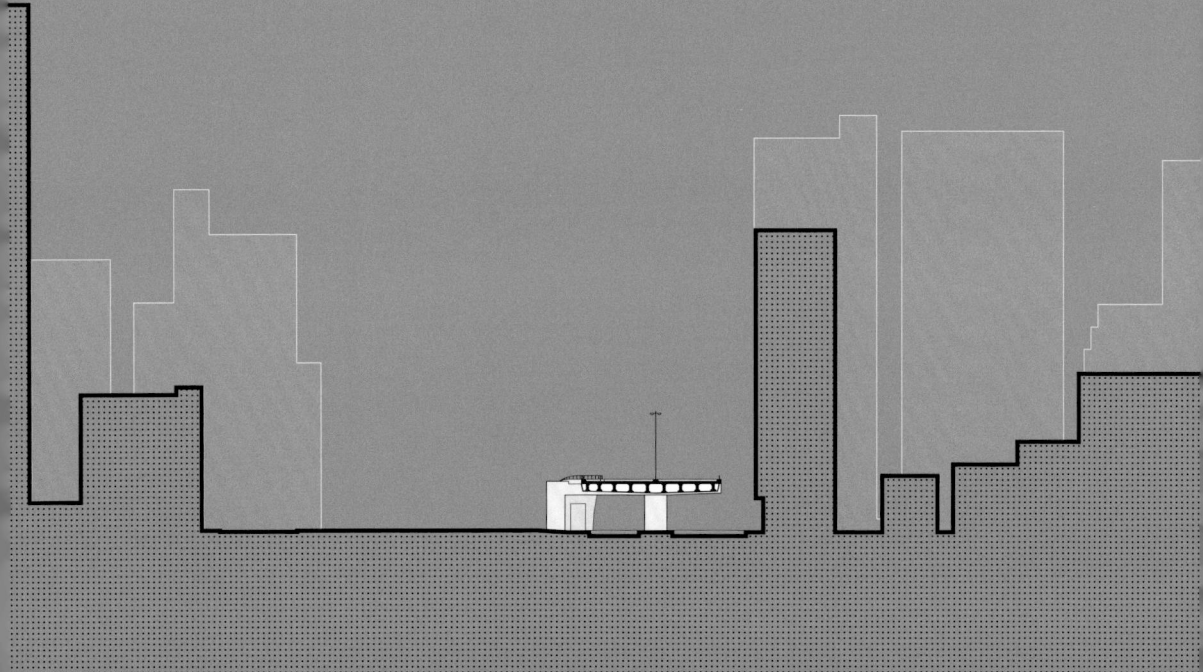

On weekends, as well as between 9.30 p.m. and sunrise, various activities can be observed. Besides walkers and joggers, many users move along on bicycles, in-line skates and skateboards. Localised uses include improvised sports and play areas, sunbathing, reading and celebrating. Photo shoots and mobile vending of drinks and snacks also take place at the site. Depending on the season, organised events such as dance evenings or theatre performances[21] are also held.

Over the course of the route, the aforementioned uses intermingle, taking into account areas with particularly beneficial conditions (position of the sun and shade from surrounding buildings, distance from access ramps, seating facilities, etc.). Since lanes, area markings and established rules of conduct do not exist, the various users each consider the needs of others and avoid disruptions. On the viaduct, a highly specific space for congregation has developed and is frequented by different social groups.[22]

The height of the Elevado averages roughly 5.5m - viewed from the ground level, the space beneath the structure appears oppressive and rather narrow. In contrast to the leisure activities, traffic and transit uses still intermingle here. Residents cross below the route to get to other quarters, wait at bus stops, or use shops and services in the vicinity. The canopied area is popular with homeless people for sleeping, inhabiting and protection from the weather.

RECEPTION AND CONFLICTS

The overpass is perceived as an inanimate and unsafe place, especially in the evening and at night. Forming a break in urban space, the route and the spaces below it have a negative effect on their surroundings. This assessment is associated, among other things, with the informal and partially illegal activities taking place beneath the structure.

Those surveyed had varying levels of knowledge regarding the impending developments and the transformation options for the route. Many welcome the conversion of the Elevado into a park. Given the shortage of open urban spaces, they expect the new park to add meaningful and necessary uses. The rise in visitors to the route also increases the appeal of the neighbourhood.

Some also question the suitability of the route as a public space, since shaded areas are missing. There are also concerns that the uses from underneath the structure will gradually shift to the park level and cause disruption there in the medium term. However, a permanent closure of the overpass was also met with incomprehension by some of those surveyed. In the face of chronic capacity overloads of traffic spaces, they expect further spikes in traffic levels.

Some neighbours surveyed voiced concerns that the upgrading of the area would mainly serve the economic interests of the real estate industry and lead to a displacement of low-income strata. In some areas, rising rents were already reported.

9 **Stadtkulisse**
Urban backdrop
Fotoshooting
Photo shooting

10 **Grüne Fassaden**
Green facades
(S. 164 / p. 164)

21 Some of the theatre performances take place behind the windows of adjacent buildings. The audience is on the street.

22 Schröder, Carta, Ferretti, Lino (2017): p. 143

CENTRO CULTURAL SÃO PAULO

RAUM UND GESTALT

Das Centro Cultural São Paulo (CCSP) besetzt eine topografisch und verkehrsräumlich exponierte Lage. Es liegt an der Schnittstelle der vier Stadtteile Paraíso, Aclimação, Liberdade und Bela Vista. Der Entwurf reagiert auf die topografischen Eigenarten des Ortes.[1] Das Gebäudevolumen ist eingebettet in die bestehende Hangkante zum inzwischen verrohrten Rio Itororó und betont die Längsausrichtung des Grundstücks. Der Erhalt der Bestandsbäume sowie ein grün geprägter Dachgarten tragen zusätzlich zur Integration in den Talraum bei.[2]

Das Gebäude liegt zwischen der Avenida 23 de Maio und der Rua Vergueiro, zwei auf unterschiedlichen Niveaus liegenden Straßen. Als Schnellstraße belegt die Avenida das ehemalige Flussbett des Rio Itororó. Die Kanalisierung des Flusses zwischen der Rua João Julião und der Rua do Paraíso ist Teil des Avenida Itororó-Projekts.[3] Der Umbau des Talraums erfolgt im Zuge der Umsetzung des Plano de Avenidas von Prestes Maia in den Jahren zwischen 1951 bis 1969. Der Fluss liegt inzwischen kanalisiert unterhalb der Schnellstraße. Der Entwurf des CCSP verbindet den landschaftsräumlichen Kontext des Flusstals mit dem kleinteiligen Maßstab von Stadt und Fußgängern. Dabei präsentiert sich das Gebäude bewusst zurückhaltend und will als besonderer Ort beiläufig ‚entdeckt' werden. Erkennungsmerkmal ist die langgestreckte, betretbare Dachfläche. Größe und Komplexität des Gebäudes erschließen sich erst beim Annähern.

Die Nutzflächen des Gebäudes sind über vier Geschosse, inklusive Dachgeschoss, organisiert. Dabei nimmt lediglich die Tiefebene die gesamte Grundfläche ein. Die beiden darüber liegenden Ebenen berühren jeweils nicht die Hangkante. Zwischen den Ebenen bestehen unterschiedliche räumliche und visuelle Verbindungen.

Dazu gehören Lichtöffnungen sowie Rampen- und Treppenanlagen. Die Dachfläche wird ebenfalls über Treppen und Rampen erschlossen.

Das Gebäude ist offen und durchlässig konzipiert, um möglichst viele Nutzungen und Aktivitäten sichtbar zu lassen. Auch zwischen den einzelnen Nutzungseinheiten wird auf geschlossene Flächen oder Trennwände weitgehend verzichtet.[4] Zum offenen Charakter des Gebäudes tragen Konstruktion und Materialzusammenstellung bei. Dazu gehören schlanke Betonstützen und Rampen, filigrane Metallkonstruktionen sowie ein großer Glasanteil. Die Trennelemente für geschlossene Räume wie das Theater und die Konzertsäle bestehen aus transparenten Materialien.

NUTZUNG UND BESPIELUNG

Das CCSP versteht sich als Alternative und Ergänzung zu bestehenden öffentlichen Räumen. Es ist niedrigschwellig zugänglich und richtet sich damit bewusst an Nutzer, die selten mit Bildungs- und Kulturangeboten in Berührung kommen.

Das Gebäude ist über unterschiedliche Zugänge mit der Stadt verbunden. Bodengleiche Zugänge befinden sich jeweils an den Kopfseiten im Norden und Süden des Gebäudes. Sie sind jeweils mit kleinen Platzsituationen verbunden.

Grob unterscheiden lassen sich die selbstorganisierten Nutzungen, feste Nutzungen sowie Programmangebote. Zu den informellen Nutzungen gehören Tanzen, Treffen und Austausch sowie Entspannen, Lesen und Lernen. Dazu bietet das CCSP einen hohen Anteil an offenen, unbelegten Flächen, die flexibel bespielbar sind.[5] Ihr Zuschnitt und ihre Disposition lassen ein Nebeneinander selbstorganisierter Nutzungen zu.

---

1 Offene Innenräume
Open interiors

[1] Nascimento, Teixeira (2014): S. 141 f.
[2] Nascimento, Teixeira (2014): S. 142 f.
[3] Lei 3209, de 31 de Julho de 1928 do Município de São Paulo
[4] Matera (2018): S. 160 ff.
[5] SIAA Arquitetos Associados (2018): S. 29

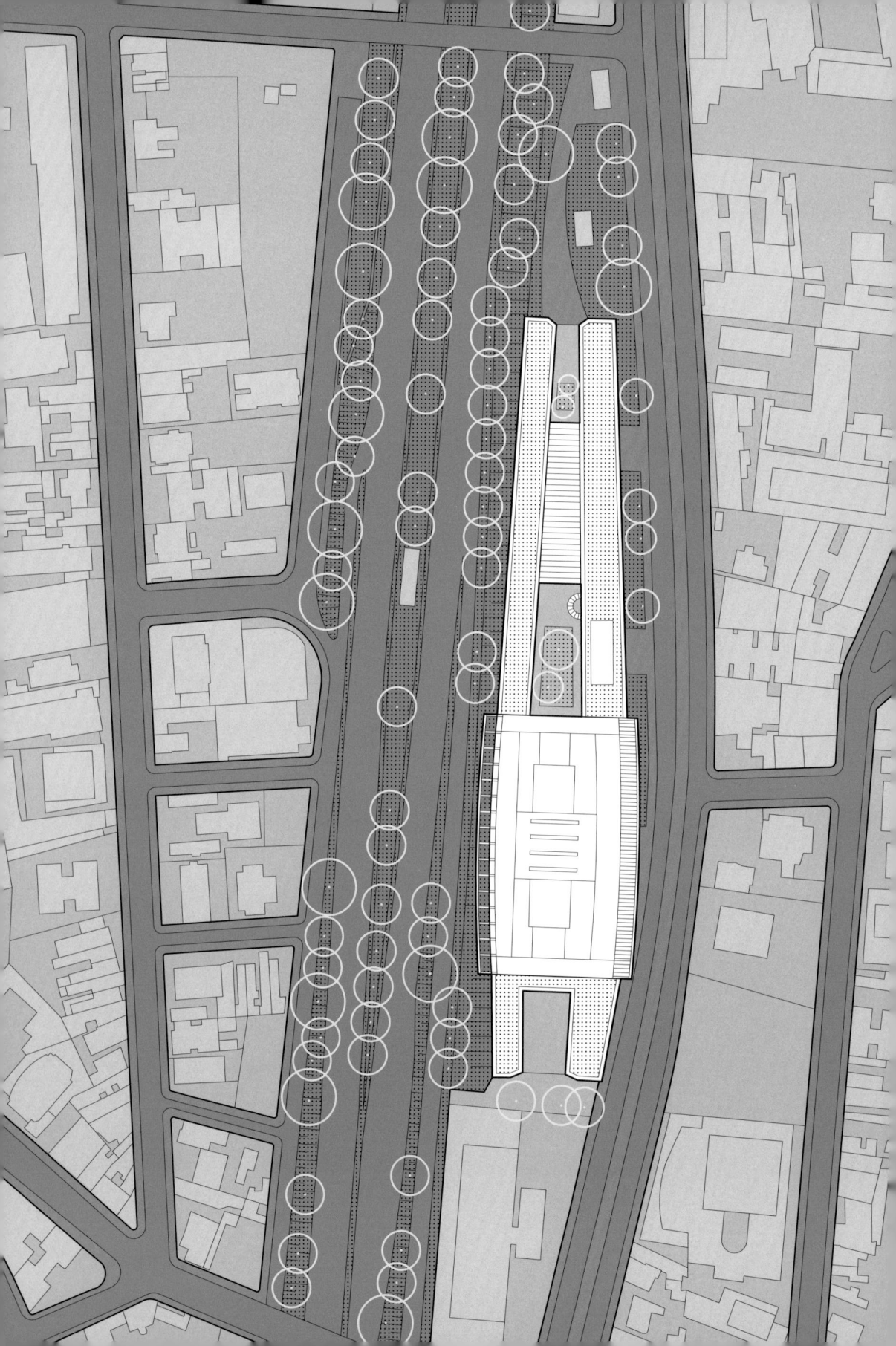

Ruhigere Bereiche liegen in der Nähe der Bibliothek; auf der gleichen Geschossebene befinden sich zusätzlich ein Kino, eine Konzerthalle, ein Theater und eine Kindertagesstätte. Dagegen sind Flächen für laute Aktivitäten wie Musik und Tanz auf den darüberliegenden Ebenen angeordnet. Im zweiten Untergeschoss sind eine Druckerei, das FabLab als eine offene Werkstatt sowie die Administration untergebracht.

Die Nutzer des CCSP kommen aus dem gesamten Stadtgebiet. In den vergangenen Jahren ist das Gebäude zu einem beliebten Treffpunkt für Tanzinteressierte geworden. Manche Nutzer nehmen bis zu zwei Stunden Fahrtzeit in Kauf um das CCSP zu erreichen. Zur Zeit treffen sich die Gruppen in der Nähe des Hauptzugangs zur Rua Vergueiro sowie auf der oberen Ebene entlang der Korridore. Beliebt sind diese Orte aufgrund ihrer Glasfassaden. Die Flächen spiegeln die Bewegungsabläufe und erlauben so ein individuelles Prüfen und Korrigieren der eigenen Tanzbewegungen. Um den Grad an Spiegelung zu erhöhen, hat die Gebäudeverwaltung die Glasscheiben nachtönen lassen.

Die meisten Tanzgruppen üben an arbeitsfreien Zeiten. Entsprechend sind die Flure am späten Nachmittag und am Wochenende besonders stark belegt. Aktuell denkt die Leitung des CCSP darüber nach diese Form der Bespielung aufgrund ihrer besonderen Beliebtheit stärker zu fördern.

Der Dachgarten wird gerne als Treffpunkt, zum Entspannen und als Lernort genutzt. Die Fläche bietet eine besonders Aussicht, liegt aber gleichzeitig geschützt. Sie ermöglicht Picknicken, Sonnenbaden und Lesen mit Rundumblick über die Stadt. Im Norden, entlang der Rua Vergueiro bilden Hecken eine Barriere zwischen Straße und Grundstück. Durch Gehölzbestand und Dachüberstand ist dieser Ort zusätzlich sonnengeschützt. Der Bereich wird gerne von Yoga- und Lesegruppen genutzt.

Neben den selbstorganisierten Nutzungen bietet das CCSP auch ein umfangreiches Programm an, das von der Ação Cultural e Educativa (Aktion für Kultur und Bildung) organisiert wird. Es umfasst Angebote in den Bereichen bildende Kunst, audiovisuelle Medien, Tanz, Literatur, Musik und Theater. Darüber hinaus finden regelmäßig besondere Aktivitäten und Veranstaltungen statt, die neue Besucher für das CCSP gewinnen sollen. Für Konzerte, Filme und Vorträge sind jeweils unterschiedliche Kuratoren zuständig.

Ein weiterer Schwerpunkt bilden die Bibliothek und die angeschlossenen Lernbereiche. Die Einrichtung ist gut ausgestattet und uneingeschränkt zugänglich. Lange Öffnungszeiten, eine gute Anbindung sowie eine Vielzahl an nahegelegenen Bildungseinrichtungen tragen zusätzlich zu ihrer Beliebtheit bei. Trotz der eher lauten Umgebung wird das Lernumfeld intensiv genutzt. Teilweise weichen Lernende auch in den Südgarten, den Vorgarten oder ruhigere Korridorabschnitte aus.

ENTSTEHUNG

Ende der 1970er Jahre wird das U-Bahn-System in São Paulo erweitert.[6] Parallel dazu findet ein Wettbewerb statt, der zwischen Avenida 23 de Maio and Rua Vergueiro auf einer Fläche von 80.000 m² eine Nachverdichtung durch Hochhäuser vorsieht.[7] Kritiker verbinden mit dem Projekt negative Auswirkungen auf die umgebenden Stadtteile.

Als Alternative schlägt São Paulos Bürgermeister Olavo Setúbal im Jahr 1975 vor, die Zentralbibliothek São Paulo Vergueiro am Nord-Süd Korridor zu errichten. Er stellt dem Projekt dazu eine rund 22.000m² große Fläche zur Verfügung, die sich im Besitz der Stadt befindet. Der Vorschlag greift Planungen auf, die eine Dezentralisierung von Kultureinrichtungen außerhalb des Stadtzentrums vorsehen. Dies umfasst Gebäude mit dem Fokus auf Bildung, Gesundheit, Kultur und Sport. Sie sollen als Schnittstellen zwischen dem Zentrum und der städtischen Peripherie dienen.[8] Das Projekt wird zwischen 1975 und 1985 konzipiert und umgesetzt. Das Team besteht aus den Architekten Luiz Benedito de Castro Telles und Eurico Prado Lopes in Zusammenarbeit mit PLAE Arquitetura SC Ltda.

Der Entwurf berücksichtigt die Topografie des ehemalige Flusstal und die Nähe zur angrenzende Schnellstraße. Ein wichtiges Anliegen der Entwurfsautoren ist es, einen traditionellen Bibliotheksbau zu vermeiden, der die Tätigkeiten der Nutzer auf Suchen und Lesen beschränkt. Stattdessen soll das Gebäude die Besucher anregen das Flächenangebot für sich in Anspruch zu nehmen. Es soll Begegnungen ermöglichen und dabei ohne Barrieren auskommen.[9] Damit soll auch ein beiläufiger und niedrigschwelliger Zugang zu Bildung und Kultur initiiert werden.[10]

2 Lageplan
Site plan
1:2000

6 Companhia do Metropolitano de São Paulo - Metrô und Empresa Municipal de Urbanização (EMURB)

7 Anelli (2007) in Nascimento, Teixeira (2014): S. 140

8 Anelli (2019) in Lepik, Talesnik (2019): S. 20

9 Telles (2002): S. 1

10 Wissenbach (1981): S. 33

Die Planung ist das Ergebnis einer intensiven Auseinandersetzung zwischen Entwurfsteam und Stadtverwaltung. Bis zu seiner Eröffnung 1982 muss das Projekt über die Planungs- und Bauphase hinweg zahlreiche Änderungen überstehen. Die mit dem Projekt verbundenen Vorstellungen unterlaufen die Ziele der brasilianischen Militärregierung. Hinzu kommen Bauunterbrechung sowie Probleme mit den ausführenden Firmen. Aus politischen Gründen wird das Gebäude bereits im Mai 1981 eingeweiht, obwohl erst 70% des Gebäudes fertiggestellt sind.[11]

REZEPTION UND KONFLIKTE

Das Gebäude wird als Fortsetzung der Straße verstanden - als Teil eines überraschenden Stadtspaziergangs. Im Stadtraum wird es als ‚grüne Insel' wahrgenommen. Dabei laden die unterschiedlichen Erschließungselemente zum Auskundschaften ein. Viele der Befragten schätzen die Großzügigkeit und die Vielfältigkeit des Gebäudes.

Das CCSP wird als ein offener und sicherer Ort wahrgenommen, der allen Bevölkerungsschichten zur Verfügung steht - ein Schutzraum ohne Diskriminierung, Vorurteile und Gewalt. Darüber hinaus richten sich bestimmte Angebote und Veranstaltungen, wie Kinofestivals und Ausstellungen an bestimmte Minderheiten.

Wohnungslose gehören selbstverständlich zur Nutzergruppe. Für die Betroffenen bietet das CCSP vor allem Schutz und Normalität. Sie erhalten Zugang zu Sanitärräumen, Schlafgelegenheiten, die Möglichkeit zu entspannen und Anderen bei ihren Aktivitäten zuzuschauen. Allerdings schränken die inzwischen nachträglich eingefügten Tore und Türen den Zugang zum Gebäude ein. Auch der Eingangsplatz zwischen Bibliothek und der Avenida 23 de Maio ist nicht mehr frei zugänglich. Sicherheitspersonal prüft zudem das Einhalten der Hausordnung.

Die Ausrichtung des Kulturzentrums als lebendiger und vielfältiger Ort hängt ab von der Haltung und den Schwerpunktsetzungen der jeweiligen Leitung. Aktuell sind mit der Wirtschaftskrise und den politischen Veränderungen Einschnitte bei der Finanzierung verbunden. Zudem wird darüber nachgedacht, Teilbereiche zu privatisieren. Einige der Befragten befürchten, dass das CCSP damit seinen Charakter als offener Ort verliert.

3 Nach Innen gerichtet
Inward orientation

Abschirmung zu den Straßen
The building shields itself from the street

[11] Wissenbach (1981): S. 31

4 Grundriss EG
  Floor plan GF
  1:1500

5 Schnitt West-Ost
  West-east section
  1:1500

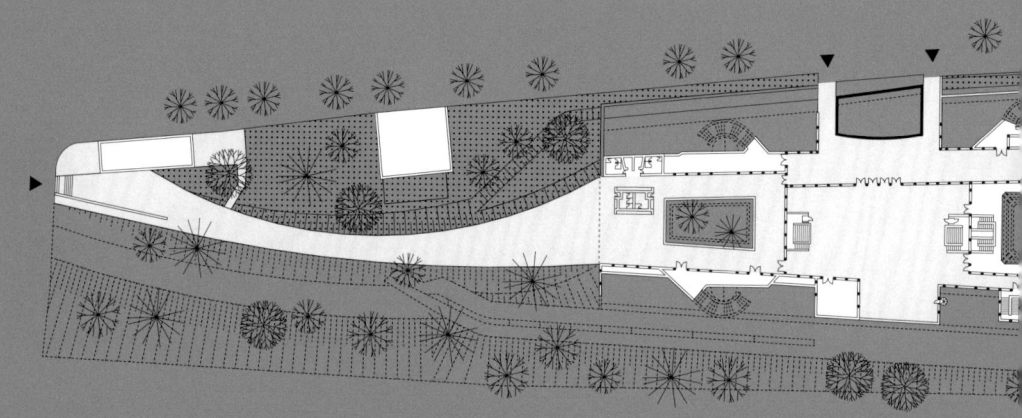

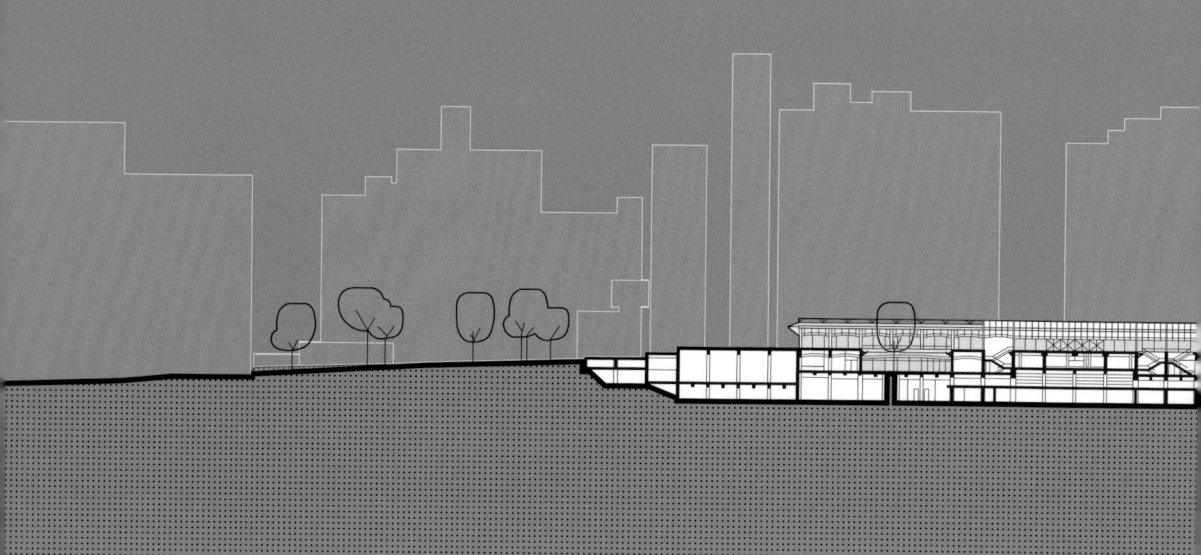

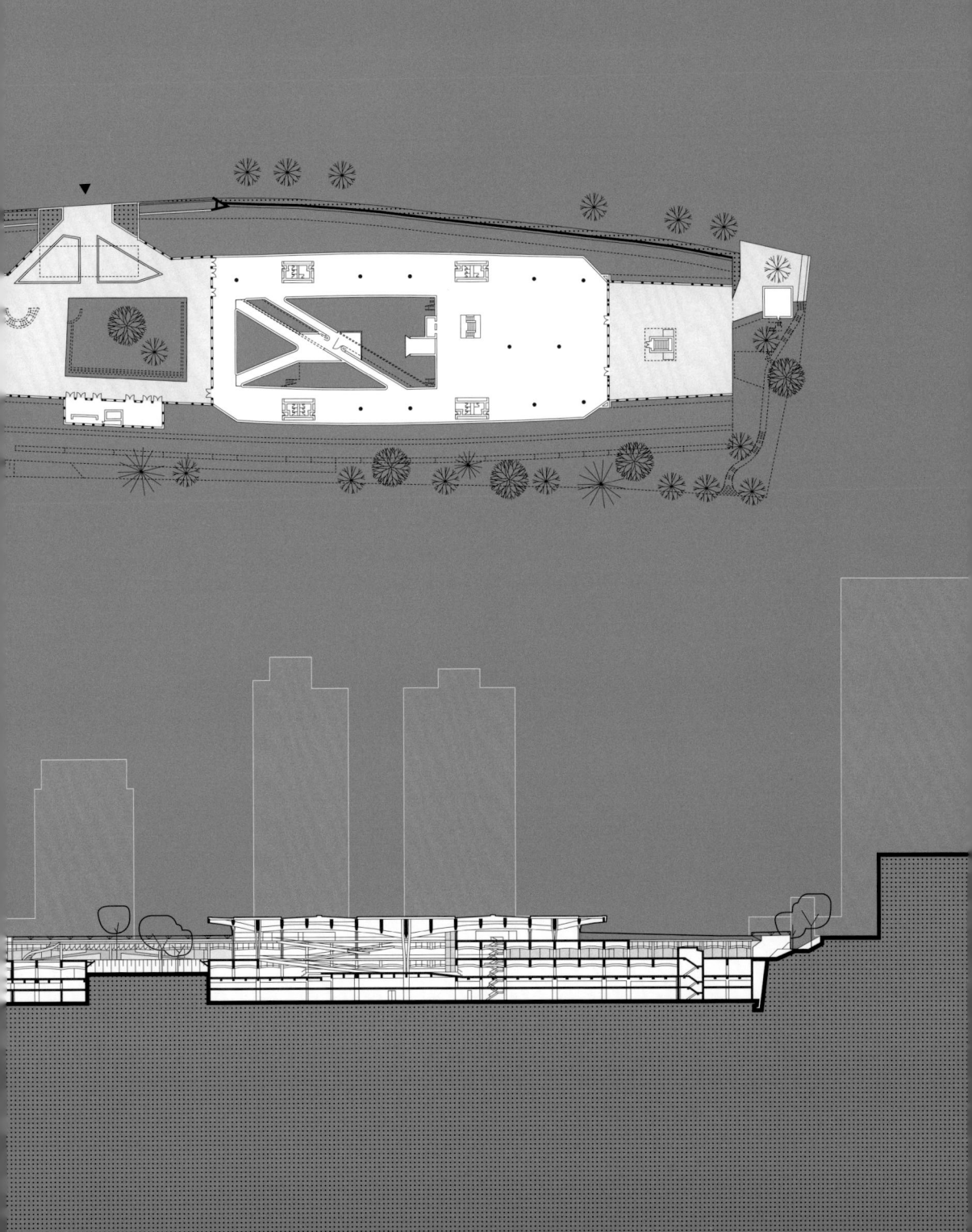

CENTRO CULTURAL SÃO PAULO

SPACE AND FORM

The Centro Cultural São Paulo (CCSP) occupies an exposed location in terms of topography as well as traffic at the intersection of the four quarters Paraíso, Aclimação, Liberdade and Bela Vista. The design reacts to the topographical peculiarities of the location.[1] The building volume is embedded into the existing edge of the slope to the now canalised and covered Rio Itororó and emphasises the longitudinal orientation of the property. The conservation of the existing trees as well as a verdant rooftop garden additionally contribute to the building's integration into the valley area.[2]

The building is located between Avenida 23 de Maio and Rua Vergueiro, two streets situated on different ground levels. The Avenida, a motorway, occupies the former riverbed of the Rio Itororó. The river's canalisation between Rua João Julião and Rua do Paraíso is part of the Avenida Itororó project.[3] In the context of the Plano de Avenidas by Prestes Maia, the space of the valley was reshaped between 1951 and 1969. Nowadays, the river flows underneath the motorway in a canalised way. CCSP's design combines the landscape context of the river valley with the small-scale components of urban fabric and pedestrians. The building's appearance is intentionally restrained, aiming to be 'discovered' randomly as a special place. Its identifying feature is the elongated, accessible roof area. Only upon closer inspection, the building's complexity becomes apparent.

Its usable space is organised across four floors, including the top floor. Only the bottom level takes up the entire building area. The two levels above it each do not touch the edge of the slope. Between the levels, there are various visual and spatial connections. Those include light openings as well as ramps and stairways. Access to the roof is also facilitated via stairways and ramps.

The building concept is open and permeable to display as many uses and activities as possible. Even between the individual usage units, the design mostly does without closed areas or visual barriers.[4] Structure and material composition contribute to the open character of the building. They involve slender concrete supports and ramps, delicate metal structures as well as a large portion of glass. Separating elements for closed spaces such as the theatre and the concert halls are made of transparent materials.

USE AND UTILISATION

The CCSP is intended as an alternative and a supplement to existing public spaces. It provides low-threshold access, targeting mainly users who rarely encounter educational and cultural offers.

The building is connected to the city via various entrances. Ground-level access points are located at the front sides to the building's north and south. Both are connected with small square environments which invite people to stay and linger.

In total, the share of open spaces in the CCSP is very high compared to buildings with similar use. The intent behind that is to make the areas as flexible as possible in terms of utilisation.[5] Their layout and disposition facilitate a coexistence of various informal uses. Quiet areas are located close to the library; the same floor level also houses a cinema, a concert hall, a theatre and a childcare facility. In contrast, areas for loud activities such as music and dance are arranged on the level above. The second basement floor contains administrative rooms, a printing press as well as the FabLab as an open workshop. A rough distinction can be made between self-organised uses and arranged programmes. Informal uses include dancing, encounters and exchanges as well as relaxation, reading and studying.

---

6   **Zugang Dachgarten**
      Access to the roof garden

7   **Ausblick Stadtlandschaft**
      View cityscape
      (S. 176 / p. 176)

---

[1] Nascimento, Teixeira (2014): p. 141 f.
[2] Nascimento, Teixeira (2014): p. 142 f.
[3] Lei 3209, de 31 de Julho de 1928 do Município de São Paulo
[4] Matera (2018): p. 160 ff.
[5] SIAA Arquitetos Associados (2018): p. 29

8 Grundriss EG
Floor plan GF
1:1500

9 Schnitt Ost-West
East-west section
1:1500

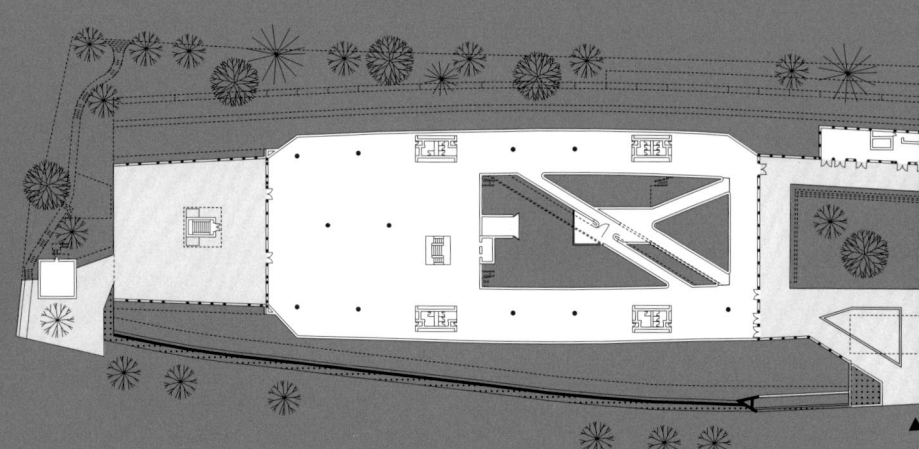

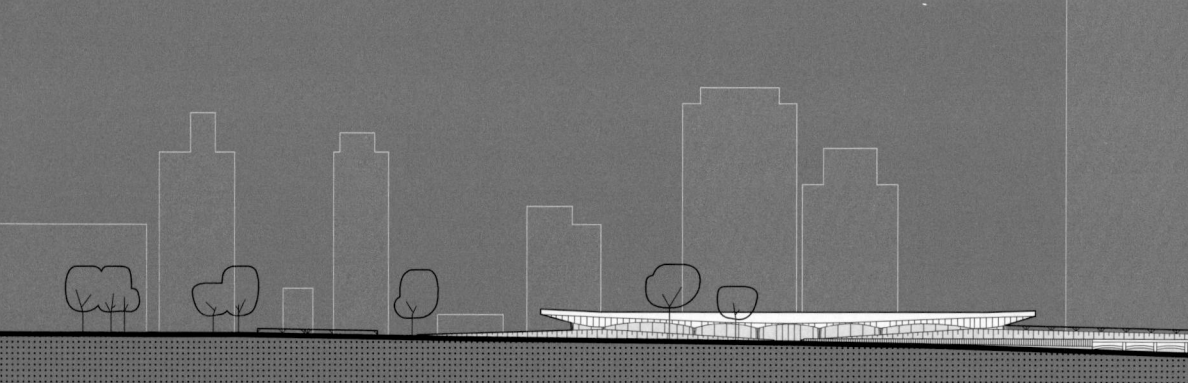

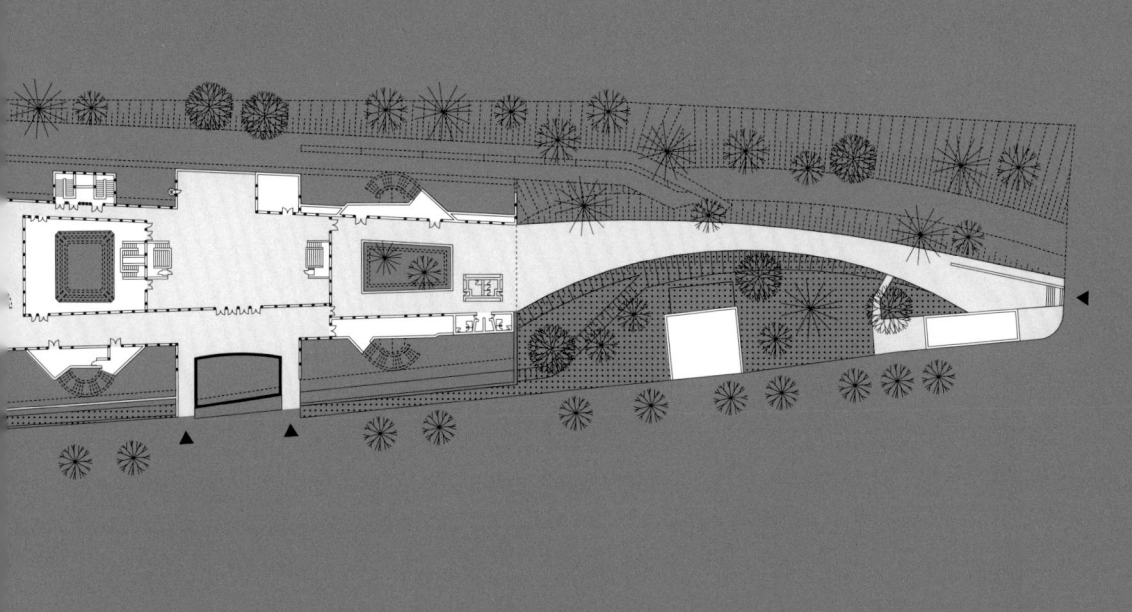

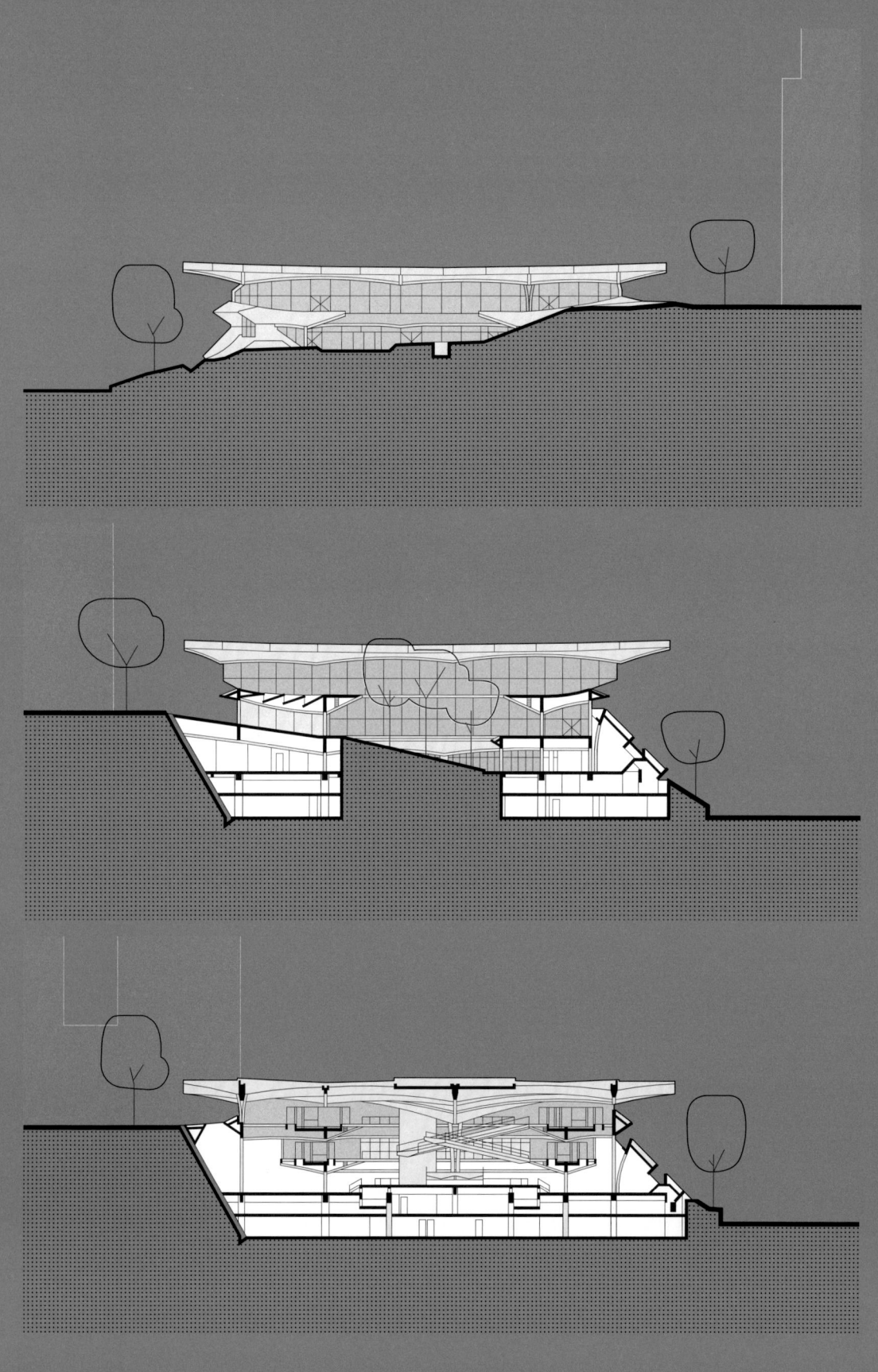

CCSP users arrive from all over the city area. Over the past years, the CCSP has become a popular meeting point for dance enthusiasts. Some users travel up to two hours just to reach the CCSP. At the same time, groups gather around the main entrance on Rua Vergueiro as well as on the top floor along the corridors. These spots are popular due to their glass surfaces. The facades mirror motion sequences and thus facilitate individual checking and correcting one's own dance moves. To increase their degree of reflection, the building administration had the glass panes tinted retroactively.

Most dancing groups use the building during time off as well as on Friday afternoons and during the weekend. Accordingly, the corridors are used particularly intensively starting in the late afternoon hours and on bank holidays. Currently, the administration is contemplating promoting this form of use further.

The CCSP is popular as a meeting point, for relaxing and as a space for studying. A particularly popular feature is the rooftop garden. The area is sheltered and allows for picnics, sunbathing and reading with a 360-degree view of the city. To the north, along Rua Vergueiro, hedges form a barrier between the property and the street. The area is popular with yoga and reading groups. Thanks to the grove and the roof overhang, it is particularly well-shielded from the sun.

Besides self-organised uses, the CCSP also features an extensive programme organised by the Ação Cultural e Educativa (culture and education campaign). It involves visual arts, audiovisual media, dance, literature, music and theatre. In addition, special activities and events take place regularly to attract new visitors to the CCSP. Different curators are responsible for concerts, films and lectures.

Another focal point of the programme consists of the library and its adjacent study areas. The facility is well-equipped and offers unrestricted access. Extended opening hours, good transport connections as well as a multitude of education facilities nearby contribute to its popularity. In spite of the rather loud and chaotic surroundings, the study space is used intensively. In part, those intent on studying also retreat to the quieter southern garden, the yard or the corridors.

ORIGIN

In the late 1970s, São Paulo's underground railway system was expanded and updated.[6] In parallel, a competition was held for an 80,000sqm lot between Avenida 23 de Maio and Rua Vergueiro to further densify the area with high-rise buildings.[7] Critics associated the project with negative effects on the surrounding urban structure.

As an alternative, São Paulo's mayor Olavo Setúbal suggested in 1975 to erect the São Paulo Vergueiro central library at the north-south corridor. He provided an area of 22,000sqm of municipal property for the project. This suggestion picked up on planning efforts intended to decentralise cultural facilities outside of the city centre. Such efforts included buildings with an emphasis on education, health, culture and sports. Those were supposed to serve as interfaces between the centre and the urban periphery.[8] The project was designed and realised between 1975 and 1985. The team consisted of architects Luiz Benedito de Castro Telles and Eurico Prado Lopes in cooperation with PLAE Arquitetura SC Ltda.

The design factors in the former river valley and the neighbouring motorways. One important concern to the architects was to avoid a library building that limited visitors to browsing and reading. Instead, the building was to inspire its visitors to make their own use of the provided areas. It was to facilitate encounters and to manage without barriers.[9] The aim was to target people with limited access to education and culture in particular. For the architects, this clearly puts the indoor spaces into focus.[10]

The design is the result of intensive debate between the design team and the municipal administration. Until its opening in 1982, the project had to overcome numerous modifications throughout its design and construction phase. Ideas connected to the project undermined the goals of the Brazilian military government. It was plagued by interruptions in construction, conflicts with the municipal administration as well as difficulties with the executing business. For political reasons, the building was inaugurated as early as May 1981 even though it was merely 70% completed.[11]

10	Blick auf die Autobahn View to parkway (S. 182 / p. 182)	
11	Ansicht Süd South view 1:750	
12	Schnitt Ost-West East-west section 1:750	
13	Schnitt Ost-West East-west section 1:750	

[6] cf. Companhia do Metropolitano de São Paulo - Metrô and Empresa Municipal de Urbanização (EMURB)
[7] Anelli (2007) in Nascimento, Teixeira (2014): p. 140
[8] Anelli (2019) in Lepik, Talesnik (2019): p. 20
[9] Telles (2002): p. 1
[10] Wissenbach (1981): p. 33
[11] Wissenbach (1981): p. 31

RECEPTION AND CONFLICTS

The building is perceived as a continuation of the street - part of a surprising city stroll. Many of those surveyed appreciated the complexity and the generosity of the building. In the urban fabric, it is experienced as a 'green island'. Its various access elements promote approaching.

For those surveyed, the CCSP is an open and safe place accessible to all social strata - a safe space without discrimination, prejudice or violence. Beyond that, certain offers and events such as cinema festivals and exhibitions address certain minorities.

Homeless people are a natural part of the user group. Those concerned are mainly provided with protection and normalcy by the CCSP. They have access to sanitary facilities, sleeping spaces and the possibility to relax and to watch others performing their activities.

However, retroactively installed gates and doors do restrict access to the building. The entrance square between the library and Avenida 23 de Maio is also no longer accessible. Also, uniformed security staff check for compliance with house rules.

The positioning of the cultural centre as a lively and diverse location depends on the attitude and the focus of the respective administration. Currently, the economic crisis as well as political changes are associated with funding cuts. There are considerations of privatising parts of the building. A change in direction is also evaluated for the centre. Some of those surveyed fear that this will cause the CCSP to lose its character as an open space.

14   Freibespielbare Flächen
     Multipurpose spaces

3
ANHANG
APPENDIX

QUELLEN SOURCES

- Acrópole Nr. 259/4 (1960); Revista mensal, São Paulo.
- Aleixo, Cynthia (2005); Edifícios e galerias comerciais, arquitetura e comércio na cidade de São Paulo, São Paulo.
- Andreoni, Federica (2017); The thickness of the ground: Four micro-stories on the project of the open urban ground floor in São Paulo from 1892 until nowadays, Barcelona.
- Andreoli, Elisabetta; Forty, Adrian (2004); Brazil's Modern Architecture, London.
- Anelli, Renato (2012); Urban planning, urban design and architectural design in São Paulo during the Military Regime; in: 15th International Planning History Society Conference, São Paulo, FAU USP.
- Artigas, Rosa (Hrsg.) (2008); Caminhos do Elevado Memória e Projetos, São Paulo.
- Augé, Marc (2012); Nicht-Orte, München.
- Autores, Vários (2009); Desenhando São Paulo. Mapas E Literatura 1877-1954, São Paulo.
- Batista, Liz (2015); Era uma vez em SP... Belvedere Trianon, www.acervo.estadao.com.br/noticias/acervo,era-uma-vez-em-sp-belvedere-trianon,11165,0.htm, abgerufen am 29.07.2019.
- Bo Bardi, Lina; Ferraz, Marcelo Carvalho (2018); Lina Bo Bardi, Instituto Bardi, Casa de Vidro, São Paulo.
- Caffey, Stephen Mark; Campagnol, Gabriela (2015-1); Construction of the Museu de Arte de São Paulo; in: 5th International Congress on Construction History, Chicago.
- Caffey, Stephen Mark; Campagnol, Gabriela (2015-2); Dis/Solution: Lina Bo Bardi's Museu de Arte de São Paulo; in: Journal of Conservation and Museum Studies, London.
- Cenzatti, Marco (2008); in: De Cauter, Lieven; Dehaene, Michiel (Hrsg.); Heterotopia and the City - Public Space in a Postcivil Society, London, New York.
- Costa, Sabrina Studart Fontenele (2010); Relações entre o traçado urbano e os edifícios modernos no centro de São Paulo. Arquitetura e Cidade, São Paulo.
- Costa, Sabrina Studart Fontenele (2014); Edifícios modernos e o traçado urbano no centro de São Paulo, São Paulo.
- Costa, Sabrina Studart Fontenele (2015); A "promenade architecturalle" in modern galleries of São Paulo downtown; in: ReUSO Libro Comunicaciones, Valencia.
- Coy, Martin (2001); São Paulo: Entwicklungstrends einer brasilianischen Megastadt; in: Geographica Helvetica, Jg. 56 2001/Heft 4, Innsbruck.
- Cunha Jr., Jaime (2007); Edifício Metrópole: Um diálogo entre arquitetura moderna e cidade, São Paulo.
- Corradini, Juliana; Alves José (2006), Prêmio Prestes Maia de Urbanismo: www.vitruvius.com.br/revistas/read/projetos/06.067/2689?page=3, abgerufen am 21.02.2019.
- De Cauter, Lieven; Dehaene, Michiel (Hrsg.) (2008); Heterotopia and the City - Public Space in a Postcivil Society, London, New York.
- Diniz, Pedro (2019); Rei da noite, Facundo Guerra marca a ascensão e queda do centro paulistano; in: Folha de S.Paulo, São Paulo www1.folha.uol.com.br/ilustrada/2019/01/rei-da-noite-facundo-guerra-marca-a-ascensao-e-queda-do-centro-paulistano.shtml; abgerufen am 29.07.2019.
- Estêvão, Bertoni (2016); O que é e para que serve o Minhocão?, www.nexojornal.com.br/expresso/2016/10/11/O-que-%C3%A9-e-para-que-serve-o-Minhoc%C3%A3o, abgerufen am 25.09.2019.
- Fanucci, Francisco; Ferraz, Marcelo; Cartum, Marcos (Hrsg.) (2013); Praça das Artes - Performing Arts Centre - São Paulo, São Paulo.

- Fanucci, Francisco; Ferraz Marcelo (2016); Praça das Artes: Urbanism Made of Architecture; in: ARQ 92, 2016, Santiago.
- Faubion, James D. (2008); Heterotopia: an ecology: in: De Cauter, Lieven; Dehaene, Michiel (Hrsg.); Heterotopia and the City - Public Space in a Postcivil Society, London, New York.
- Feldtkeller, Andreas (1995); Die zweckentfremdete Stadt - wider die Zerstörung des öffentlichen Raums; 2. Aufl., Frankfurt am Main.
- Fernández Galiano, Luis (Hrsg.) (2015); Museo de Arte de São Paulo, 1957-1968; in: AV Monographs 180, 2015; Lina Bo Bardi 1914-1992, Madrid.
- Ferraz, Marcelo Carvalho (1994); Lina Bo Bardi, Mailand.
- Ferriss, Hugh (1929); The metropolis of tomorrow, New York.
- Ferroni, Eduardo (2008); Aproximações sobre a obra de Salvador Candia, São Paulo.
- Ferroni, Eduardo; Shundi Iwamizu, Cesar (2013); Salvador Candia, São Paulo.
- Folha de São Paulo (1989), Minhocão passa a ser interditado mais cedo, www.acervo.folha.com.br/leitor.do?numero=10792&anchor=4092656&origem=busca&_mather=71651da49cc54692, abgerufen am 25.09.2019.
- Folha de São Paulo (1990), Como fugir do Minhocão interditado, www.acervo.folha.com.br/leitor.do?numero=10976&anchor=4905591&origem=busca&_mather=71651da49cc54692, abgerufen am 25.09.2019.
- Foucault, Michel (1966[2013]); Die Heterotopien, Der utopische Körper - Zwei Radiovorträge, 3. Aufl., Berlin.
- Foucault, Michel (1978); Discipline and Punish - The Birth of the Prison, New York.
- Foucault, Michel (1992); Andere Räume; in: Barck, Karlheinz (Hrsg.); Aisthesis - Wahrnehmung heute oder Perspektiven einer anderen Ästhetik, Leipzig.
- Fraser, Nacy (1992[1993]); Rethinking the public sphere in Calhoun, Craig (Hrsg.); Habermas and the Public Sphere, Cambridge.
- Gehl, Jan (2012); Leben zwischen Häusern, Berlin.
- Gonsales, Patricia Cecilia (2016); Sérgio Milliet e a metrópole paulistana: Crítica, urbanismo e cultura (1920-1958), São Paulo.
- Habermas, Jürgen (1965); Strukturwandel der Öffentlichkeit - Untersuchungen zu einer Kategorie der bürgerlichen Gesellschaft; 2. durchgesehene Aufl., Neuwied am Rhein, Berlin.
- Instituto Odeon (2019); www.institutoodeon.org.br/, abgerufen am 25.09.2019.
- Jacobs, Jane (1963); Tod und Leben großer amerikanischer Städte; Bauwelt-Fundamente, Berlin.
- Karfeld, Kurt Peter (1955); São Paulo, São Paulo.
- Klanten, Robert; Borges, Sofia (2016); The Tale of Tomorrow: Utopian Architecture in the Modernist Realm, Los Angeles.
- Koolhaas, Rem (1999); Delirious New York: Ein retroaktives Manifest für Manhattan, Rotterdam.
- Lepik, Andres; Bader, Simone (2014); Lina Bo Bardi 100: Brasiliens Alternativer Weg in die Moderne, São Paulo.
- Lepik, Andres; Daniel, Talesnik (2019); Access for All: São Paulo's Architectural Infrastructures, Altenburg.
- Leme, Maria Cristina da Silva (1990); Revisão do Plano de Avenidas: um estudo sobre planejamento urbano, 1930, São Paulo.
- Leme, Maria Cristina da Silva (Hrsg.) (1999); Urbanismo no Brasil 1895-1965, São Paulo.
- Leme, Maria Cristina da Silva (2010); Transforming the modern Latin American city: Robert Moses and the International Basic Economic Corporation; in: Planning Perspectives 25, Nr. 4, 2010, São Paulo.

- Lobato, Maurílio Lima (2009); Considerações sobre o espaço público e edifícios de uso misto modernos no centro de São Paulo, Ano de Obtenção, São Paulo.
- Machado, Joana Sarue (2008); O Lugar das Galerias do Centro de São Paulo - Relações entre Espaço Público e Privado, São Paulo.
- Matera, Sergio (2018); Transformação e apropriação do território, In estratégias do vazio: Construção e desenho do solo público: O projeto moderno na arquitetura contemporânea paulista, São Paulo.
- Mungioli, Arlindo (2017); Projeto: Nov/Dez 17 (Ausgabe 440), São Paulo.
- Muzzio, D.; Muzzio-Rentas, J. (2008); 'A kind of instinct': the cinematic mall as heterotopia: in: De Cauter, Lieven; Dehaene, Michiel (Hrsg.); Heterotopia and the City - Public Space in a Postcivil Society, London, New York.
- Nascimento, Gislaine Moura do; Azevedo Teixeira, Katia (2014); Paisagem urbana, arquitetura e representação, São Judas Tadeu.
- Niemeyer, Oscar (1982); in: Módulo Nr. 72, 1982; Centro Cultural São Paulo, São Paulo.
- Nosek, Victor (Hrsg.) (2013); Praça das Artes - Performing Arts Centre, São Paulo.
- Oliveira, Olivia de (2014); Lina Bo Bardi - Obra construida - Built work, Barcelona.
- Operação Urbana Centro (1997); Lei 12.349 de 6 de Junho de 1997 do Município de São Paulo; www.prefeitura.sp.gov.br/cidade/upload/783a3_Lei_N_12.349-97_Estabelece_programas_de_melhorias.pdf, abgerufen am 30.07.2019.
- Peng, Zhiyuan (2019); Öffentlicher Raum Heterotopie (Masterarbeit), Hannover.
- Petrov, Arkady (2019); Landmark Museum asks São Paulo to help protect structure from large crowds; The Rio Times: www.riotimesonline.com/brazil-news/sao-paulo/landmark-museum-asks-sao-paulo-to-help-protect-structure-during-crowded-events/, abgerufen am 30.07.2019.
- Pitanga do Amparo Arquitetura & Arte (1987), www.pitangadoamparo.com.br/images/obras/minhocao/minhocao1.htm, abgerufen am 25.09.2019.
- Prestes Maia, Francisco (1930); Estudo de um Plano de Avenidas para a Cidade de São Paulo, São Paulo.
- Prestes Maia, Francisco (1945); Os melhoramentos de São Paulo, 2.tiragem atualizada, São Paulo.
- Quintella, Sérgio (2019); Prefeitura anuncia a construção do Parque Minhocão, www.vejasp.abril.com.br/cidades/minhocao-capa-projeto-verde/, abgerufen am 25.09.2019.
- Ribeiro, Patricia (2016); Facundo Guerra conta sobre o Mirante 9 de Julho e seu novo projeto: um bar no subsolo do Teatro Municipal: www.passeiosbaratosemsp.com.br/facundo-guerra-conta-sobre-o-mirante-9-de-julho-e-seu-novo-projeto-um-bar-no-subsolo-do-teatro-municipal/, abgerufen am 29.07.2019.
- Riodel, Vicente (2010); Beyond Brasília: Contemporary urbanism in Brazil, Gainesville.
- Rolnik, Raquel (2008); São Paulo zwischen Wachstum und Schrumpfung. Eine chronologische Stadtgeschichte; in: Arch+ n.190, 2008, Zeitschrift für Architektur und Urbanismus, Aachen.
- Rupf, Lilian (2015); Lugares públicos: a dimensão cotidiana no centro de São Paulo, São Paulo.
- Schäfer-Biermann, Birgit; Westermann, Aische; Vahle, Marlen; Pott, Valérie (2016); Foucaults Heterotopien als Forschungsinstrument - Eine Anwendung am Beispiel Kleingarten; 1. Aufl., Wiesbaden.
- Schröder, Jörg; Carta, Maurizio; Ferretti, Maddalena; Lino, Barbaro (2017); Territories, Rural-urban Strategies, Berlin.
- Segurança Imobiliária S.A. (1962); Hoje: Lançamento na rua Nova Barão! - A nova rua paralela à Rua Marconi in o estado de S. Paulo (Jahrgang 1962), São Paulo.

- Sennett, Richard (1998); Verfall und Ende des öffentlichen Lebens - die Tyrannei der Intimität, Frankfurt am Main.
- Serapião, Fernando (2018); Centro de São Paulo, São Paulo's Downtown; in: Monolito, Ausgabe 39/40, 2018, São Paulo.
- SIAA Arquitetos Associados (Hrsg.) (2018); Centro Cultural São Paulo - Cartografia de usos.
- Siebel, Walter (2004); Die europäische Stadt; Orig.-Ausg., 1. Aufl., Frankfurt am Main.
- Somekh, Nadia (1997); A cidade vertical. E o urbanismo modernizador. Cidade Aberta, São Paulo.
- Telles, Luiz (2002); CCSP - Centro Cultural São Paulo, um projeto revisitado, Universidade Presbiteriana Mackenzie.
- Theatro Municipal (2019); www.theatro-municipal.org.br/espaco/praca-das-artes/#, abgerufen am 25.09.2019.
- Toledo, Benedito Lima de (1996); Prestes Maia e as origens do urbanismo moderno em São Paulo, São Paulo.
- Waschinkski, Georg Paulus et al. (1954); Eis São Paulo, Editora Monumento, São Paulo.
- Welsch, Wolfgang (2010); Ästhetisches Denken, Stuttgart.
- Wissenbach, Vincent (1981); Arquitetura planejamento. Desenho industrial construção; in: Projeto, 1981, São Paulo.
- Zahiri, Cyrus (2013); Zwischen Reglement und Laissez-Faire: Zum Phänomen der Unschärfe im städtebaulichen Entwurf, Kassel.

INTERVIEWS INTERVIEWS

GALERIA METRÓPOLE

- 01: Architekt
- 02: Ladenbesitzer
- 03: Ladenbesitzer
- 04: Sicherheitsdienst
- 05: Architektin / Forscherin
- 06: Nutzer
- 07: Nutzer
- 08: Nutzer
- 09: Touristin und Tourist
- 10: Nutzerin und Nutzer
- 11: Nutzer
- 12: Nutzer
- 13: Nutzer
- 14: Shopeigentümer
- 15: Hausbewohner
- 16: Architekt
- 17: Stadtplanerin

GALERIA DO ROCK

- 01: Manager (Galeria do Rock)
- 02: Verkäuferin
- 03: Rezeptionist
- 04: Tätowiererin
- 05: Verkäufer
- 06: Nutzer
- 07: Fußgänger
- 08: Verkäuferin
- 09: Sicherheitspersonal
- 10: Rezeptionist
- 11: Rezeptionistin

GALERIA NOVA BARÃO

- 01: Hausmeisterin
- 02: Ladenbesitzerin
- 03: Kunde
- 04: Ladenbesitzerin
- 05: Besitzerin Friseursalon
- 06: Sicherheitsdienst
- 07: Besucher
- 08: Angestellte
- 09: Sicherheitsdienst

SESC 24 DE MAIO

- 01: Architektin (SESC 24 de Maio)
- 02: Nutzerin
- 03: Nutzer
- 04: Nutzerin
- 05: Nutzerin
- 06: Sozialarbeiter
- 07: Bademeister
- 08: Fahrstuhlführerin
- 09: Reinigungskraft
- 10: Angestellte
- 11: Krankenschwester

PRAÇA DAS ARTES

- 01: Architektin (Praça das Artes)
- 02: Nutzerinnen
- 03: Nutzerin
- 04: Nutzerin
- 05: Gruppe Studierende
- 06: Tanzgruppe
- 07: Besucher
- 08: Gruppe Studierende

MASP / MIRANTE

- 01: Angestellte
- 02: Verkäufer
- 03: Wohnungsloser
- 04: Wohnungsloser
- 05: Fahrradkurier
- 06: Fotograf
- 07: Verkäuferin
- 08: Verkäuferin
- 09: Unternehmer
- 10: Touristinnen
- 11: Verkäufer
- 12: Verkäufer
- 13: Besucherin
- 14: Besucher
- 15: Sicherheitspersonal
- 16: Besucher
- 17: Besucherin
- 18: Angestellte
- 19: Musikerin
- 20: Besucher
- 21: Besucher
- 22: Besucher
- 23: Besucherin und Besucher
- 24: Wohnungsloser
- 25: Besucher
- 26: Musiker

- 27: Besucher
- 28: Gruppe Besuchende
- 29: Gruppe Besuchende
- 30: Manager (Mirante)

MINHOCÃO

- 01: Jogger
- 02: Restaurantinhaber
- 03: Spaziergängerin
- 04: Radfahrer
- 05: Spaziergängerin
- 06: Taxifahrer
- 07: Straßenverkäufer
- 08: Nutzerin
- 09: Nutzerin
- 10: Gruppe Nutzende
- 11: Spaziergängerin
- 12: Spaziergängerin
- 13: Tourist

CENTRO CULTURAL SÃO PAULO

- 01: Architekt (CCSP)
- 02: Fahrradmechanikerin
- 03: Gärtner
- 04: Besucherin
- 05: Pfadfinder
- 06: Rezeptionist
- 07: Rezeptionistin
- 08: Gruppe Studierende
- 09: Sicherheitspersonal
- 10: Musikerin
- 11: Wohnungsloser
- 12: Besucherin und Besucher

BILDQUELLEN IMAGE SOURCES

ÜBERBLICK

1. Praça Pedro Lessa
   rasantes Stadtwachstum
   rapid urban growth
   Prestes Maia, F. (1930): Estudo de um Plano de
   Avenidas para a Cidade de São Paulo, São Paulo,
   Companhia Melhoramentos, fig. 56.

2. Hybridbau mit Terrasse
   Perspektive
   Hybrid building with terrace
   Perspective
   ebd., fig. 47.

3. Trennung Verkehrsarten
   Querschnitte
   Separation of transport modes
   Cross sections
   ebd., fig. 78.

4. São Francisco Viadukt
   Längsschnitt
   São Francisco Viaduct
   Longitudinal section
   ebd., Estudo.

5. Hybridbau auf Viadukt
   Ansicht
   Hybrid building on viaduct
   View
   ebd., fig. 44.

6. Plano de Avenidas da Cidade de São Paulo
   Erschließungsschema
   Traffic scheme proposal
   ebd., fig. 37.

7. Plano de Avenidas da Cidade de São Paulo
   Vorstudie
   Preliminary study
   ebd., Estudo.

8. Tunnelmund Mirante Avenida Anhangabaú
   Entwurf
   Tunnel entry Mirante Avenida Anhangabaú
   Proposal
   ebd., PL. VII-a, fig. B.

9. Erdarbeiten
   Anhangabaú-Tal
   Earthworks
   Anhangabaú valley
   ebd., fig. e.

10. Belvedere do Trianon
    Aussicht zum Anhangabaú-Tal
    View facing the Anhangabaú valley
    ebd., fig. 190.

11. Entwurfszeichnung
    Tunnel und Mirante Trianon
    Proposal
    Tunnel and Mirante Trianon
    ebd., fig. 3 .

12. Belvedere do Trianon
    Tunnelmund und Aussichtsturm
    Tunnel entry and observation tower
    Georg Paulus Waschinski, 1954; in:
    Waschinski, G. P. (1954): Eis São Paulo, São Paulo.
    Trotz umfangreicher Recherche konnte ein/e Urheber*in
    nicht ermittelt werden. Wir sind dankbar für alle
    Hinweise auf die Person.
    Despite extensive research, the author could not be
    identified. We are grateful for any information
    about the person.

13. Galeria Metrópole
    Blick aus dem bepflanzten Innenhof
    in die Galeria Metrópole
    View from the planted courtyard
    into the Galeria Metrópole
    Ricardo Lima, 2005; in:
    Cunha. J. Jr. (2007): Edificio Metrópole - um diálogo
    entre arquitetura moderna e cidade, São Paulo.

14. Planung Galeria de Crystal
    Jules Martin (1898)
    Perspektive
    Perspective
    Jules Martin, 1898; Projeto de Galerias de Cristal
    em São Paulo, apresentado à Intendência Municipal.
    October 22, 1898. Ilustrations. Fonds Câmara Municipal
    de São Paulo, Series Obras Públicas Arquivo Histórico
    Municipal de São Paulo; in: Toledo, Benedito Lima de
    (1996): Prestes Maia e as origens do urbanismo moderno
    em São Paulo, p. 60 - 61.

15. Darstellung Galeria de Crystal
    Jules Martin (1898)
    Lageplan
    Site plan
    ebd.

16. Grandes Galerias
    Werbeanzeige
    Advertisement
    Alfredo Mathias, 1960; in: Folha de São Paulo, 1.a, 2.a e
    3.a ediçãoes, 14 June 1962, Nr. 140 year 40, p. 16
    Trotz umfangreicher Recherche konnte ein/e Urheber*in
    nicht ermittelt werden. Wir sind dankbar für alle
    Hinweise auf die Person.
    Despite extensive research, the author could not be
    identified. We are grateful for any information
    about the person.

17. Grandes Galerias
    Innenraum Werbeanzeige
    Inner space Advertisement
    Alfredo Mathias, 1960; ebd., p. 17
    Trotz umfangreicher Recherche konnte ein/e Urheber*in
    nicht ermittelt werden. Wir sind dankbar für alle
    Hinweise auf die Person.
    Despite extensive research, the author could not be
    identified. We are grateful for any information
    about the person.

18. Galeria Nova Baraõ
    Werbeanzeige
    Advertisement
    Alfredo Mathias, 1962; in: O Estado de São Paulo:
    pages from the issue of 29 July 1962, p. 2
    Trotz umfangreicher Recherche konnte ein/e Urheber*in
    nicht ermittelt werden. Wir sind dankbar für alle
    Hinweise auf die Person.
    Despite extensive research, the author could not be
    identified. We are grateful for any information
    about the person.

19. Centro Novo
    Lageplan
    Site plan
    böhm benfer zahiri, 2019

GALERIA METRÓPOLE

1. Atrium als Mittelpunkt
   Atrium as focal point
   böhm benfer zahiri, 2019

2. Lageplan
   Site plan
   böhm benfer zahiri, 2019

3 Offenes Treppenhaus
Open staircase
böhm benfer zahiri, 2019

4 Schnitt Süd-Nord
South-north section
böhm benfer zahiri, 2019

5 Punkthochhaus
Solitary high-rise
böhm benfer zahiri, 2019

6 Dachgeschoss der Galerie
Gallery top floor
böhm benfer zahiri, 2019

7 Grundriss EG
Floor plan GF
böhm benfer zahiri, 2019

8 Grundriss 2. OG
Floor plan 2F
böhm benfer zahiri, 2019

9 Grundriss DG
Floor plan TF
böhm benfer zahiri, 2019

10 Terrassen und Stadtraum
Terraces und urban context
böhm benfer zahiri, 2019

GALERIA DO ROCK

1 Offene Galerie
Open gallery
böhm benfer zahiri, 2019

2 Lageplan
Site plan
böhm benfer zahiri, 2019

3 Blickbeziehungen
Visual relations
böhm benfer zahiri, 2019

4 Eingangssituation
Entrance
böhm benfer zahiri, 2019

5 Übergangsraum
Transition area
böhm benfer zahiri, 2019

6 Grundriss EG
Floor plan GF
böhm benfer zahiri, 2019

7 Grundriss 1. OG
Floor plan 1F
böhm benfer zahiri, 2019

8 Schnitt Nord-Süd
North-south section
böhm benfer zahiri, 2019

9 Blick
View
Largo do Paissandú
böhm benfer zahiri, 2019

10 Galerieebenen
Gallery floors
böhm benfer zahiri, 2019

11 Ausblick
View
Rua Vinte e Quatro de Maio
böhm benfer zahiri, 2019

GALERIA NOVA BARÃO

1 Eingang
Entrance
Rua Barão de Itapetininga
böhm benfer zahiri, 2019

2 Lageplan
Site plan
böhm benfer zahiri, 2019

3 Blick von der Galeriebrücke
View from the gallery bridge
böhm benfer zahiri, 2019

4 Schnitt Süd-Nord
South-north section
böhm benfer zahiri, 2019

5 Blick
View
Rua 7 de Abril
böhm benfer zahiri, 2019

6 Grundriss EG
Floor plan GF
böhm benfer zahiri, 2019

7 Grundriss 1. OG
Floor plan 1F
böhm benfer zahiri, 2019

8 „Platz'
'Square'
böhm benfer zahiri, 2019

9 Balkon mit Aussicht
Balcony with a view
Rua Barão de Itapetininga
Jacob Fielers, 2019

SESC 24 DE MAIO

1 Dachschwimmbad
Pool at the rooftop
böhm benfer zahiri, 2019

2 Lageplan
Site plan
böhm benfer zahiri, 2019

3 Dachschwimmbad
Pool at the rooftop
Zhiyuan Peng, 2019

4 Grundriss EG
Floor plan GF
böhm benfer zahiri, 2019

5 Grundriss 2. OG
Floor plan 2F
böhm benfer zahiri, 2019

6 Grundriss 11. OG
Floor plan 11F
böhm benfer zahiri, 2019

7 Grundriss DG
Floor plan TF
böhm benfer zahiri, 2019

8 Zugang
Accessibility
Zhiyuan Peng, 2019

9 Schnitt Ost-West
East-west section
böhm benfer zahiri, 2019

10 Stadtpanorama
City panorama
böhm benfer zahiri, 2019

11	Planschbecken Stadtsilhouette Wading pool Cityscape böhm benfer zahiri, 2019
12	Rahmung historische Fassade Framing a historical facade böhm benfer zahiri, 2019
13	Blickbeziehungen Visual relationships böhm benfer zahiri, 2019
14	Blickbeziehungen Visual relationships böhm benfer zahiri, 2019
15	Vertikale Promenade Vertical promenade böhm benfer zahiri, 2019

PRAÇA DAS ARTES

1	Blick Anhangabaú-Tal View into Anhangabaú valley böhm benfer zahiri, 2019
2	Lageplan Site plan böhm benfer zahiri, 2019
3	Übergang Anhangabaú-Tal Anhangabaú valley transition böhm benfer zahiri, 2019
4	Bezug Anhangabaú-Tal Link Anhangabaú valley Rua Conselheiro Crispiniano böhm benfer zahiri, 2019
5	Grundriss EG Floor plan GF böhm benfer zahiri, 2019
6	Grundriss 2. OG Floor plan 2F böhm benfer zahiri, 2019
7	Passage und Gebäudebrücke Passage und building bridge böhm benfer zahiri, 2019
8	Sitzgelegenheiten Seating arrangements Anton Fischer, 2019
9	Schnitt Ost-West East-west section böhm benfer zahiri, 2019
10	Schnitt West-Ost West-east section böhm benfer zahiri, 2019
11	Blick Anhangabaú-Tal View Anhangabaú valley Rua Conselheiro Crispiniano böhm benfer zahiri, 2019

MASP UND MIRANTE

1	Blick MASP und Mirante View MASP and Mirante Anton Fischer, 2019
2	Lageplan Site plan böhm benfer zahiri, 2019
3	MASP Stadtrahmen MASP city frame böhm benfer zahiri, 2019
4	Grundriss 2.OG Floor plan 2F böhm benfer zahiri, 2019
5	Blick Treppenanlage zum Café Mirante View Staircase to Café Mirante Anton Fischer, 2019
6	Beziehung Avenida Paulista und MASP Relation Avenida Paulista and MASP Anton Fischer, 2019
7	Schnitt Nord-Süd North-south section böhm benfer zahiri, 2019
8	Sicherheitskräfte Security forces böhm benfer zahiri, 2019
9	Überbaute Platzfläche Roofed plaza böhm benfer zahiri, 2019
10	Schnitt Ost-West East-west section böhm benfer zahiri, 2019
11	‚Stadtbalkon' 'Urban balcony' Anton Fischer, 2019
12	Café Mirante Anton Fischer, 2019

MINHOCÃO

1	Hochstraße als Freiraum Elevated road accessible as open space Leander Olkner, 2019
2	Lageplan Site plan böhm benfer zahiri, 2019
3	Verbindungen Stadtebene Connections to the city level Leander Olkner, 2019
4	Schnitt Süd-Nord South-north section böhm benfer zahiri, 2019
5	Spur und Stadtlandschaft Track and city scape böhm benfer zahiri, 2019
6	Nutzungsmuster Patterns of use Leander Olkner, 2019
7	Stadtpromenade City promenade Leander Olkner, 2019
8	Schnitt Ost-West East-west section böhm benfer zahiri, 2019
9	Stadtkulisse Urban backdrop Photo shooting Leander Olkner, 2019
10	Grüne Fassaden Green facades Leander Olkner, 2019

CENTRO CULTURAL SÃO PAULO

1 Offene Innenräume
   Open interiors
   Milan von Moeller, 2019

2 Lageplan
   Site plan
   böhm benfer zahiri, 2019

3 Nach Innen gerichtet
   Abschirmung zu den Straßen
   Inward orientation
   The building shields itself from the street
   Milan von Moeller, 2019

4 Grundriss EG
   Floor plan GF
   böhm benfer zahiri, 2019

5 Schnitt West-Ost
   West-east section
   böhm benfer zahiri, 2019

6 Zugang zum Dachgarten
   Access to the roof garden
   Milan von Moeller, 2019

7 Ausblick Stadtlandschaft
   View cityscape
   Lina Reulecke, 2019

8 Grundriss EG
   Floor plan GF
   böhm benfer zahiri, 2019

9 Schnitt Ost-West
   East-west section
   böhm benfer zahiri, 2019

10 Blick auf die Autobahn
   View to parkway
   Lina Reulecke, 2019

11 Ansicht Süd
   South View
   böhm benfer zahiri, 2019

12 Schnitt Ost West
   East-west section
   böhm benfer zahiri, 2019

13 Schnitt Ost-West
   East-west section
   böhm benfer zahiri, 2019

14 Freibespielbare Flächen
   Multipurpose spaces
   Anton Fischer, 2019

IMPRESSUM
IMPRINT

AUTOREN Katja Benfer, Ulrike Böhm, Cyrus Zahiri
AUTHORS Rita Leal, Anna Vogels, Milan v. Moeller

LEIBNIZ UNIVERSITÄT HANNOVER
INSTITUT FÜR LANDSCHAFTSARCHITEKTUR

Herrenhäuser Straße 2A
30419 Hannover

UNIVERSITÄT STUTTGART
STÄDTEBAU-INSTITUT

Keplerstraße 11
70174 Stuttgart

HOCHSCHULE BREMEN
SCHOOL OF ARCHITECTURE

Neustadtwall 30
28199 Bremen

REDAKTION Rita Leal, Anna Vogels
EDITING

KOORDINATION Luiza Pereira, Rita Leal, Anna Vogels
COORDINATION

GRUNDLAGEN Luiza Pereira, Rita Leal, Milan v. Moeller,
RESEARCH Zhiyuan Peng, Anton Fischer, Camille Régimbart

GRAFIK, LAYOUT Anton Fischer, Milan v. Moeller, Jennifer Münner,
GRAPHICS, LAYOUT Zhiyuan Peng, Camille Régimbart, Amadeus Theimer

KOOPERATION UNIVERSIDADE DE SÃO PAULO
COOPERATION FACULDADE DE ARQUITETURA E URBANISMO

Ana Castro, Prof. Dr., Eduardo Costa, Dr., Sabrina Studart
Fontenele Costa, Dr., Marcelo Baliú Fiamenghi, Maria Luiza
Belo, Luísa Gonçalves, Elis Macedo, Marina Rigolleto,
Gabriela Yumi Takase

ESCOLA DA CIDADE
FACULDADE DE ARQUITETURA E URBANISMO

Sebastian Beck, Prof. Ms., Juliane Bellot Rolemberg Lessa,
Prof., Pedro Beresin, Prof. Ms., Joana Andrade, Sofia Boldrini,
Tamara Crespin, Paula Mattos, Luísa Moreno, Beatriz Oliveira,
Louise Rodrigues

DRUCK Spree Druck Berlin GmbH
PRINT www.spreedruck.de

STÄDTEBAU-INSTITUT
UNIVERSITÄT STUTTGART **SI**

INSTITUT FÜR LANDSCHAFTSARCHITEKTUR
LEIBNIZ UNIVERSITÄT HANNOVER **IL/·**

SCHOOL OF ARCHITECTURE
HOCHSCHULE BREMEN **HSB**

Öffentliches und Privates, Verkehr und Freiraum, Geplantes und Spontanes – unsere Stadtvorstellung ist geprägt durch Gegensätze. Dagegen zeigen die Beitragenden in dem zweisprachigen Band, dass sich diese Pole auch bewusst verknüpfen lassen. Die Stadtbausteine aus São Paulo präsentieren unerwartet eigenwillige Stadtszenenz: Tanzende entlang der Schnellstraße, Flanierende durch das Steinarchipel, Planschende vor der Stadtsilhouette…

Viele der vorgestellten Projekte sind verknüpft mit den Ideen des brasilianischen Stadtplaners Francisco Prestes Maia. Schon in den 1930er Jahren entwickelte er Konzepte, die Verkehr, Freiraum und Architektur zusammendenken – ein überraschend aktueller Ansatz.

Public and private, traffic and open space, planned and spontaneous – our idea of a city is characterised by opposites. However, the contributors to this bilingual book show that these poles can also be consciously connected. The urban building blocks from São Paulo present surprisingly idiosyncratic city scenes: People dancing along the motorway, strolling through the stone archipelago, splashing around in front of the city skyline…

Many of the case studies are linked to the ideas of the Brazilian urban planner Francisco Prestes Maia. As early as in the 1930s, he developed concepts that combine traffic, open space and architecture – a surprisingly contemporary approach.

[transcript]